University Reform in Nineteenth-Century Oxford

Crayon drawing of Henry Halford Vaughan by G. F. Watts
Reproduced by permission of Mr. H. J. Vaughan

University Reform in Nineteenth-Century Oxford

A Study of Henry Halford Vaughan

1811–1885

E. G. W. BILL

OXFORD

AT THE CLARENDON PRESS

1973

Oxford University Press, Ely House, London W. 1

GLASGOW NEW YORK TORONTO MELBOURNE WELLINGTON
CAPE TOWN IBADAN NAIROBI DAR ES SALAAM LUSAKA ADDIS ABABA
DELHI BOMBAY CALCUTTA MADRAS KARACHI LAHORE DACCA
KUALA LUMPUR SINGAPORE HONG KONG TOKYO

*Printed in Great Britain
at the University Press, Oxford
by Vivian Ridler
Printer to the University*

TO MARGARET

Acknowledgements

In writing this account of Henry Halford Vaughan, I have been fortunate in gaining access to his papers through the generosity of the late Mrs. Elizabeth Vaughan, the widow of his only surviving son William Wyamar Vaughan, and without her enthusiastic support I should not have had the temerity to attempt it. From other members of the family, in particular from Professor Quentin Bell, Sir Gyles Isham, the late Miss Emma Vaughan, Mr. Halford Vaughan, Dame Janet Vaughan, and Mr. John Vaughan, I have received invaluable help which I could not have hoped to obtain elsewhere, and my debt to them is great. My thanks are also inevitably and gratefully due to the Bodleian Library, the British Museum, Lambeth Palace Library, the Public Record Office, St. Deiniol's Library, the libraries of All Souls, Balliol, Christ Church, Magdalen, and Oriel Colleges, and the Keeper of the University Archives in Oxford. Finally, but not least, I am indebted to many private owners of documents concerning Vaughan and his times, in particular to Mrs. A. Coatalen for letters of W. F. Hook, the Marquess of Dalhousie for the diary of James Ramsay, Sir Walter Moberly for a letter by Thomas Arnold, Lord Saye and Sele for letters of Edward Twisleton, and Mrs. D. Garnett, Mrs. N. Henderson, Mrs. I. Parsons, and Mrs. R. L. M. Synge for Leslie Stephen's Mausoleum Book. Vaughan's papers have now been placed in the Bodleian Library.

E. G. W. B.

Contents

1. Parentage and Early Years

THE nineteenth century witnessed many reforms in political, administrative, and educational institutions, and from this process the universities were not immune. Oxford University was the subject of two royal commissions, and, directly or indirectly, of many Acts of Parliament. The period of reform which commenced with the Royal Commission appointed in 1850 and concluded with the Oxford Act of 1854 was in many respects the most significant because during these years the university was confronted with a choice between reform and what without unduly stretching the meaning of the word may be described as revolution, between retaining and improving its existing institutions and receiving new ones, between reforming its traditional tutorial system of education and replacing it by an intellectual oligarchy of professors.

Owing principally to the wisdom and political sagacity of Gladstone in successfully implementing a programme of radical conservative reform, which had the support of almost all shades of opinion, the nature of the challenge facing the university has been obscured. Historians have generally discriminated three main groups in the spectrum of reform: the opponents of change, the moderate reformers of the Tutors' Association, and a more radical group which gathered round Francis Jeune, the Master of Pembroke. Considerable differences divided them, but they shared a fundamental unity of purpose, and indeed without such a common ground the compromise effected by Gladstone would not have been possible.

But there was in addition a small and highly articulate group of reformers, amongst whom were many of the best men in the university, who advocated very radical solutions to the problems of university reform. Some of them were greatly influenced by the scientific and intellectual movements of the time, and proposed sweeping changes in education and learning. Some were strongly opposed to clerical influences, which had not declined with the Tractarian Movement, and some desired to establish a secular university largely freed from its dependence on the Church of England, pursuing a new kind of liberal education, and governed by professors who advanced standards of learning previously almost unknown in Oxford.

Although they dominated the Royal Commission of 1850 and had ready access to the sympathetic ear of Lord John Russell, and although in 1854 they conducted a bitter and relentless campaign to impose their ideas on the university by force through Act of Parliament, they exerted little immediate influence on events, except in one important particular which occurred fortuitously and had little to do with their programme. By their support of the professorial system and the extreme views they held on this and other questions, they incurred great hostility and engendered a mistrust of the professorial system which has still not completely disappeared from Oxford. The failure of their proposals, the enmity which was raised against them, the success of Gladstone's legislation, and the extent of the support he received from the university, have all conspired to cause this small group of radicals to drop into oblivion. Yet their ideas on education and learning and on the nature of a university were and remain worthy of consideration, and it is an irony of history that a generation later many of them were the common currency of reformers.

Had they succeeded in persuading the government and the university to accept their ideas, the history of Oxford in the last hundred years would have pursued a very different course. But they failed to persuade for many reasons. Some of their ideas were too far ahead of the times; the existing system was too deeply entrenched; they believed that it was enough that their ideas should be intellectually convincing, and compromise, which the political situation in which they found themselves demanded, was unknown to them. Perhaps above all they failed because of the religious climate in which they acted. Their antagonism to the clergy infected them with such distrust of the colleges and tutors that they proposed to introduce reforms, which were often good and reasonable in themselves, by force, and the chosen instrument through which force was to be applied was the professoriate.

One of the principal leaders of this group of radical reformers, perhaps the principal leader, was the Regius Professor of Modern History, Henry Halford Vaughan. Despite his great gifts and an original and powerful mind, his life by the yardstick of achievement was a failure, and the unbounded promise which his contemporaries discerned in him remained unfulfilled. Yet almost alone among university reformers he possessed a considered and coherent view of the nature and purpose of education and learning. It is the object of this account to restore him to the attention of posterity, to reveal the forces which moulded him, and to assess the contribution he made to the perennial debate on the great issues which occupied him.

Henry Halford Vaughan, or Halford Vaughan as he preferred to be known, was born on 27 August 1811 at 1 Montague Place near Russell Square in London. He was the second son of John Vaughan, Serjeant-at-Law and Recorder of Leicester, by his wife Augusta, daughter of the twelfth Baron St. John of Bletso. The Vaughans came originally from Devonshire, where Hugh Vaughan was steward to the Earl of Bedford in the early part of the seventeenth century.[1] His fourth son, William, studied medicine at Leyden, and became Censor of the Royal College of Physicians and eventually physician to William and Mary. In the nineteenth century, William Vaughan's parentage was not known, but the fact of his birth in the year after the marriage of Henry Vaughan, the Silurist, occasioned an obstinate family tradition that he was the son of the poet. It was a tempting legend, but one of which in the absence of positive proof Halford Vaughan always maintained a scrupulous scepticism. The tradition of medicine started by William Vaughan has been followed with distinction by many members of the family to the present day.

[1] I am indebted for this information to Sir Gyles Isham.

His son Henry entered the Church and settled at Leominster where he died in 1753, but his grandson, also named Henry, was a surgeon at Leominster where he too died in 1779, and his great-grandson James Vaughan, grandfather of the subject of this memoir, studied at Edinburgh before setting up a very lucrative practice at Leicester.

James Vaughan was a physician of some distinction and the real founder of the family fortunes. His medical skill was such that it moved William Munk to strains of lapidary lyricism. 'His doses of medicine', wrote Munk, 'are said to have been large, but they were administered with a confidence and success which afforded ample proof of his sagacity and their correctness.'[2] By his marriage to Hesther, the daughter of William Smalley, alderman of Leicester, and of his wife Elizabeth, the daughter of Sir Richard Halford, of Wistow, James Vaughan raised his family in social position and wealth. With great singleness of purpose he resolved that the best gift he could confer on his children was a good education rather than a financial inheritance, and accordingly he sent six of his sons to Rugby and then to Oxford or Cambridge. As one of them later recalled, he applied 'the annual produce of his profession in affording them the advantage of a liberal education, whereby they might be enabled to make their own fortunes, rather than to accumulate resources not to be made available for any purposes of theirs until his death'.[3] In his aim he was highly successful, for most of his sons achieved distinction in medicine, scholarship, diplomacy, or in law. Sir Henry Halford, his second son, who changed his name from Vaughan in 1809 on inheriting a substantial fortune from Lady Denbigh, widow of his mother's cousin Sir Charles Halford, was the leading medical practitioner of his day. He became a baronet in 1809 and was elected President of the Royal College of Physicians in 1820. He was physician in ordinary to George III, George IV, William IV, and Queen Victoria, and one of the doctors in attendance on George III during his long years of insanity. If the royal family was attached to Sir Henry, he for

---

[2] W. Munk, *Roll of the Royal College of Physicians* (1878), ii. 236.
[3] Quoted ibid. 237.

his part returned that attachment with interest, for when in the reign of George IV he was employed to open the coffin of Charles I he removed one of the vertebrae of that unfortunate monarch, had it suitably mounted, and thereafter circulated it with the port for the edification of his friends and guests. When Queen Victoria heard of the ignominious fate of her ancester she was displeased, and in 1874 the royal relic was hastily returned to Windsor in a brown paper parcel and reunited with its owner. Peter Vaughan, the fourth son of James Vaughan, had an equally distinguished if less spectacular career, and became Warden of Merton College, Oxford, in 1810 and Dean of Chester in 1820. His younger brother, Sir Charles Richard Vaughan, was a Fellow of All Souls and minister-plenipotentiary in Spain and the United States of America.

John Vaughan, the father of Halford, was the third son of James. When he became Serjeant-at-Law in 1799 he was believed to be the youngest ever known, and his practice was so extremely successful that at one time he was reputed to be earning £15,000 a year. He was appointed Baron of the Exchequer in 1827, was knighted in the following year, and became Justice of Common Pleas and Privy Councillor in 1834. Opinions about his professional abilities varied, and the rumour that he owed his elevation to the bench to the influence of his courtly brother Sir Henry Halford, the physician, caused it to be said that he was a judge *by prescription*. One hostile critic described him as 'celebrated for possessing not the slightest notion of law',[4] and even his American friend Charles Sumner admitted that 'he is reputed to have the smallest possible allowance of law for a judge'.[5] It was, on the other hand, generally allowed that he possessed 'strong sense and a knowledge of the practice of courts, and of the human character',[6] and 'a bold, rough and ready style of address, which made him a great favourite with juries'.[7] Whatever the truth may be, Sir John enjoyed his work and had a great capacity for it. He once wrote to his wife, 'I am supposed to have passed

---

[4] J. Arnould, *Memoir of Lord Denman* (1873), i. 58.
[5] *Memoir and Letters of Charles Sumner*, ed. E. L. Pierce (1878), ii. 28.
[6] Ibid. i. 334. [7] J. Arnould, op. cit., i. 59.

one of the most eloquent sentences of death (eloquent because natural and full of feeling) that ever was heard in a Court of Justice.'[8] The law's delays were unknown to Sir John. 'They are all astonished', he wrote, 'at my endurance of hard work. I was in court yesterday from eight o'clock in the morning until between twelve and one this morning.' His industry and expedition were remarked on even by his colleagues on the bench. Sir Nicholas Tindal, for example, wrote to him with grim humour:

I cannot but congratulate you on the celerity with which you drove the team of the Common Pleas, compared with mine. I appear to myself like a hearse driver, who carried only four bodies to their long and distant homes during the whole of my sittings at Westminster and London—two of them being four day jobs, very slow and solemn indeed. You on the contrary, mount the box with all the vigour and alacrity of the driver of an omnibus. You crack your whip, stop at the corner of the first street, down goes one passenger and in jumps another; and so, according to the newspaper, you clear half the paper of the causes that are standing idling all the day.[9]

Although Sir John lamented that 'my ermine is likely to be dyed with blood in every criminal court in which I sit throughout the circuit',[10] and although the barbarity of the law could not be laid at his door, there was perhaps a certain insensitivity in a man who once adjourned the slaughter at the Court of Common Pleas to ride fifteen miles while recovering from a broken leg to slaughter pheasants instead. In other respects he was a plain, forthright man, well endowed with common sense, not without a sense of humour, a lover of Shakespeare. His domestic life was tranquil and contented. He married twice. His first wife, Augusta, died in 1813, when her son Halford was only two years old, but the ladies of the St. John family exercised a hypnotic influence on the judge and in 1823 he married Louisa St. John, widow of the thirteenth baron, aunt by marriage of his first wife and sister-in-law of Barbara St. John, who was the wife of his brother

---

[8] Sir John Vaughan to his wife [1828].
[9] Letter to Sir John Vaughan, 4 Mar. 1839.
[10] Sir John Vaughan to his wife [1828].

Sir Henry Halford. Through his father's first marriage, Henry Halford Vaughan acquired four sisters and a brother, and through the second marriage a half-sister and two half-brothers. Despite the judge's evidently unremitting application to his marital duties, the offspring of his second litter were too removed in age to provide suitable companions for Halford Vaughan, and he spent a lonely childhood, his mother dead and his father, of whom he was very fond, frequently absent. He was thrown much into the society of his sisters Barbara and Augusta, the former of whom subsequently married her cousin, Sir Henry Halford, the second baronet, but the family circle was dominated by his successful and ambitious uncles.

2. Rugby

IN 1822, at the age of eleven, Vaughan was sent to Rugby. He entered School House, and later recalled that for his last two or three years he occupied a study 'on the top passage next but one to the fireplace, looking into the school close'.[1] Rugby represented a family tradition a generation old, for not only his father but no fewer than five of his uncles had attended the school, among them Peter Vaughan, who had been an assistant master until his election as Warden of Merton, and Sir Henry Halford, who was to become a trustee in 1825. The choice of Rugby did not depend on sentiment or local connection alone, for during the century prior to Arnold's appointment the school had steadily increased in reputation, and in 1818 stood second in size among public schools. When Vaughan went to Rugby the headmaster was John Wooll, a good scholar and teacher and an athletic disciplinarian who once flogged an entire class of thirty-eight boys in the space of a quarter of an hour. From Wooll he received a sound education in classical learning. 'I never was so hard worked in my life as I am now', he wrote to his father, 'and from a quarter after seven till ten o'clock which is bedtime I literally shall hardly stir off my chair. I have just shewn in a theme of forty lines in length, and have got a copy of verses to do to-night as well as learn my lessons for tomorrow, and if this is not enough I do not know what is.'

Vaughan held Wooll in high esteem, and felt that his achievements had been unjustly overshadowed by the fame and influence of Arnold. 'Do you', he asked a witness before the Public Schools Commission in 1864, 'share my impression that as to the state of the school before the time of Dr. Wooll's leaving some

---

[1] Vaughan to W. W. Vaughan, 15 Feb. 1879.

misapprehension has prevailed?'² Having at his own request been allowed by his father to remain at Rugby for a further year after Arnold's appointment in 1828 he was in a position to compare the two men. He believed that Arnold's contribution to the academic reputation of Rugby, and, perhaps more important, his reform of the moral character of the school were commonly overestimated. In 1855 he described his lasting impressions of Wooll and Arnold to the wife of his friend Edward Twisleton.

He seems [she wrote] to have felt very strongly the influence of his [Arnold's] earnest, excellent character, and the change from the routine and formality of the former master to the vital spirit Dr. Arnold waked up; but he thinks he was not a first-rate scholar, though very frank about his own deficiencies, so that they never did him any harm with the boys; and as to his efforts where we should think them most essential, Mr. Vaughan merely says that he does not see that Arnold's system has produced finer characters than that which went before.³

Writing in 1881 to Lord Selborne, his contemporary at Rugby, he remarked, 'Wooll was a gentleman and treated the boys as gentlemen to a greater degree than might be supposed by one perusing Stanley's life of Arnold',⁴ and in a further letter discussing the changes in the curriculum introduced by Arnold he noted that 'Arnold introduced the "vulgus" as you describe it when he first came to Rugby. At *that* time he had but little feeling otherwise for Latin poetry. He once told me himself at dinner . . . that he could not see anything to admire in the classical verses of Virgil, Ovid and others . . . he put an end to all learning by heart as *childish*. This was his word. . . . Yet I believe that he changed his opinion.'⁵ In 1853 Richard Congreve, the English Positivist and a close friend of Vaughan's Oxford years, was present with Vaughan, Goldwin Smith, and others at a dinner when the subject of Arnold came up.

They all spoke of Arnold as morally great [he wrote], [but] differed as to his intellectual [powers] very widely. His remarkable influence they seemed to trace in very great measure to this, that he was only

---

² *Report of the Public Schools Commission* (1864), iv (Evidence, pt. 2), 274.
³ *Letters of the Hon. Mrs. Edward Twisleton* (1925), 294.
⁴ Lambeth Palace Library MS. 1867, f. 233ᵛ.   ⁵ Ibid., MS. 1868, f. 11.

fresh, not new—that in the positions he took up he was but a slight way in advance, and therefore easily appreciable by his contemporaries who were near him, whereas a man really in advance of his time is shut up, cannot work on them, except in isolated cases . . . I do not blame him, said Vaughan, but I think in discussion if beaten, and he did not get or take time to reflect, it was his tendency to fall back on the solution that it was a moral fault in his opponents not seeing the conclusions he saw.[6]

Matthew Arnold once told Liddell that his father considered Vaughan the most able boy he had had under him at Rugby.[7] His school career was crowded with distinction, and almost fifty years later his accomplishments remained in the memory of his friend, T. L. Bloxam, who wrote to him in 1870 'It seems only yesterday since you were reciting Achmet in Barbarossa at the school speeches, and reciting your Prize Poem of Christ healing the sick in the Temple.'[8] In 1829 Vaughan's first historical work was published, a prize essay entitled *Of the alleged decline of literature between the first and sixth centuries and the principal causes to which it may be attributed*. It was a precocious and well-written work, and in its analysis of the injurious consequences which followed the development of a 'narrow circle of theological discussion' among early Christians, not without interest for Vaughan's subsequent intellectual development. 'It was', he wrote, 'impossible that a refined and liberal taste could be united to a strong sectarian spirit.' A few months later Vaughan left Rugby with an exhibition of £60 a year for seven years.

On his departure, Arnold wrote to Baron Vaughan in the following terms:

As I expect to leave home on the very first day of the vacation, I must anticipate a little the period of your son's leaving Rugby to express to you my great regret at losing him, and to assure you that my opinion of him is in no respect lessened during the last half year, but increased as far as regards his advancement in knowledge, particularly during the last two or three months. I think in many respects

---

[6] Bodleian Library MS. Eng. lett. c. 181, f. 60.

[7] MS. recollections of Vaughan by H. G. Liddell in Christ Church.

[8] Letter 23 Sept. 1870. The verses were occasioned by Benjamin West's picture similarly entitled.

it will be a good thing for him to leave school as he has here no competitor, nor any who approaches him in brilliant talent, and this circumstance makes him less aware of his actual deficiencies in acquired knowledge, which are remarkable when we consider his great natural talents and fondness for reading. But I think you will agree with me that his knowledge of general literature, of history, geography, and matters of common life and conversation is not such as it might be. And this when he is removed to the university he will soon find, and then labour, I think, to remedy. What I shall urge upon him, before I part with him, is to desire improvement more for its own sake, and with less reference to external stimulants, such as Classes, prizes etc. To a mind so vigorous as his, its exercise is naturally delightful in itself, and he would soon find it so, but the stimulants of prizes etc., like other stimulants, is apt to be followed by a distaste for ordinary and healthful incitement, and this is a danger which I wish him to guard against.[9]

[9] T. Arnold to Sir John Vaughan, 29 June 1829.

3. Christ Church

VAUGHAN spent the summer of 1829 travelling on the continent, mainly in Switzerland where he took lodgings in Lausanne, and in the autumn he matriculated at Oxford as a commoner of Christ Church. The college recruited its members mainly from Westminster, Eton, and Harrow, and had little connection then or subsequently with Rugby, though Vaughan's uncle Sir Henry Halford had been an undergraduate there. The choice of the richest, grandest, and most aristocratic college in the university may have been due to Sir Henry, or it may have reflected Sir John's rising position in society, or since Vaughan was intended by his father for the law it may have been influenced by the large number of Studentships at Christ Church tenable by men studying the law in London after taking their degrees. Whatever the reason, the choice of Christ Church seems to have left its mark on Vaughan's subsequent contribution to university reform at Oxford in two ways. It was the probable source of some of his ideas, and it may well have been the reason why of all the reformers of the 1850s he was less interested in the reform of the colleges than in the reform of the university.

In 1829 Christ Church was still at the peak of a long period of sustained brilliance and achievement, and Vaughan's contemporaries included a future prime minister, Gladstone, and two governor-generals of India, Charles Canning and James Ramsay. It had never sufffered from the intellectual inertia described by Gibbon, and in the early nineteenth century had taken a leading part in the reform of the examination system, which it then proceeded to dominate for several decades. Many of the abuses common in other colleges were unknown at Christ Church. It had no obsolete statutes because it had no statutes at all. Its 101 Studentships were not filled by open competition, but neither were they closed to founder's kin or to particular localities. Except for those statutorily elected from Westminster, the Students were nominated by the Dean and Canons, frequently on the recommendation of the Censors, from the whole body of the undergraduates of the college (except the servitors), and this was always large enough to supply a wide choice of suitable candidates. From the manner of their election these Students were known as Canoneers.

In its tutorial system, Christ Church was particularly fortunate. Whereas many colleges had difficulty in finding one or two tutors, Christ Church invariably had five or six, and until Gaisford became Dean the number was often increased by resident B.A.s. There were also readers in Divinity, Rhetoric, Logic, Greek Philology, and eventually a mathematical lectureship created by Gaisford. With so many tutors, the large classes undifferentiated by ability, which were common elsewhere, were rare at Christ Church, except in elementary mathematics and logic where demonstration was required. In 1831, for example, Charles Wordsworth had four pupils, and when H. G. Liddell, the lexicographer and future Dean, was appointed to a tutorship he had only a dozen.[1] In most colleges a single tutor was often obliged to teach every subject in the curriculum, but at Christ Church not only were there enough tutors to allow some division of labour, but, according to Pusey, 'the pupils of one Tutor might attend the lectures of any other in any branch in which he was understood to excel.'[2]

Except in logic and its ancillary subjects, such as mathematics, a tutorial, or lecture as it was called, usually consisted of the reading and construing of Greek and Latin authors. The frequency with which an undergraduate saw his tutor varied, but the experience of W. F. Hook, who matriculated in 1817, was not uncommon. He relates that in his first term he saw his tutor only twice, 'which is generally as often as he sends for a man in one

[1] Lambeth Palace Library MS. 1824, f. 50ᵛ. See also Sir Algernon West's *Recollections* (1899), for the position a few years later.

[2] *Report and evidence . . . presented to the Board of Heads of Houses and Proctors* (1853), Evidence, 79.

term', but in his second year he read Thucydides three hours a week with three other undergraduates, Aeschylus for one hour, and Aristotle for a further three hours with another tutor.[3] Only a limited number of authors could be studied in the time available for tutorials, and the more ambitious students, particularly those seeking honours, were expected to read more widely without tutorial supervision. Hook states that 'in classical reading we are left almost entirely . . . to ourselves, for you merely read one book with your tutor'.[4] When he asked his tutor for advice about his reading, he was told that he should read whatever he liked. Although the system encouraged the better student to read more extensively than has perhaps been possible at any time subsequently, its shortcomings were correctly described by Charles Wordsworth when he said that it did not communicate stores of knowledge or create an interest in the subjects of study, but ensured that everyone did a minimum amount of work. In consequence, tutorials were often no more than 'schoolboys' lessons', and unprofitable to the better students, particularly to those who came well prepared from school.[5]

At the end of each term at Christ Church the ordeal of Collections took place. The holding of Collections in the college may be traced with certainty to the latter part of the seventeenth century, and the vigour and increasing regularity with which they were conducted from the time of Dean Markham in the following century accounts as much as any single factor for the freedom of Christ Church from the intellectual torpor of the time. The examination was held before the Dean and Censors, and the Collection Books record not only the books presented but the comments, often pungent and occasionally scabrous, of the examiners. In his old age, Ruskin remembered with feelings of dread his own experience, and recalled Gaisford, 'scornful at once, and vindictive, thunderous always, more sullen and threatening as the day went on'.[6]

---

[3] W. F. Hook to his father. Letter in the possession of Mrs. A. Coatalen.
[4] Ibid.
[5] C. Wordsworth, *Annals of My Early Life* (1891), 39.
[6] *Praeterita*, ed. E. T. Cook and A. Wedderburn (1908), 193.

The comparatively high academic standards at Christ Church tended to strengthen the predominance of the college at the expense of the university. To Dean Gaisford the college examinations were more important than the university examinations, and he went so far as actively to discourage men from seeking university honours. But during his tenure of the Deanery an important change took place in the public examinations. Originally they were oral in character as were those held in colleges. Keble, who had been an examiner, told Hook that 'the greatest stress is laid upon the manner in which a man construes, and not upon his sciences [i.e. Aristotle's *Ethics* and *Rhetoric*]'.[7] In 1830, owing principally to an increase in the number of candidates, the examinations began to be conducted on paper, and candidates for honours were separated from those seeking only a pass degree. Simultaneously the examinations changed in content as the importance of philosophy and composition, which were written exercises, increased, and construing, which was oral, diminished. The effect of these changes was gradually to raise the academic standard of the university. Whereas the examination statutes of 1800 and 1807 did not so much impose a standard of attainment as recognize one which already existed in the better colleges, the statute of 1830 was in its results the imposition by the university of a new standard on the colleges. Perhaps without fully realizing the consequences, the university possessed in its power to control the public examinations a potent instrument for altering the traditional relationship between the colleges and the university.

This was the educational system which awaited Vaughan on his arrival at Christ Church. The record of his Collections shows that he read Herodotus, Thucydides, Livy, Polybius, Homer, Virgil, a good deal of Cicero, Xenophon, some Plato, and the plays of Euripides, Aeschylus, Sophocles, and Terence, and the inevitable Euclid and Aristotle. He also read a course of logic and theology, which included Butler's *Analogy of Religion*. The leading schools, such as Rugby, sent their pupils well prepared to the university, and most of the books which Vaughan presented at Collections

[7] Letter in the possession of Mrs. A. Coatalen.

had been read by him at school. A similar fate befel Clough who came up to Oxford, also from Rugby, in 1836. In the sixth form, he records, he had read most of Thucydides and Herodotus, some parts at least three times, five plays of Sophocles, four of Aeschylus (several of them two or three times), four or five of Euripides, and parts of Aristophanes. He had also read most of the *Odyssey*, about a third of the *Iliad*, most of Virgil and all of Horace, one or two dialogues of Plato, a lot of Livy and Tacitus, the *Rhetoric* and two or three books of the *Ethics* of Aristotle.[8] Gladstone, for whom the proper use of time was an obsession, built on the similar foundation laid at Eton and read widely. Whether Vaughan, faced by equal familiarity with the curriculum, did likewise, or sought to improve the knowledge of literature, history, and geography in which Arnold had found him deficient, is less certain, but there are indications that he was bored by the system rather than stimulated by its opportunities, and in 1832 his friend and contemporary James Ramsay wrote in his diary, 'Vaughan came into my room in the evening and made me quite idle for two hours. He is about the most idle fellow in Christendom himself and does his best to make others equal him.'[9]

In 1831 Vaughan successfully competed for a Fell Exhibition, which was worth £40 a year and was not infrequently the prelude to a Studentship.[10] In his case, however, a Studentship did not follow. The idea that places on the foundation of a college ought to be awarded for intellectual ability as a result of competition was only gradually accepted at Oxford in the nineteenth century. At Christ Church the traditional view that they afforded assistance to poor scholars continued well into the century, and Studentships

[8] A. H. Clough, *Prose Remains* (1888), 399–402.

[9] Unpublished diary in the possession of the Marquess of Dalhousie.

[10] Gladstone wrote to Helen Gladstone on 2 Nov. 1829 after winning a Fell Exhibition, 'We had an examination on Thursday, Friday and Saturday last, much the same as the Scholarship Examinations in its nature but not so difficult, and the competition of course not nearly so extended. We had, I think, thirteen candidates altogether, and five exhibitions were disposed of. All these thirteen however were chosen from among the Christ Church commoners and servitors, and not even the whole of those—only from those of a certain standing being qualified to go in for the examination. So as the choice is small the honour is very small also.' Hawarden Letters, St. Deiniol's Library.

were regarded rather as aids to education than as prizes. In 1854
the Dean and Chapter publicly disclaimed any intention of
awarding them solely for what they contemptuously dismissed
as 'mere intellectual merit'.[11] With a scholarship from Rugby
and a Fell Exhibition, Vaughan could hardly be said to stand
in financial need. Although a Studentship did not necessarily
imply any considerable academic distinction and did not confer
the power in the government of the college which Fellowships
enjoyed elsewhere, it had advantages not lightly to be disregarded.
Tutors were chosen from the Students, for those entering the
law it provided support and security, and for those entering
the Church it offered a choice of the ninety odd livings in the
patronage of Christ Church.

Although Vaughan's failure to obtain a Studentship does not
thus reflect adversely on his abilities, it requires explanation. Since
he contemplated a career in the Law or the Church, the advantages
of a Studentship were considerable, while for its part the college
needed to appoint the best of its undergraduates if only to secure
able tutors, and from this point of view Vaughan was a good
candidate. The award of Studentships to Gladstone and to other
wealthy undergraduates suggests that his comparative affluence
was not the only reason for his being passed over. It was, however,
an advantage of the Christ Church system of election that an
undergraduate was not normally elected to a Canoneer Studentship until he had been resident for a considerable period of time,
often a year or more, during which his tutors were able to form
a reasonable estimate of his capacity. It is possible that by the
time Vaughan sat for the Fell, the Censors had formed a not
entirely favourable estimate of his powers of application and of
his general conduct. 'I quite agree with Vaughan', Ramsay wrote
only a month after the examination, 'that one of the punishments
of a Censor in Purgatory must be the eternal tickling and smother-
ing of the slips of impositions—those Sibylline leaves which so
much abound in his [Vaughan's] rooms.'[12] He was inclined to
a youthful arrogance which cannot have endeared him to his

11 *The Dean and Chapter of Christ Church, Oxford, to Lord Palmerston*, 1854.
12 Diary.

elders. Ramsay once complained that his serene dogmatism extended to Aristotle, and that 'with his brazen voice and still more brazen face [he] lays down the law on every syllable'.[13] In argument he was disposed to silence rather than to convince. Towards the end of his life he referred in a letter to his son to this irritating characteristic and infallible method of provoking resentment. 'It is', he wrote with feeling, 'a good rule, although very far from one which I have followed always in life myself, not to humiliate others by proving your superiority to others . . . I have *often and often* regretted that my father never gave me warning and advice in such matters.'[14] Amongst those he wittingly or unwittingly offended was Dean Gaisford, and whatever the cause the effect was of a lasting nature. When Vaughan was a candidate for the chair of moral philosophy in 1846, the recollection of ancient injury stirred the Dean, who was one of the electors, to violent and unseemly wrath.[15]

Vaughan's intellectual exuberance found a more congenial outlet in the social life of Christ Church. Although he once told his son that he was not prone to join societies, during his undergraduate years he belonged to many such bodies. Having failed to gain a Studentship, which would have admitted him to the Senior Common Room, he became a founder member of the first Junior Common Room at Christ Church. It was established in 1832 by Charles Wordsworth in the house of a tailor named Tribe situated opposite Christ Church, and its members, of whom there were ten, predictably called themselves The Ten Tribes. All of them, said Wordsworth, had some claim to be reading men.[16] Besides Vaughan himself, they included Benjamin Harrison, later Archdeacon of Maidstone; Herbert Kynaston, later High Master of St. Paul's; Walter Hamilton, who was to become Bishop of Salisbury; Henry Jeffreys, a future Honorary Canon of Canterbury; Henry Denison, subsequently a Fellow of All Souls; James Hope, better known as Hope-Scott, who was

---

[13] Diary.

[14] Vaughan to W. W. Vaughan, 26 Feb. 1882.

[15] See p. 64.

[16] C. Wordsworth, *Annals of My Early Life* (1891), 121.

to join the Church of Rome; Sir Francis Doyle, subsequently Professor of Poetry, and H. G. Liddell, the future Dean. Very different in character was the famous Essay Society founded by Gladstone, which held its first meeting on the evening of Saturday, 31 October 1829.

Our new Society [Gladstone wrote], nameless as yet, held its first regular meeting on Saturday last, when the first Essay was read 'On the union of moral and intellectual powers'. There was a little disposition to quarrel, but confined to one individual. The essay was a very good one, on sound principles and displaying great research and likewise much beauty of style. Anstice, who got the Newdigate Prize last year, was its author. Our numbers were then enlarged, or rather our limiting number was extended to sixteen, rather against my will, for I think *that* a number rather unwieldy to meet in a private room. It seems likely to become the fashion to give tea and coffee to the members after the business is over. We elected one member more upon the spot, and there are I believe two more who wish to get in.[17]

With its second and third meetings, the society began to show signs of its political tendencies with debates on natural and political freedom, and on the degree of change required in the system of education.[18] Vaughan became an early member of the society, though he was not one of the original twelve.[19]

Vaughan was never on a footing of close intimacy with Gladstone, but in 1831, when Gladstone was busily canvassing opinion in the university against reform, he was thrown much into his company. In the summer term of that year Gladstone drew up a petition with the help of Henry Denison and another Christ Church undergraduate named Charles Thornton, and in his diary for 9 June he noted that most of the previous night had been spent arguing about it with Vaughan.[20] Vaughan, however, was not at this time nor subsequently very politically inclined. He was elected to the recently formed Oxford Union

---

[17] Hawarden Letters. W. E. Gladstone to Helen Gladstone, 2 Nov. 1829.

[18] Ibid. The same to the same, 19 Nov. 1829.

[19] *Memoir of Sir Thomas Acland*, ed. A. H. D. Acland (1902), 23.

[20] *The Gladstone Diaries*, ed. M. R. D. Foot (1968), i. 363. The petition is printed in the Commons' *Votes and Proceedings*, 1831, xi. appendix 51.

on 17 June 1830, and to the committee on 3 November in the
following year, but the two debates in which he is known to
have spoken give little clue to his political opinions. On 10
February 1831, he spoke against the motion, which was defeated
by 35 votes to 81, 'That the extent to which the Liberty of the
Press is now carried is injurious to the peace and welfare of
Society'. On the following 20 October, Arthur Acland of Christ
Church proposed the motion 'That to punish sheep stealing with
death is a greater crime than to steal sheep', and Robert Lowe,
later Viscount Sherbrooke, proposed the amendment 'That to
punish sheep stealing with death is inexpedient'. Both the original
motion and the amendment were opposed by Vaughan and
negatived without a division.

At about this period in his life, Vaughan developed an absorbing
interest in natural science, but he decided on entering Christ
Church not to read for the School of Mathematics and Physics,
and his father, acquiescing in his wish to read only for classical
honours, agreed that he should 'forego the more perilous enterprise of a double first that you might not have to complain of too
heavy a load'.[21] In Easter Term 1833 he was accordingly placed
in the First Class in the School of Literae Humaniores. Of thirteen
Firsts, five, including Liddell, Robert Scott, and C. J. Canning, in
addition to Vaughan, came from Christ Church. In a letter to
his uncle Sir Charles Vaughan, he described the examination,
and his account shows the effect of the recent statute.

The matter of examination consists of four subjects, Scholarship,
History, Theology, and the Moral Sciences. The time usually occupied
in the paper work is about six days. All the candidates are locked up
in a very large room. They have separate tables and as much ink and
paper as they choose to call for.

They are tried in the scholarship department by having hard passages
from the most valuable Greek and Latin authors placed before them
which they are required to translate into English and to accompany
with notes explanatory of peculiarities in construction and of such
allusions to local customs as may occur. Passages are also selected from
the best English writers which they are required to turn into Latin and

[21] Sir John Vaughan to Vaughan, n.d.

Greek . . . and this branch of the examination is finished by giving a set of questions on the nicest and most critical points in the Greek language, calling for the opinions of the most approved critics upon the subject. The examination in history is conducted chiefly by questions of all sorts, involving not only a knowledge of facts but an acquaintance with the constitution of each nation, her relation to those around her, her commercial and military resources, her maxims of policy with the causes of her grandeur and decay. A subject is generally given also for an essay upon some point in history.

The third and perhaps one of the most important divisions of the examination is that of the moral sciences, embracing ethics, rhetoric and logic. Our text book upon these subjects is usually Aristotle, an accurate acquaintance with whose treatises is quite indispensable. Nor indeed is a man likely to acquit himself very well in this branch unless he has given considerable time to the study of English writers upon the same subject, Locke, Butler, Cudworth, and a host of dry Scotch metaphysicians. This is, I think, more trying than any other subject. It usually displays the most strong headed men and proves a stumbling block to the weaker. The trial is conducted by questions and an essay as in the historical department. After the paper work there is a day of viva voce examination for each candidate. He has four examiners who take him severally in the three branches above mentioned which are pursued in the viva voce examination in order to try the candidate in points where his papers may have betrayed any weakness, or where he may not have sufficiently explained himself. The Divinity is conducted viva voce only. The candidate is expected to know the Articles of our Church, to be able to support them by quotation from Scripture. He is also examined upon the history of the Bible.[22]

How far Vaughan's ideas on university reform were influenced by his experiences at Christ Church must be conjectural, but it is

[22] Vaughan to Sir C. R. Vaughan, 12 Nov. 1833, All Souls College. The only surviving paper for this examination is in logic, but in 1845 Vaughan published a correspondence with J. T. H. Peter concerning the examination from which it appears that there were questions on the rapid growth of the arts in Athens, on the power of the Roman senate, and a compulsory paper of dates. Peter, who became a Fellow of Magdalen, and as Junior Proctor earned a reputation for valour by pursuing an errant undergraduate of Christ Church into the college Hall and the presence of the irascible Gaisford himself, was, according to Provost Hawkins, 'generally considered a semi-maniac' (H. G. Liddell to Vaughan, 23 Oct. 1845).

possible to note parallels between what he found in the college and what he advocated twenty years later. There is, for example, a resemblance between his support of the professoriate and the state of the professoriate at Christ Church, which, in its chairs of Divinity, Hebrew, and Greek, and its readership in Anatomy, possessed more professorships than any other college in the university. His belief in the endowment of chairs with Fellowships is paralleled at Christ Church by the example of Gaisford, who held a Studentship with the professorship of Greek for twenty years before receiving a canonry, and his advocacy of the appointment of professors by the Crown by the system which prevailed in the college. His belief in the government of the university by an oligarchy of professors may have been influenced by the practice at Christ Church, where the governing body was appointed by the Crown and almost half its members were professors. Finally, the comparative excellence of the tutorial system at Christ Church may have accounted in part for his interest in university rather than in college reform.

4. Oriel

VAUGHAN was undecided whether to make a career in the law or the Church, but while this doubt remained unresolved he began the study of law in his father's chambers in Serjeant's Inn towards the end of 1833. A legal education then demanded a year or more in the chambers of a conveyancer followed by a similar period with a draftsman for those called to the Chancery Bar or a year or perhaps two with a special pleader for those intending to practise Common Law. Vaughan entered the chambers of Richard Preston, who had the reputation of being one of the best conveyancers in England, but the experience was not a happy one. 'Preston used to lay hold of me on my first appearance in the morning', he wrote to Roundell Palmer, 'and made me wear away my finger-ends in writing opinions, which he dictated so fast that my mind never entertained a single proposition as it went down to the paper; and he could not bear to be stopped by any questions whatever. After about a week of this, I put off going until 12 o'clock and after about five weeks ceased to repair there at all.'[1] The longer he studied law the clearer it became that what interested him was the philosophy rather than the practice of law. In a facetious but perceptive letter, Peter Payne, an Oxford friend, imagined Sir John Vaughan asking his clerk 'Where is Mr. Halford?' and answering his own question 'in a half sarcastic, half-despairing tone' with the words 'gone to learn the law *his own* way'. Meanwhile, Payne added, Vaughan himself was 'pacing round the Court House, or sitting at home, delving in cogitation to the root of some all *comprehensive principle of universal law*'.[2] A clue to the way his mind was

[1] Vaughan to R. Palmer, 13 Nov. 1835. Lambeth Palace Library MS. 1861, f. 14ᵛ. Quoted in R. Palmer, *Memorials, Family and Personal* 1889, i. 124.

[2] P. S. H. Payne to Vaughan, 27 Mar. 1838.

moving at this time is provided by a paper he wrote entitled 'Thoughts on Law'. The thoughts are not very profound but are of some interest as evidence of the influence of utilitarianism on him. Injustice, he says, is the infliction of 'gratuitous pain', by which he understands pain which 'the human mind generally' is not prepared for. Pain inflicted on those whose minds are prepared for it may be evil but it is not injustice. Law therefore is a body of rules 'which assigns good and evil according to general anticipation', and the basis of these rules consists in the universality of certain feelings and opinions. When the facts are so complicated that the mind is unable to recognize the principles behind them, they are clarified by 'the ordinary process of association, viz., by which the *mind* travels from one object to those which resemble it', and out of this process new rules develop.

Vaughan's search for a philosophy of law which would elucidate the nature of good and evil strengthened his growing preoccupation with moral philosophy and increased his hesitation in choosing between a career in the law or the Church. In order to think things over, he went to reside in Oxford in August 1834, and during this time decided to stand for a Fellowship at Merton, where one of his uncles, Peter Vaughan, had been Warden, and another, Sir Charles Vaughan, an undergraduate. The value of such family connections was demonstrated in the following January when Sir Charles Vaughan successfully canvassed the vote of the senior Fellow, T. E. Capel, who had been made a Fellow in 1793 when he himself entered the college. Liddell was enraptured at the thought of Vaughan's permanent return to Oxford, and urged him to employ his uncle's interest to the full. 'All canvassing from him would have weight', he wrote, 'and be so managed as to secure you from all dangers of overdoing the matter.'[3] Liddell himself was not inactive and approached W. K. Hamilton, who had been elected a Fellow from Christ Church in 1832, and on his advice sent the following note on how best to solicit the Fellows:

Mr. Griffith. Lord A. Hill or any of that family.
Whish is a *Reading* (town) man—not very accessible.

[3] H. G. Liddell to Vaughan, 29 Mar. 1835.

Tyndall [Sub Warden]. A Bristol man. Per Messrs Miles (father and son) M.P.s for Bristol and W. Somerset [E. Somerset].

Ricketts [Dean]. Ld. St. Vincent.

Wortley. Pupil of Saunders [of Christ Church] son of Ld. Wharncliffe.

Calvert. Pupil of Saunders. Sir H. Verney.[4]

In 1835 there were two vacancies, and one of the Fellows, J. R. Hope, was about to take Orders, so Liddell thought, which would improve Vaughan's chances because it would be less important for the college to elect 'clerici'. The judge was not sanguine of success, but before the matter could be put to the test Vaughan had decided to try for a Fellowship at Oriel.

The Fellowships at Oriel and Balliol were the most coveted academic distinctions in Oxford. Under Eveleigh and his successor Copleston the Oriel Fellowships had been opened to competition by the whole university, and in 1821 the last restriction on them was removed.[5] The result was a sustained series of brilliant elections—Keble and Whately in 1811, Arnold in 1815, Newman in 1822, Hurrell Froude and Robert Wilberforce in 1826. The Fellowship examination was always held in Easter week and lasted four days. The written papers, of which the most important were the translation of English into Latin prose and the English essay, were followed by two oral examinations before the Provost and assembled Fellows in which candidates were required to translate Greek and Latin texts. The examination was not primarily a test of scholarship, and sought, as Mark Pattison put it, to ascertain not what a man had read but what he was like, and above all to discover originality.[6]

Within a few years of the election of Edward Hawkins as Provost in 1828, Oriel was split by internal dissension. In 1831 there occurred the famous quarrel between Hawkins and the three tutors, Newman, Hurrell Froude, and Wilberforce. The tutors proposed to introduce new books into the curriculum and to reorganize the course of instruction for the benefit of the better undergraduates. This apparently innocuous scheme was bitterly opposed by the Provost because, according to Tom

[4] H. G. Liddell to Vaughan, 29 Jan. 1835.
[5] D. W. Rannie, *Oriel College* (1900), 185. [6] M. Pattison, *Memoirs* (1885), 77.

Mozley, it would have taken control of tuition out of his hands and the introduction of new books would have prevented him from taking Collections. Coming so close on the heels of the university examination statute of 1830, the tutors' proposals were evidently designed to meet the higher academic standards it demanded, but the real cause of the dispute lay in Newman's belief in the pastoral nature of the relationship between tutor and pupil, which, so Pattison believed, would have turned the college into 'a mere priestly seminary'.[7]

Hawkins eventually took the drastic step of dismissing the three Fellows from their tutorships, though their Fellowships were beyond his reach. The dispute occurred before the Tractarian Movement had really got under way, but once this had taken place a new and more bitter element of partisanship appeared with prejudicial effect on elections to Fellowships. 'I hear it reported', wrote Whately in 1836, 'that inferior men are brought forward and sometimes with success as candidates at Oriel on the strength of party-cabal.'[8] Pattison, himself an unsuccessful candidate, was even more forthright. 'The elections to fellowships', he wrote, 'for the ten years, from about 1830, were struggles between Newman endeavouring to fill the college with men likely to carry out his ideas and the Provost endeavouring, upon no principle, merely to resist Newman's lead. Newman did not lose sight of the old Oriel principle of electing for promise rather than for performance; only, instead of looking for promise of originality, he now looked for promise of congeniality.'[9]

Vaughan's decision to stand for Oriel was welcomed, though for different reasons, by the Provost and by the Newmanites. Both scented an ally. His younger sister Hesther had married Francis Hawkins, the Provost's brother, and a cordial friendship existed between the two families. Vaughan's uncle, Sir Henry Halford, had obtained for Francis Hawkins the position of Physician to the Royal Household and also the Professorship of Medicine at King's College, London.[10] The Provost, whose

---

[7] M. Pattison, *Memoirs* (1885), 87.

[8] Oriel Letters, no. 216.   [9] M. Pattison, op. cit., 99.

[10] Mrs. Amelia Hughes to Sir C. R. Vaughan, 26 July 1830. All Souls College.

prevailing characteristic, according to his brother, was affection for his family,[11] was in turn instrumental in securing Sir Henry's appointment as a trustee of Rugby. Newman had different reasons for approving of his candidature. 'I suppose we shall have a good election', he wrote to Froude. 'Perhaps Vaughan of Ch.Ch. will stand; a clever man, a friend of Denison, a connexion of the Provost's . . . Vaughan is going to the law, yet last Long Vacation, for love of Oxford, took up his abode here, and attended daily service at St. Mary's. Rogers says that he is *his own forming*.'[12]

By all accounts, Vaughan's election was a brilliant occasion. His legal studies and his indecision whether to stand for Merton or Oriel had prevented him from much preparation, and in view of the nature of the examination this was probably to his advantage. It was said that he read nothing in the vacation before he stood except Bacon's *Advancement of Learning*.[13] Liddell remembered a remarkable incident, which, but for its circumstantial detail, recalls Dean Church's account of the election of James Mozley.[14]

When [he wrote] he stood for the Oriel Fellowship, he wrote only a few lines on the subject given for the Essay; and so discontented was he with what he had done that he threw them down and left the room. He told me that he [had] given up all hope of success. But Frederic Rogers, afterwards Lord Blachford, one of the examining Fellows, picked up the despised paper and brought it before his brother examiners. They were so struck by the vigour and thought displayed in the little that was done that taken (I suppose) with his other work, they recommended him for election. The Essay, however, was understood to be the chief thing that determined an Oriel election.[15]

Far from settling the question whether he should enter the Church or the law, the Oriel Fellowship postponed the time of decision. It was obligatory for all but three of the Fellows to take Holy Orders when they were of six years standing from their

[11] J. Burgon, *Twelve Good Lives* (1888), i. 438.
[12] *Letters and Correspondence of J. H. Newman*, ed. A. Mozley (1891), ii. 74.
[13] M. Pattison, op. cit., 159.
[14] H. P. Liddon, *Life of E. B. Pusey*, 1893, i. 67.
[15] H. G. Liddell's recollections of Vaughan.

Regency. None of the three lay Fellowships was vacant in 1835, and Vaughan stood for and was awarded a clerical Fellowship. He could thus either take Orders when the statutory time arrived, or he might transfer to a lay Fellowship if the opportunity offered in the meantime. In view of the course events were to take, it is worthy of note that the implication of his candidature was made known to him in a letter which the Provost wrote to Francis Hawkins, who sent it to Vaughan.

Pray tell Halford Vaughan [he wrote] that to me personally it will be a great satisfaction to have him a Fellow of Oriel. I did not know till I received your letter that he thought of standing, but I find that it was on his account Denison had consulted me about his being already a student of the law. He fully understands, therefore, I believe, that this is no technical objection, though it may very possibly constitute an objection to him such as I should imagine would be sure to tell against him in anything like a caeteris paribus case. But it is impossible to say beforehand how far such objections may be felt by the electors on any particular occasion. He knows of course that it is not the mere fact of the study of the law which is any objection but the circumstance that we have at present rather more than our complement of lawyers. We can have *two* law Fellows and *one* physician, or during the time that we have no medical Fellow (we have none now) one more lawyer instead. We have at this time three lawyers so that we are quite full. But no Fellow is obliged to take Orders until he is of six years standing from his *Regency*.[16]

It was after the election that Vaughan accompanied by Liddell paid his first visit to Germany. He went to Heidelberg, and in view of the charges subsequently levelled against him of seeking to Germanize Oxford, it is of interest that he went, according to Liddell to learn the language rather than to study the organization of the university. He had a poor knowledge of spoken German, but read the language fluently,[17] and his library contained a number of historical works in German. He admired German scholarship, but never possessed much knowledge of German universities, and when in 1854 he crossed swords with Pusey

---

[16] E. Hawkins to F. Hawkins, 19 Feb. 1835.
[17] H. G. Liddell's recollections of Vaughan.

on the professorial question he needed to call on the knowledge of Stanley and Bunsen. A second visit to Germany also with Liddell was planned, and probably executed, in 1841, but its object was to travel down the Rhine admiring the beauties of nature and to visit Munich to see 'the new Art of Germany',[18] rather than to visit the universities.

Returning to Oxford, Vaughan won the Chancellor's English Essay Prize in 1836 for an essay on 'The effects of a national taste for general and diffusive reading'. It was an accomplished piece of writing, and half a century later the author of the obituary notice of Vaughan which appeared in the *Oxford Review* described it as 'one of the few prize compositions which have succeeded in arresting something more than an ephemeral notice, owing to the unsparing thoroughness and profundity of its treatment'.[19] When Hurrell Froude's unsuccessful essay for the prize was published in 1838,[20] Mark Pattison wrote:

Vaughan's is a much better Essay, both intrinsically and πρός τι. It is not so confined as Froude's to the inculcation of one particular theory, but takes a comprehensive view, passing along from topic to topic through the whole subject. Not that it is merely a well arranged collection of observations—a logical unity pervades the whole, as well as a close train of thought each branch of the subject—yet it is anything but a mere barren argumentative dissertation—but full to overflowing of matter—he seems to have emptied out his whole mind, his whole stock of principles in morals, metaphysics and criticism, yet every one introduced with so vital and close a bearing upon the point as never to seem out of place. Nothing appears brought in for its own sake because it was a fine thing to say—the eye of the writer seems fixed upon his goal throughout.[21]

The philosophical basis of the essay confused two critics so perceptive as Pattison and Sir Charles Vaughan. To Pattison, the principles laid down were only strong, forcible restatements of the ordinary Butlerian Aristotelian doctrines,[22] but Sir Charles

[18] H. G. Liddell to Vaughan, 28 July 1841.

[19] *Oxford Review*, 13 May 1885.

[20] *Essay on the age favourable to works of fiction*, printed in *Remains of R. H. Froude* (1838), i. 145–63.

[21] Bodleian Library, MS. Pattison 6, f. 14.   [22] Ibid.

Vaughan recognized 'marks of the utilitarian school and I rejoice to see it. It is in that school that you have your battle to fight and I delight to see that your armour is of the proper temper.'[23] Both in a sense were right. A taste for diffusive reading, Vaughan declared, favoured those branches of knowledge which depended on observation and experiment, on deduction rather than induction, because a great variety of ideas was rapidly conveyed by the senses to the memory as the mind passed from one subject to another. Certain consequences followed. For example, the spread of general knowledge in society caused certain faculties to develop, amongst them the powers of definition, division, systematization. New skills and crafts were thereby developed, and a new political element was created. Because truth of all kinds was the natural possession of every rational being, society became opposed to the aristocratic and paternalistic principle in government. On the moral state of society, the effect of diffusive reading was to weaken the authority of moral principle because it tended to encourage irresponsible opinion, and in religion it led to incredulity because it widened experience and men granted or withheld belief according to the extent of their experience.

Although Vaughan welcomed the spread of knowledge and power over the material world, and the reduction of ignorance and prejudice, he concluded that the consequences of what he called the sensual philosophy or the philosophy of general knowledge far outweighed the good. He argued that the higher reaches of philosophy formed abstractions of which 'no account can be given but that they are native of the intelligence which contains them'. Where knowledge was valued for its practical results, those who pursued it for its own sake were disparaged and neglected. In a passage very characteristic of views he expressed when defending the professoriate at Oxford, he wrote of them: 'Not urging very anxiously the chase after any particular result, they are free to follow the gleams of truth from whatever direction they may play upon their path, and delighting mainly in the energy of labour they are prevented by no timid economy of strength from sifting old principles and grasping at higher laws.'

[23] Sir C. R. Vaughan to Vaughan, 13 Aug. 1836.

Vaughan was twenty-five when he wrote the essay. It made no important contribution to philosophy, nor perhaps could it be expected to do so, but it displayed the presence of a vigorous and questioning intelligence. It also displayed evidence of the conflict in his mind which was leading towards religious crisis. Any thoughts he had of a career in the Church were rapidly receding, and it was with evident relief that Sir Charles Vaughan wrote to him: 'After the repeated proofs which you have now given at Oxford of your powers of mind, take care, and let me never again be annoyed by hearing that you think the Church and not the Law opens a better field for their display. Remember that the world has always exacted from the preachers and professors of *faith* a surrender of their reasoning powers.'[24] Many years later, Vaughan alluded to his state of mind at this period when he commented on the famous case of the Reverend Charles Voysey, who was deprived for deistical beliefs. It was not enough, he remarked, for a clergyman to have sympathy for the beliefs and hopes of his flock, there ought to be a common basis of faith in which the leading convictions of the clergyman and his parishioners coincided. 'I felt thus', he said, 'at 24 years of age. I would not then consent to bind myself *through life* to the articles of the Church of England, even though interpreted with all reasonable latitude.'[25]

The central question which troubled him was the nature of authority in religion. It was the question which lay at the heart of the Tractarian Movement, but Vaughan approached it less through theology and history than through logic and science. In the Chancellor's Essay he had remarked that scientific studies often led to incredulity, and it is perhaps no accident that the crisis in his own faith coincided with the emergence of an enthusiasm for natural science. In nothing, he told his son in 1880, did he envy modern youth so much as in their training for the acquisition of such knowledge.[26] The sale catalogue of his library, which was dispersed in 1886, provides illuminating evidence of

24 Sir C. R. Vaughan to Vaughan, 13 Aug. 1836.
25 Vaughan to John Halford, 1 June 1871.
26 Vaughan to W. W. Vaughan, 10 May 1880.

his interest, and enables its most active period to be dated with some certainty. Most of his numerous scientific books were published between about 1832 and 1844, and since nearly all were manuals or introductory works such as a student entering on the subject for the first time might acquire, it is a reasonable assumption that they were the most recent available and that in many instances they were acquired at the time of publication. He possessed many books on physiology and anatomy. Although most were manuals, there were also specialized works on the stomach, urinary diseases, diseases of the eye, deafness, and two copies of Samuel Cooper's *First Lines of the Practice of Surgery* published in 1836. He also owned books on chemistry, physics, including Faraday's *Experimental Researches in Electricity*, botany, astronomy, and geology. Simultaneously, the foundations of faith were being eroded from another quarter, for philosophically Vaughan came under the powerful influence of David Hume, who, according to Roundell Palmer, became his master.[27] 'Do not fail', wrote Sir Charles Vaughan to his brother the judge, 'to read with attention the first page of the Life of Hume. There you will see a picture of Halford's dispositions. The likeness he has entirely confessed himself.'[28]

Vaughan once told Frederic Rogers that we never have the history of men in the most interesting period of their life, from eighteen to twenty-eight or thirty.[29] This is largely true in his own case, and he never cared to reveal the course of his religious doubts or their eventual resolution, if resolved they were. In the spring of 1837, Rogers told Newman that Vaughan had retired to Hampstead in the company of Edward Twisleton to think out principles. 'He said he had taken his views for some time on authority, and wanted to satisfy himself for himself.'[30] The first step was to divest himself of Arnold's influence. It took five years, he once remarked, to recover from the mental and moral distortion of Arnold's teaching.[31] In May of the following year,

[27] R. Palmer, *Memorials, Family and Personal* (1889), i. 144.
[28] Sir Charles to Sir John Vaughan, 5 Oct. 1838.
[29] *Letters and Correspondence of J. H. Newman*, ed. A. Mozley (1891), ii. 237.
[30] *Letters of Lord Blachford*, ed. G. E. Marindin (1896), 42.
[31] W. Tuckwell, *Reminiscences of Oxford* (1900), 211.

he went to stay with Arnold who was greatly alarmed at his state of mind and feared that it would lead him to Newmanism.

Halford Vaughan [he wrote to W. K. Hamilton] has just been staying with us for four or five days, and a most interesting person he is. Still there seems to me to be a sort of atmosphere of unrest and paradox hanging around many of our ablest young men of the present day which makes me very uneasy. I do not speak of religious doubts, but rather of questions as to great points in moral and intellectual matters; where things which have been settled for centuries seem to be again brought into discussion. This restless love of paradox is, I believe, one of the main causes of the growth of Newmanism; first directly, as it leads them to dispute and oppose all the points which have been agreed upon in their own country for the last two hundred years, and to pick holes in existing reputations; and then when a man gets startled at the excess of his scepticism and finds that he is cutting away all the ground under his feet, he takes a desperate leap into a blind fanaticism. I cannot find what I most crave to see, and what still seems to me no impossible dream—inquiry and belief going together, and the advance to truth growing with increased affection, as follies are more and more cast away.[32]

If, as Arnold believed, excess of scepticism led to Newmanism, the Newmanites for their part felt that Vaughan was drifting towards infidelity. In July 1838 W. G. Ward had a long and important conversation with him, the substance of which he reported in a letter to Arthur Clough.

I had [he wrote] a long talk with Vaughan of Oriel last night who has thought a good deal of these matters: he says he is perfectly certain of this, that there is no mean between Newmanism on the one side and extremes far beyond anything of Arnold's on the other; that Arnold and all Anglican Protestants are in a false position: for his own part he trusts himself to the progress not knowing whither it will carry him, but not feeling confident that any part of Xtianity will remain, except the truth of the main facts (miracles and Resurrection of our Lord) and those virtues (humility, forgiveness, etc.) which though first brought to light by Xtianity, carried their own evidence with them. Neither the canonicity nor authority of Scripture he thinks

[32] T. Arnold to W. K. Hamilton, 5 May 1838. Original in the possession of Sir Walter Moberly.

will remain: further he thinks Newman seems to see the real bottom
of the question, the degree of evidence for and against, and the way of
thinking of infidels better than any Xtian alive . . . Arnold he thinks on
the contrary understands neither the grounds of the infidel nor of the
Newmanist and will never give himself the trouble to understand
them: still admiring Arnold very highly. Also he has always thought
and still fully thinks that Stan[ley] will end in being a Newmanist . . .
as he thinks any enquiring person must, who is not prepared to give up
very much which every person Xtianly educated has been taught to
hold most sacred.[33]

It was amongst those beset by similar doubts and questionings
that the Newmanites frequently found their converts. Theirs was
a state of mind well understood by Newman himself, who had
once thanked God that He had shielded him morally from what
intellectually might easily have become general scepticism. But
there was never any real likelihood that Vaughan would be
drawn intellectually into the Newmanite circle. Arnold, Newman,
and Vaughan were all in their different ways concerned with
the quest for authority. Arnold found it in the Scriptures, and
Newman in the Church: both found it within Christianity.
Vaughan, on the other hand, appears to have rejected Revelation,
and, it would seem to follow, the inspiration of the Scriptures.
As an explanation of morality, Revelation was not only difficult to reconcile with the deductive principles of his new-found
enthusiasm for natural science, but it was historically inaccurate,
for, according to Ward, he believed that moral virtues 'though first
brought to light by Christianity carried their own evidence with
them'. If morality preceded Revelation in time, it also preceded
the creation of the Church, and thus the terms of reference to
which Newman and Arnold appealed were not available to
Vaughan. His religious experience therefore differed from that
of such men as Clough and Pattison, who were drawn towards
Newmanism. For them, as Froude expressed it, 'as one Church
only professed to be infallible, we must become Romans or un-
believers'.[34] It was a dilemma Vaughan never had to face.

[33] *Correspondence of A. H. Clough*, ed. F. L. Mulhauser (1957), i. 81.
[34] W. H. Dunn, *James Anthony Foude* (1961), i. 94.

A disbelief in Revelation and the inspiration of the Scriptures did not necessarily imply a denial of the existence of God, but rather that God had not revealed himself to man except through Nature. The study of Nature, therefore, revealed the nature of God. Vaughan looked to science, which was the study of nature, for religious authority, and to history to give moral meaning to science. He was never lured into general scepticism, but the path he followed was long and tortuous and could be found only by endless and patient inquiry. He believed that truth could not be bound by dogma or doctrine, and that the Church was not only unnecessary to religious belief but often an obstacle to its discovery. From such opinions it was a short step to a passionately held anticlericalism.

To have resisted successfully the influence both of Arnold and Newman says much for Vaughan's intellectual strength and independence. The crisis of his religious experience finally convinced him that he could not make a career in the Church, and in 1837 he resumed his legal studies in London and took up residence in Devereux Chambers in the Strand. He was called to the Bar on 7 May 1838. His uncle Sir Charles Vaughan dismissed his leanings towards philosophy as a temporary aberration, and was confident that he would now embark on a legal career. After a discussion with him he wrote to the judge:

The result of our conversation is that he has determined to decide before March next when the Circuits commence, either upon going on Circuit (and by the advice of friends he is more than half inclined to choose the Northern) or at once to go to the Chancery Bar. The motive for hesitating between the Circuit and the Chancery Bar is that the latter is the least expensive, and as you have declared that the sums which you must be called upon to advance to him in the further prosecution of his profession will be deducted from the sum which may be left to him ultimately by your will, he has not that liking to his profession nor that confidence in his success to venture to hazard so serious a diminution of the fortune upon which he is ultimately to depend by going a most expensive circuit, if the Northern, the amount of which may be spared by going to the Chancery Bar. You may however depend upon this that next March he will without fail be upon the circuit or at the Chancery Bar, and I trust that he will not,

like Hume, make a feeble trial for entering into the active scenes of
life . . . I think he has a fine intelligent head and a most excellent heart.
He may be led into anything but coerced into nothing. The first time
his ambition is stirred by a successful fight at the Bar, there will be an
end of his Philosophy and his theories about study and rigid frugality
and retirement.[35]

But within a few months of this conversation, Vaughan finally
decided against a career either in Chancery or the Common
Law. On 15 January 1839 he was appointed Clerk of Assize for
the South Wales Circuit. The appointment was in the hands of his
father as senior justice, and the patent is signed and sealed by him,
and witnessed by Edward Twisleton. The judge, it is said, wept
to think what a lawyer was going to be lost.[36] The Clerkship,
although an important office in the administration of the law,
was not one which led to preferment, but it ultimately provided
Vaughan, who held it until his death, with an income of £500
a year in addition to fees. When his father died later in 1839 he
inherited the sum of £4,000, which would have been spent on
his legal career had he pursued it as originally intended, and his
father's library. From these sources he had an adequate income,
and the periodic duties of the Clerkship enabled him to apply
himself to other and more congenial activities.

What perhaps decided Vaughan to take the Clerkship was the
imminent revival of the Praelectorship of Logic at Oxford. When
university reform became a political issue in the 1830s, the
university had maintained a respectable record of academic reform
from the beginning of the century. Faced with Lord John
Russell's threat to issue a royal commission of inquiry in 1837,
and with Lord Radnor's motion for a committee on college
statutes, the Hebdomadal Board was stirred to continue what had
been successfully begun and set about a general revision of the
statutes of the university.[37] Although eventually little came of it,
some attempt was made to deal with the professorial system,

[35] Sir Charles Vaughan to Sir John Vaughan, 5 Oct. 1838.
[36] G. Smith, *Reminiscences* (1911), 275.
[37] W. R. Ward, *Victorian Oxford* (1965), 105.

which, being an instrument of the university rather than of the colleges, could be reformed without trespassing on college rights. Moreover, the professoriate was thought by some to offer the means of imparting that higher level of attainment which reform of the public examinations had demanded but which the colleges in general were unable to supply. Except in religion, the professorships were for the most part badly integrated with the educational system of the university. Many, particularly the more recent foundations, existed in subjects excluded from the curriculum, and in some subjects such as Latin, which were important in the curriculum, there was no professorship. Attendance on professorial lectures, unlike tutorial lectures, was not compulsory, and the difficulty experienced by many professors in assembling classes was a conspicuous cause of their non-residence.

A modest scheme was eventually submitted to Convocation, but met with scant success. On 31 March, Peter Payne reported,

All was rejected except the clause obliging the present professors to lecture. The part compelling undergraduate attendance fell to the ground. Also the part which established two new professors— metaphysics and logic and grammar and rhetoric. . . . The university seems well satisfied, as appears by its vote, to make the professors lecture, but will do nothing to secure them a class. And I think the general feeling is against granting distinctions, at all events classes, for any acquirements besides those at present favoured. Hussey proposes that honorary certificates of proficiency should be given by each professor, which would be making a great step.[38]

In another letter written at this time, Payne complained that what people called the principle of professors lecturing was passed, but that they were still excluded from the business of the university, and that compulsory attendance, which would have placed them on a vantage point by making them necessary for a degree, was thrown out.[39]

In one point only was a measure of reform achieved, when, after initial doubts, the Praelectorship of Logic was revived.[40] It was a modest victory for the reformers, for a reader in logic

[38] P. S. H. Payne to Vaughan, 31 Mar. 1839.
[39] The same to the same, Mar. 1839.
[40] Subsequently the Wykeham Professorship of Logic.

was already required by the university statutes, though no appointment had been made for many years.

The election of the Praelector took place in Convocation, which, since the prosecution of Hampden, had been the traditional arena of conflict between the Tractarians and their opponents. In the contentious atmosphere of the times it was perhaps inevitable for party strife to enter the election. By his prolonged absence in London, Vaughan had avoided becoming involved in Oxford politics, but politics and religion were inextricably combined, and his decision to stand for election exposed his religious opinions, which might otherwise have remained a source of private unease to his friends, to a searching examination by the Newmanites. By the end of the contest he was disgusted by the party's treatment of him and had moved noticeably towards the party of political liberal reform in the university.

The suggestion that he should stand came from Liddell, and was enthusiastically supported by Payne. Although Tait's support waivered, he too was anxious to get Vaughan to Oxford, and in March had asked Payne to sound him about the regius chair of modern history which might become vacant as Nares was rumoured to be dying.[41] Thus at the start of the campaign Vaughan, who had little taste and less aptitude for the guerilla warfare of university politics, found himself in association with the anti-Tractarian party, for in the previous year Liddell had supported that ingenious measure designed to discredit the Tractarians, the Martyrs' Memorial,[42] and Tait was soon to lead the opposition to Tract XC.

The readership had undeniable attractions for Vaughan. It offered him a field in which to develop his philosophical interests and legal training. He had no specialized skill in logic, but none was required. Henry Wall, who was elected in 1849, informed the Royal Commission that the holder must be at least M.A., B.C.L., or Bachelor of Medicine, but that no special qualification was needed.[43] The duties were not onerous and consisted of

41 P. S. H. Payne to Vaughan, Mar. 1839.
42 H. L. Thompson, *Henry George Liddell* (1899), 45.
43 *Report of the Oxford University Commission* (1852), Evidence, 151.

one course of lectures in the first year and two in subsequent years. If Vaughan hung back it was because of the question of residence. In theory the duties could be discharged by a non-resident reader, and for financial reasons he preferred not to reside. The stipend was only £247. 15s. 0d. raised from a small tax on all members of the university below the degree of M.A., except servitors, and was insufficient if he resigned his Clerkship or lost his Fellowship at Oriel. The question of non-residence speedily became an issue, and Payne told him that he had a very fair chance of success if only he would agree to reside. Several Christ Church men, he said, would vote for him, but 'Hussey sticks at your non-residence'.[44] A few days later he wrote again urging Vaughan to come to Oxford and stating that Hampden would support him if he would clarify the position on residence.[45]

While Vaughan continued to hang back, other candidates came forward in plenty. The leading contender was Richard Michell, a Fellow of Lincoln, Bampton Lecturer, and later an opponent of Mark Pattison. Also in the field were Henry Wall, a Fellow of Balliol with reforming tastes; T. W. Lancaster, a former Fellow of Queen's, and like Michell a Bampton Lecturer, but unlike him the author of a pamphlet against Hampden; C. W. Stocker, former Vice-Principal of St. Alban Hall, who became White Professor of Moral Philosophy in 1841; John Hill of St. Edmund Hall, the Evangelical candidate, and Robert Lowe, later Viscount Sherbrooke and in 1839 a distinguished private tutor.

There was as yet no Newmanite candidate. The party was in no hurry, for its strength in Convocation was derived from the country clergy rather than from the resident members of the university and was more easily canvassed. It was favoured by the large number of candidates, and Michell informed Liddell that if all of them went to the poll many residents would decline to vote and the election would be carried by the 'outvoters' [i.e. the Newmanites].[46] The Newmanites, however, could not ignore Vaughan's candidature, for his position as a Fellow of

---

44 P. S. H. Payne to Vaughan, 17 May 1839.
45 The same to the same, 31 May 1839.
46 H. G. Liddell to Vaughan, 24 May 1839.

Oriel obliged them to decide whether to grant or withhold the support of that part of the college which followed Newman. At first, in spite of his liberal sponsors, they were disposed in his favour, and when his name was brought forward Frederic Rogers, a close friend of Newman, entertained no scruples of his fitness, and told Liddell 'that he thought you [Vaughan] the fittest man not excepting Sewell who is thought likely to stand but he said he did not see how you could be elected without residing'.[47] But three days later, on 20 May, he wrote to Vaughan in a very different vein.

I am afraid I am going to write you a very annoying letter, but I do not see how I can help it. I only hope you will give me credit for feeling as much pain at having to write it as you can at receiving it. Liddell spoke to me some days since about your standing for the Logical Professorship, and I have been thinking about it very anxiously ever since, and the more I think the more I feel that, *with my present notions* of what you feel and think I cannot conscientiously vote for you.

Perhaps the most frank and clearest way will be to say at once what I feel of you, though it may give what I say a presumptuous appearance, which I hope you will pardon. I cannot help thinking that you are in a way to doubt of all strictly *Revealed* Religion, if indeed you do not do so already, and that not as a person whose conviction is strong enough practically to repel his doubts, but deliberately and so as to influence your actions. I should be almost surprised to find that you, even now, *felt yourself fixed* in a belief of the Inspiration of Scripture, its permanent obligation, perhaps of the Trinity, and I have certainly long felt (most painfully at times) that you had got hold of a view of things in general which you were too able not to carry out, which led straight that way, and which you yourself indistinctly felt to do so. . . . If these are fancies of mine I need hardly say how *exceedingly* glad I should be to have them dispelled, though I really can hardly say at this moment what would and what would not make me easy in voting for you. It is possible, though I confess I scarcely hope it, that you may be able to set the matter at rest at once.[48]

What happened in those three days to cause such a complete volte-face by Rogers? Vaughan suspected Arnold of having

[47] P. S. H. Payne to Vaughan, 17 May 1839.
[48] F. Rogers to Vaughan, 20 May 1839.

circulated rumours of his religious opinions, but this was strongly denied by Arnold, who had reasons of his own for thinking that the Newmanist definition of heresy was too refined.

> I neither have nor have had [he wrote] any suspicion of your being an unbeliever or being disposed or likely to become so, or of your disbelief of the Scriptures, or of the Trinity. I have and have had, no suspicion of your disbelief or danger of disbelieving any of these in my sense of the terms, and in what I hope and think is still the general sense of them. But I have no doubt that in the Newmanite sense I am myself an unbeliever, and in fact Newman said publicly some years since that I was a very doubtful Christian, which he explained afterwards by saying that no true Christian could think as I did about the Inspiration of the Old Testament and the lives of the Patriarchs.[49]

A day later Arnold wrote again to say that his fear for Vaughan had not been the danger of unbelief but on the contrary the possibility that he would become a Newmanite. His letter contained a shrewd insight into the attraction of Newmanism, but revealed his blindness to Vaughan's real state of mind.

> I may [he wrote] have expressed my sense of your being too little impressed with the certainty of moral truths independent of Revelation, a tendency which I certainly never thought likely to lead you to religious unbelief, but exactly the opposite—to Newmanism. Palmer of Magdalen, William Palmer not Roundell, quite startled me with his scepticism, which in him and in several other men whom I have known, leads them to an unreasoning reliance on authority, inasmuch that if ever I see a young man over sceptical I think him likely, if he be morally well disposed and goes to Oxford, to become a Newmanite. I believe that I said something of this kind to you when you were here, but I do not remember having said it to any one else, and certainly if I did my meaning has been most utterly misconstrued, for if I had a fear for you it was much more lest you should become a Newmanite than an unbeliever, and I rather rejoiced to hear from your cousin that they had disgusted you by their conduct on the present occasion, for the danger, as far as I thought you in danger at all, lay to my mind all on that side.[50]

49 T. Arnold to Vaughan, 30 May 1839.
50 The same to the same, 31 May 1839.

It was not Arnold but Ward who had caused Rogers's sudden change of opinion, though Vaughan was not to know this for some time. Ward's account of his conversation with Vaughan in the previous July, which he now communicated to a meeting of Newman and his friends in Oriel, thoroughly alarmed the Newmanites, who immediately embarked on a campaign to persuade Vaughan to withdraw from the contest. They proceeded with the utmost secrecy. At this juncture Providence conveniently provided them with a stalking-horse in the person of William Sewell, whose ambition and disingenuousness made him a suitable and flexible instrument in their hands. Sewell, who is best remembered for burning the *Nemesis of Faith* in Exeter Hall, was not a follower of Newman. He dreamt of forming a party of moderates within the Oxford Movement, and when he refused to follow Newman to Rome, Whately contemptuously described him as 'Suillus', the little pig, because he would not go the whole hog. Sir M. E. Grant Duff described him as a 'very clever and extremely foolish Anglican leader, of whose contributions to the *Quarterly* Lockhart used to say: "They teach nothing, they mean nothing, they are nothing—but they go down like bottled velvet."'[51] Mozley's account of his candidature is well known. Sewell, he relates, feared that by jumping into the contest he might incur the opposition of Newman and his friends, and so he came to Newman with a proposal that if he were elected to the chair of logic Newman might succeed 'to his own cast-off shoes, that is, the chair of Moral Philosophy'.[52] Sewell's own lengthy account of the episode occurs in a letter to Ernest Hawkins dated 31 May and casts much light on the election and the methods of the Newmanites.

I have heard for some days past of strange stories being circulated in London about the part I have taken in this unpleasant election. But without anything very definite till to-day when I have had a letter from Vaughan, in answer to one of mine. It is the first thing which has opened my eyes to the real magnitude of the scandal, for I

[51] 'Personal Reminiscences of Oxford by Sir M. E. Grant Duff', *Trans. of the Franco-Scottish Society* (1897), 87.
[52] T. Mozley, *Reminiscences* (2nd ed. 1882), ii. 27.

can call it nothing else. And Vaughan having permitted it and indeed originated it without asking any explanation from myself, though we are friends of very old standing, has precluded himself, as I have told him, from receiving any explanation from me now. I am indeed very indifferent to common rumours, and know that in cases like the present things must take their course. But I have a value for your opinion and that of some whom perhaps you know, and though I find the [*tear*] was written to you on the subject I will trouble you with one more [*tear*]. He has told you, I believe, that even before the statute was [*tear*] immediately afterwards I was urged to come forward, and from all I could see with no reason to anticipate a contest. But I declined for many reasons, and preferred that the Praelectorship should be filled by some other person. Liddell on finding that this was my intention, mentioned Vaughan's name to me, and though I said nothing one way or the other I had resolved in my mind to give him all the support I could, provided I could satisfy myself as to certain points about his opinions quite distinct from theology, about which opinions I felt some uncertainty and doubt.

While I was in this state I found that he was in Oxford. I think it was when I was going down to Oriel to find him out that I met a mutual friend who, without saying anything of Vaughan's unfitness, though I have since found that he was strongly impressed with it, urged me to stand as a matter of duty. And in the course of conversation I told him that I intended to support Vaughan if I found reason not to question the soundness of his views, but that I could not help fancying that they were not yet settled. I declined also coming forward myself.

Before I saw Vaughan certain other persons had proposed to bring forward Newman as the fittest man in the university, and as I objected to this most strongly as tending to divide the university on a question very different from Logic, I went to the room where they were and strongly expressed my objection to it. When I was there (about 3 o'clock) (and none were present but about half a dozen of Newman's personal friends) I heard for the first time of things which alarmed me very much indeed as to Vaughan's religious opinions. They were mentioned in the most confidential way with strict injunctions to privacy, and as a reason why his college could not bring him forward, and why it was necessary for those who wished well to the university to guard against the chair falling to him. And I could assure you the opinions alluded to were not such as had reference to peculiar parties.

Without entering into them specifically they were such as to make any one very anxious. On it being found that it would not do to bring forward Newman, the next thing was to see if Vaughan, by the representation of his friends, could be brought to withdraw. And with a view to endeavour to effect this, I went myself to Liddell to urge him to advise it. I pointed out to him that Vaughan would not be supported by his college, that his own personal friends, and myself specifically, whom every one knew to be most sincerely attached to him, would feel compelled to exert themselves against him, and that if he persevered a question must occur as to his principles which would throw a slur upon them and probably injure him in his future prospect.

I fixed with Vaughan to see him between five and six that I might tell him my own feelings on the subject. And in the [course] of a long conversation I was led to urge on him, as [I had] done on Liddell, the expediency for his own sake of withdrawing. You perhaps know something of the affection which I have always felt for him as one of my first pupils, and can understand that I should feel myself not only authorised but bound to advise him, as far as it was possible in such a case. In the course of conversation I saw enough of his mode of thinking and opinions to satisfy me that they were, whether right or wrong, precisely of that kind to which I have long attributed our present mischief, and which I am resolved to battle with as long as I have a voice or pen. I conceive them to be dangerous and unsound. And so I told Vaughan, telling him at the same time that in condemning them, I did not wish to say or imply anything respecting his religious notions. But they were the principles which he would have to bring forward in his lectures, and however he might hold them conscientiously and be secured against their natural conclusions by his own personal piety, they could not be promulgated without doing great harm.

I left him about six having walked with him to the Angel, and came back without dreaming either that any proposition would be made to me to stand or of consenting to it. About seven a person came to me to say that there was a great wish that I should come forward, and on looking into all the circumstances I agreed to it. My first wish was to prevent the chair from being made an instrument, as I conceived, of great mischief, even if no suspicion attached to Vaughan's theological opinions. My second that in coming forward myself I might give those who refused to support him in his own college and elsewhere, on the ground of his unsettled state of mind, an ostensible reason for not supporting him, without entering into that question—a reason which they could not have had except some one of a certain position in the university was brought forward. And these were I assure you the reasons of those who asked me to be nominated. I had another reason, that if questions arose as to Vaughan's religious opinions (which I foresaw from his state of mind and his own complaints would probably occur) I might take a ground of opposition to him which would not compromise his character on that head—namely my conviction of his erroneous views in logical and metaphysical subjects, of which I had become convinced in conversation, and on which as professor I might be supposed [competent] to judge and bound to take a prominent part in opposing them.

I stated [this object], and we separated under a distinct agreement that every exertion should be made to avoid throwing upon him any stigma whatever, or even bringing his name into discussion, and I leave you to decide whether there was in this any thing unfriendly or unfair. I wrote Vaughan a note immediately to tell him that I intended to stand, and directed it to Twiss' where he was at dinner, and was vexed, after Vaughan had left Oxford, to find it lying unopened on Liddell's table. I must also add that I was not privy to any use being made of the notion of his resignation. I informed those who knew that I had seen him on the subject of his withdrawing that he did not intend to do it while there seemed a probability of success but that I could not help hoping he would do so ultimately. This was told them before as well as after I was induced to stand, but certainly with no intention, nor apparent probability of influencing votes. I do not believe it was so employed.

I must also add that if the question of Vaughan's theological opinions has been publicly mooted it has been so by himself and his friends. His opponents have studiously kept it out of sight with the most scrupulous delicacy, and as for myself I have scarcely opened my lips on the election, except to Claughton, Hope and Scott, who drew me into it as friends of Vaughan who had heard the report alluded to, and to whom I made privately and confidentially the same statement that I have made to you. They will answer best whether I spoke to them as his friend. I grieve much that Vaughan in a moment of irritation should have permitted himself and others to believe that a friend like myself could have acted with the indelicacy and want of candour which his letter implies, in urging him to withdraw while I was proposing to stand myself, and he has certainly done me an injury which it will be difficult to undo.

Sewell's letter is dated 31 May, but the crucial conversation with the Newmanites at Oriel and the subsequent conversations with Liddell and Vaughan, culminating in Sewell's decision to stand, occurred no later than 20 May, the very day in fact on which Rogers assured Liddell of his high opinion of Vaughan's suitability for the chair.[53] It would appear, therefore, that Ward's revelations about Vaughan's religious opinions had the instantaneous effect of withdrawing Tractarian support for him without any inquiry at all into the veracity of Ward's information.

It is difficult to acquit Sewell of behaving foolishly, though a more charitable view of his conduct would be possible but for his own defence of it. His sudden conversion within the space of a single day from a supporter of Vaughan into a rival candidate, his attempt to blackmail Vaughan into withdrawing by the threat that otherwise 'a question might occur as to his principles which would throw a slur upon them', his decision to stand after a conversation with Vaughan, which, by his own admission, contained no undertaking by Vaughan to retire, are the actions of a fool or a knave. Vaughan's friends were initially disposed to the first alternative. Payne thought Sewell absurd rather than dishonest, and found the possibility that he had lied difficult to believe.[54] But reflection made the difficulty easier to accept, and the suspicion grew that Sewell had decided to stand before his conversation with Vaughan.

Although Sewell's intervention had failed to secure Vaughan's withdrawal from the election it injured his chances of success by increasing the already considerable uncertainty whether he was a candidate or not. Edward Dayman, a Fellow of Exeter, told Hawkins on Sewell's authority that Vaughan would probably withdraw.[55] Sewell, moreover, was not averse to spreading suspicions about Vaughan's orthodoxy, so much so that the Newmanites could be forgiven for supposing that the most effective way of broadcasting them was to divulge them to Sewell in confidence. It was hardly for the good of Vaughan's soul that he mentioned the matter to Claughton, who subsequently

[53] P. S. H. Payne to Vaughan, 31 May 1839.   [54] Ibid.
[55] The same to the same, 29 May 1839.

called on Payne in Balliol. 'I have had a visit from Claughton this morning', Payne reported, 'to whom Sewell had been suggesting (at the same time that he expressed a belief that you would ultimately come right) that you held dangerous [and] unsettled opinions. Claughton said this made him glad to be out of the way and not vote at all.'[56]

Sewell's intervention removed Vaughan's lingering doubts, and he made known his intention of standing, much to the delight of Provost Hawkins who became his enthusiastic supporter as soon as he discovered that the Newmanites had a candidate in the field. But Vaughan's canvass proceeded slowly, and on 27 May Liddell and Hawkins calculated that he had twenty-five certain votes among the residents and could rely on perhaps another thirty from London. Michell, however, who lamented to Payne that the Newmanites would get in because of the divided votes,[57] had been actively canvassing while Vaughan still hesitated, and when Arnold tried to muster support for Vaughan among the masters at Rugby he found that he had been forestalled by Michell.

At this juncture a new and more serious threat menaced Vaughan. 'Some of the Oriel men', Payne wrote to him '(the more moderate) are not I conceive working hard against you, but one or two are in right earnest.'[58] How much in earnest they were appeared when, having failed to persuade Vaughan to withdraw by using Sewell as a catspaw, they launched a campaign to compel him to do so by making known where it would cause most harm the suspicions, previously disclosed to Sewell under conditions of strict secrecy, that they entertained of his religious orthodoxy.

In his letter of 20 May, Frederic Rogers had invited Vaughan to refute the charges against him. One way in which he might have done so was by subscribing to the Thirty-Nine Articles. Vaughan, having subscribed on taking his degree, not unnaturally resented the suggestion that he should do so again. The Articles, however, symbolized the real point at issue. To the Newmanites,

---

[56] The same to the same, 24 May 1839. Sewell too lost support, for Payne reported that Tait and Scott had decided not to vote for him.

[57] The same to the same, 29 May 1839. [58] Ibid.

who did not discover their versatility until the publication of Tract XC, they were a formula signifying assent to the essentially religious nature of the university, and the suspicion that they did not represent a man's true beliefs convicted him of perjury. Vaughan, on the other hand, maintained that 'questions as to faith were irrelevant in a matter like the present and that religious and other truth would be better arrived at by pursuing each path of knowledge independently of other paths'.[59] The objections to subscription most frequently heard were that it excluded dissenters from the university and was often performed in a spirit of cynical incomprehension, but to Vaughan it was in addition prejudicial to learning. 'Vaughan', wrote Stanley, 'maintains that the Oxford plan is destructive of learning—his opponents that the contrary plan would be destructive of religion.'[60] A few months after the election, Stanley had a conversation with Vaughan and Bunsen, and proposed that the theological professors in the university should be asked whether subscription was 'compatible or incompatible with really active, professorial, critical investigations in all lines', and whether it might have prevented the rise of German rationalism. Referring no doubt to what he had called 'the contrary plan', he suggested that they should also be asked whether it would be possible for the Articles to occupy the same position theologically as the Augsburg Confession, 'of great historical authority, yet binding on no man's conscience expressly', or alternatively whether they might not be considered, as F. D. Maurice suggested, 'not as tests but merely as conditions of thought and instruments of education'.

However ingeniously Vaughan and his friends might seek avenues of escape, his position was unacceptable not only to the Newmanites but to the majority of all Anglicans. However much the Newmanites and their enemies might squabble about theological issues, they were united in their opposition to any weakening of the Anglican position in the university. The Newmanites, therefore, found an ally in, of all people, Arnold when they made known their doubts of Vaughan's religious

[59] P. S. H. Payne to Vaughan, 24 May 1839.
[60] Lambeth Palace Library MS. Tait 76, f. 258ᵛ.

soundness. Arnold at once wrote to Vaughan in forceful terms:

I must trouble you again with a few lines in consequence of a letter which I have had from Ward of Balliol this morning. He says that you make it your avowed principle that a man's religious opinions are wholly irrelevant to the question of his fitness for a Logical Professorship. Now I owe it to you and to myself to say at once that I utterly dissent from such a principle, and could not support any man who avowed it. I thought and think you quite right in refusing to answer Rogers' questions because as every Master of Arts at Oxford has professed himself not merely a Christian generally but even specially a member of the Church of England, it seems to me that to ask him whether he is a believer in Revelation or no is an insult which nothing but some decided overt act or language on his part can justify, and the Newmanites so misconstrue and misunderstand other men's opinions and use words in so peculiar a sense that I should require some better ground than their vague suspicions before I felt myself called upon to give a profession of my faith more than my position as a Master of Arts in the university had given already. And when I heard that charges which I conceived to be wholly calumnious were circulated in part on my authority, I was anxious to show publicly my total disbelief of them by coming up and voting for you. But as to a man's Christian faith I would just as soon vote for an unbeliever to be Divinity Professor as Professor of Logic because I would not put an unbeliever into any place of instruction in a Christian university if that place implied that he was a member of the university generally and not merely called in to lecture on a particular subject. I should contradict the principles on which I have always acted and which I hold most sacred if I gave any countenance to the opposite doctrine. But as believing that you have been calumniated, and that having been asked an offensive question with no reasonable foundation for the suspicion which it implied you very properly refused to answer it, I will come up and vote for you with the greatest pleasure. Only it must be distinctly understood that I vote for you as for a Christian man who has been slanderously charged with unbelief and not as if I thought that even though the charge were true yet it did not affect your fitness for [a] Professorship in the university, if that Professorship were not directly connected with theology.[61]

61 T. Arnold to Vaughan, 2 June 1839.

Arnold and Rogers demanded assurances, the one implicitly
the other explicitly. If Vaughan accepted Arnold's vote he accepted
Arnold's condition; if he refused the vote he could hardly continue to be a candidate. Whether or not he intended to resign
from the contest, he made no immediate move and the Newmanites resolved to force his hand by making their suspicions
public. In these events W. G. Ward's part was decisive. On
5 June, three days after Arnold's letter to Vaughan, Rogers wrote
as follows:

I had a very unsatisfactory conversation with S[tephen] D[enison]
yesterday afternoon, which induces me to trouble you again about
the old most painful subject. I had intended and indeed almost
began to give him an account of a conversation which Ward of Balliol
describes himself to have had with you some time since. Without
knowing my suspicions he mentioned it to me lately as a reason why
he could not vote for you. He did not intend however to take any
further steps, but what he said quite decided me as to the duty of acting
as I did on my own independent but less definite impressions to the
same effect. I did not think, however, when it came to the point that
it was likely to do any good, and I felt particularly anxious to save
Ward (whose sister is now dying in his house) from being unnecessarily
mixed up in this most annoying question. So I did not press the matter
on Denison. I wish you however to know it. I have had one or two
accounts of the matter from Ward but that which is evidently of most
importance is a letter written by him the day after it took place to an
intimate friend of his own engaged like himself somewhat anxiously
in theological enquiries. [Rogers then quoted from the letter which
Ward wrote to Clough in July 1838.[62]] Other points of detail he
remembers with more or less clearness, but it seems more satisfactory
to refer to his impression formed at the time and independently of the
late perplexing affair. If there is any inaccuracy in his language it
must be remembered that he was writing to a friend to whom his mode
of speaking on these topics was familiar. Now I am very unwilling
to bring this statement forward if correct for your sake, and in any
case for Ward's. At the same time I feel that without doing so, not
only I myself but those who have acted with me must suffer, as they
are very heavily suffering, from a charge of adopting very grave
suspicions on frivolous and insufficient grounds, grounds, I ought to

[62] See p. 33.

remind you, which, of whatever value they may be, were not acted upon till by your refusal to answer *any* questions which you considered unconnected with the subject of your professorship, both seemed to be confirmed and the possibility of obtaining better information cut off.[63]

Throughout the affair Vaughan preserved a dignified silence and refused to discuss his religious opinions, which, he continued to maintain, were irrelevant to the election. The importance of the issue and his readiness to justify his conduct on other occasions suggest that there was truth behind the charges of the Newmanites. They for their part seem to have learnt the lesson of the Hampden Case and to have preferred private assassination to public execution. Their actions scarcely show them in a favourable light, for it is evident from Rogers's letter that they based their campaign against Vaughan on evidence no more substantial than Ward's uncorroborated account of his conversation. Unable to prove their suspicions, they nevertheless used them under a cloak of secrecy, and when this failed proceeded on the dangerous principle that silence was confession.

Before matters could go any further, Vaughan, either because of Roger's threats, or because his campaign had run into difficulties, withdrew from the election early in June. When the votes were counted Michell was elected by a large majority, even though all the clergy 'of Oriel persuasion' were brought up for Sewell, and Oakeley brought down a coach-load of supporters from London.[64] Despite the excellence of his canvass, Michell did not lead the field until late in the day. Lowe and Stocker drew support away from him, particularly the latter, who, it was said, 'hath subducted from him all St. John's',[65] but when they retired their supporters transferred their allegiance to him as the most substantial anti-Newmanite candidate. The voting was Michell 218 votes, Sewell 116, Wall 18, and Lancaster 36. A poll of 388 votes was low compared, for example, with the celebrated contest in 1841 between Isaac Williams and James Garbett for the professorship of poetry, also elected by Convocation, when

[63] F. Rogers to Vaughan, 5 June 1839.
[64] P. S. H. Payne to Vaughan, 24 and 30 May 1839.
[65] H. G. Liddell to Vaughan, 24 May 1839.

no fewer than 1,544 votes were promised,[66] and appears to confirm Michell's prediction that many residents would abstain. It also suggests that, despite rumours to the contrary, the Newmanites did not muster the 'outvoters' in force, perhaps because their principal object was not the election of Sewell but the defeat of Vaughan, which had been achieved by his withdrawal before the election day.

Roundell Palmer believed that the gossip of Newman's curate, Golightly, caused Vaughan to distrust the good faith of the Tractarian leaders,[67] but a more important cause was the treatment meted out by them during the election of 1839. The effect was lasting and exercised a powerful influence on Vaughan's approach to university reform, for the distrust he felt for the Newmanites led him to believe that reforms must be imposed by the legislature. The election influenced his developing ideas on reform in other ways. Religion had been a determining factor in deciding a question which to Vaughan was not a religious question, and the experience contributed to his belief that learning could not flourish unless the clergy were deprived of their predominant position in the university and colleges. The election thus marks an important stage in his progress towards political radicalism in university reform, and his estrangement from Anglican reformers.

A further step in his political progress occurred three years later when he was deprived of his Fellowship at Oriel. Vaughan was an empiricist whose own experience was the catalyst of his ideas. The election to the chair of logic convinced him that the ecclesiastical character of the university ought to be reduced; the deprivation of his Fellowship confirmed his belief that Fellowships ought to be freed from clerical restrictions, and their emoluments applied more generally to learned purposes.

The time was rapidly approaching when by the college statutes he would be obliged to take Holy Orders or surrender his Fellowship, but it was by now apparent to him that he could not conscientiously comply with the statutory condition. He

[66] W. R. Ward, *Victorian Oxford*, (1965,) 115.
[67] R. Palmer, *Memorials Family and Personal* (1889), i. 143.

sought therefore by a series of resourceful expedients, based on the interpretation of the statutes, to transfer to one of the three Fellowships tenable by laymen. In 1612 the college had made a statute reducing the number of law Fellowships from three to two, adding a medical Fellowship tenable by a layman in place of the third. The statute was amended in 1815 by a decree permitting a third law Fellowship where there was no claimant to the medical Fellowship. In 1841 there were three law Fellows and no medical Fellow. They were Charles Neate, elected in 1828, J. E. Walker, elected in 1831, and Frederic Rogers, conditionally elected in 1833 in the absence of a claimant to the medical Fellowship. It so happened that none of the three had been formally admitted to a law Fellowship, and Vaughan seized upon this fact to inform Hawkins that he wished to study medicine. It was a claim which could only be substantiated at the expense of his old antagonist in the election of 1839, Frederic Rogers, whose enthusiasm for the law was in so much doubt that even the Provost had to admit that 'Rogers has often told me that he does read law—whether he studies it very thoroughly is another question'.[68] For reasons which cannot now be ascertained Vaughan eventually decided not to persist in his intention to study medicine, and in the following October the college, not to be caught twice, passed the following resolution:

In this Chapter it being probable that Mr. Neate and Mr. Walker whom the College had considered as their two Law Fellows had never been formally allowed to be so, as required by the statute of 1805, the College declared that they are the two Law Fellows. Also the College declared Mr. Rogers is admitted to the 3rd Law Fellowship until a claimant in Medicine appears under the statute of 1815.[69]

The unexpectedness of Vaughan's proposal raises the suspicion that his sole object was to circumvent the regulations governing his Fellowship, but there is little doubt that he was in earnest in contemplating a career in medicine. 'I was most serious', he later informed Rogers, 'in my intentions of acting on my communications to the Provost and taking up the study, and as far as my own tastes and interests were concerned had no doubt

[68] E. Hawkins to Vaughan, 30 Mar. 1841.   [69] Oriel College Act Book.

of the propriety of the step.'[70] There is no reason to doubt this statement in view of his known enthusiasm for natural science, and his interest in medicine in particular is confirmed by the contents of his library.

Hardly had this scheme fallen to the ground when he produced a second. On 30 June 1841, his great friend Peter Payne died and in his will bequeathed to Vaughan an annuity of £45 to commence from such time as he might be obliged to surrender his Fellowship, and to continue until he should have acquired an income equal in amount to it. In order to prevent Vaughan from refusing the legacy a condition was attached which made the effect of such a refusal nugatory. If the Fellowship were not vacated, the fund out of which the annuity was to be paid passed to Payne's unmarried sister Laura, but if the Fellowship were vacated and Vaughan refused the bequest, the fund was not to pass to Laura Payne but to be divided between the members of a numerous family. Vaughan therefore made an ingenious proposal which, if accepted, would have enabled him to decline the legacy without injury to Laura Payne. 'I arranged', he relates, 'to give to one of the then lay Fellows a pecuniary equivalent for the resignation of *his* Fellowship, an agreement to which he acceded on condition that it could be carried into execution without legal difficulty.'[71] Any flexibility the Oriel statutes may have possessed, however, fell short of simony, and on the advice of the Attorney General Vaughan dropped the scheme. The Fellow to whom this curious proposal was made was J. E. Walker.

A year passed before Vaughan made his last and most desperate attempt to keep his Fellowship. He had previously sought to exploit technicalities in the statutes. He now made the bold attempt to prove that the statute by which his deprivation was threatened was illegal. The root of his contention was that the statute limiting the number of lay Fellowships to three was contrary to the original statutes of Oriel, which were declared to be inviolable, and that the Provost might create additional

[70] Vaughan to F. Rogers, n.d.
[71] Vaughan to Lord Blachford, 7 Sept. 1881. See also Oriel Letters no. 810.

lay Fellowships to a total of five or six at his discretion.[72] Hawkins was as adept as Vaughan in expounding the niceties of the constitution and disputed his interpretation of the facts. Crushingly he replied that the question at issue was not whether the college had the power to create more than three faculty Fellowships, but whether it had exercised that power. Since it had not, and since Vaughan had sworn to obey the statutes, he forfeited his Fellowship under the statute of 1805, which regulated the period when Orders had to be taken.

The original statutes of Oriel seem to have left the decision to the discretion of the Provost and Hawkins's position was unassailable. Yet if it was at his discretion, it was in theory possible for him to accommodate Vaughan by converting his Fellowship into a faculty Fellowship. The reasons he chose not to do so lie partly in his temperament and partly in the conditions prevailing in Oriel. Hawkins was zealous in his strict attention to the enforcement of college rules,[73] and he firmly believed that Vaughan's deprivation was the logical consequence of the statute of 1805. 'You and I', he wrote to him, 'are bound by the existing regulations, and the college is not at liberty to alter them for a particular occasion, the only use of regulations being to prevent our consulting our *wishes* at the expense of the permanent interests of the society.'[74] An additional faculty Fellowship could only be created by retrospective legislation, and his mind, being 'essentially legal in its texture',[75] instinctively recoiled from such a prospect. Moreover, Hawkins had warned Vaughan of the conditions attached to his Fellowship when he became a candidate, and Vaughan's attempt to interpret the statutes in his own favour did not gain in credibility by his two previous attempts to retain his Fellowship on quite other grounds.

There was another and even more compelling reason for Hawkins's opposition to the creation of another lay Fellowship.

[72] Vaughan's memorandum of his case does not survive, but in 1854, stung by a remark of Hawkins that the loss of his Fellowship had influenced his evidence to the Royal Commission, he repeated its substance in an appendix (pp. 108–11) to *Oxford Reform and Oxford Professors*.   [73] M. Pattison, *Memoirs* (1885), 83.
[74] E. Hawkins to Vaughan, 7 Oct. 1842.
[75] J. Burgon, *Lives of Twelve Good Men* (1888), i. 391.

He was experiencing great difficulty in finding enough tutors. The difficulty had started with his dispute with Newman, Froude, and Wilberforce, and had worsened as the Tractarian Movement progressed and the rift widened between him and the supporters of what he always referred to afterwards as 'the late unhappy movement'.[76] He refused to appoint J. F. Christie to a tutorship, and terminated Charles Marriott's appointment. Some, such as Tom Mozley, refused to accept a tutorship. In 1841 matters reached a crisis when R. W. Church lost his tutorship for refusing to lecture on the Articles after the publication of Tract XC. At the same time, two other tutors, Daman and Prichard, were lost through marriage.[77] To make matters even worse, no election to a Fellowship took place in 1841, and in the following year the entire tutorial work of the college was in the hands of James Fraser and E. A. Litton, the mathematical lecturer. Vaughan could hardly have timed his request at a worse moment.

Any increase in the number of faculty Fellowships would have made the tutorial position at Oriel worse by increasing the number of non-teaching Fellows because since law and medicine lay outside the ordinary curriculum the faculty Fellows did not teach undergraduates. It would have reduced the number of Fellowships tenable by divines, who, by an assumption almost unchallenged, were deemed the proper instructors of the young, particularly if Hawkins accepted Vaughan's contention that the statutes permitted as many as five or six faculty Fellowships. Hawkins believed that even as things were the effect of the statute of 1805 was to fill the college with laymen, and that in order to increase the number of clerical Fellows, and thus of tutors, Orders ought to be taken after four instead of six years. In a letter to the Oxford University Commissioners in 1855, he advocated such a change and in doing so referred to Vaughan's deprivation.

Upon the only occasion [he wrote] on which within my memory the existing rule has operated to the exclusion of a Fellow (in 1842),

[76] *Oxford Magazine*, 21 June 1905.
[77] *Letters of Lord Blachford*, ed. G. E. Marindin (1896), 105.

the late Bishop of Llandaff,[78] who knew the College, its objects and interests at least as well as any person now living, spoke of the interval of choice allowed as too long—its effect being 'to increase the number of Lay Fellows far beyond the proportion intended'. But as 'to in-increasing the number of Faculty Fellowships,' he said, 'it would be manifestly at variance with the letter and also the spirit of the original statutes'.[79]

Fellowships, said Hawkins, were not intended by the founder for monastic clergy, nor for priests to say mass for his soul, nor for 'merely learned academic' clergy, but for 'a learned clergy qualified to teach the people by their life and doctrine'.

Although in his correspondence with Vaughan the Provost contrived to combine erudite exposition of the college statutes with amiable domestic gossip about his brother Francis, he did not permit family piety to interfere with his duty, and on 15 October 1842 he declared Vaughan's Fellowship vacant.

Vaughan's deprivation was something of a *cause célèbre*. Men might from time to time lose their Fellowships for immorality, but they seldom lost them for the morality of following their consciences. On the development of Vaughan's ideas on university reform, the episode had considerable impact. It may seem ironical that he should have championed the inviolability of college statutes, for the impediment to change which they represented was to become a principal argument of reformers for the intervention of Parliament in university affairs. Yet on closer examination it is evident that he was not defending statutes in themselves. Rather he was expounding a radical view of the nature and purpose of college endowments, and he was not the first or the last reformer to defend innovation as a return to an earlier state of uncorrupted innocence. In discussing the loss of his Fellowship in *Oxford Reform and Oxford Professors*, he stated that college endowments did not exist primarily for the purpose of educating undergraduates, which was the view held by

---

[78] Edward Copleston, Provost of Oriel, 1814-28. His letter to Hawkins is dated 9 Oct. 1842.

[79] E. Hawkins to the Oxford University Commissioners, 25 Sept. 1855. Correspondence in Oriel Treasury.

Hawkins, but for study. He thus anticipated the arguments advanced by Mark Pattison in his celebrated pamphlet *Suggestions on Academical Organisation* in 1868. Vaughan believed that a larger proportion of Fellowships, at Oriel perhaps as many as a third of the total number, should be devoted to learning. In 1842 he was not defending the view that they should be aids to enable men to prepare for the professions, for his own Fellowship had already discharged such a function when he was called to the Bar in 1839, and he was in effect demanding that his Fellowship should be applied to secular learning not necessarily or directly related to the educational needs of the university.

His conception of the purpose of Fellowships at Oxford brought him into further conflict with the traditional Anglican conception of the university, for an increase in the number of Fellowships devoted to secular learning would reduce the clerical element and eventually alter the nature of the institution. He developed the argument in his evidence to the Royal Commission in 1852. The obligation laid on Fellows to take Orders, he complained, 'has already prevented laymen who may have distinguished themselves in their academical career, from obtaining the due reward for their industry; it has prevented some from devoting themselves to literary and scientific pursuits, who may have had a real call to such occupations, without feeling any such call to "preach the gospel" as ordination presupposes.'[80] The preponderance of the clergy had not only exposed the university to the shock of ecclesiastical disputes, it had produced a jealousy and fear of sciences which a university ought to encourage. The relation of the clergy, he added, to learning, literature, science, the arts and professions was utterly different from what it used to be. Vaughan's experiences at Oriel lit a train of gunpowder which was to explode a decade later.

[80] *Report of the Oxford University Commission* (1852), Evidence, 90.

5. Appointment as Regius Professor of Modern History

In December 1842, two months after his deprivation, Vaughan was invited by Edwin Chadwick to serve as a special assistant poor law commissioner to inquire into the employment of women and children in agriculture. The inquiry was headed by the assistant commissioner Alfred Austin, and Stephen Denison and Francis Doyle, both Oxford friends and contemporaries of Vaughan and like him lawyers, were appointed special assistants. Vaughan took the counties of Kent, Surrey, and Sussex, and completed his report with great thoroughness, taking much of the evidence on oath, by March 1843. It was, however, only an interlude in his unremitting search for a professorship in Oxford. Between 1841 and 1846, he twice trembled on the brink and twice actually became a candidate. By the time he was appointed to a chair in 1848, he had stood or seriously considered doing so no less than six times. Few men can have sought a professorial chair so long and with such inflexibility of purpose.

In 1841 the chair of moral philosophy founded by Dr. Thomas White in 1621 became vacant by the retirement of Vaughan's old adversary in the election of 1839, William Sewell. The electors were the Vice-Chancellor, Philip Wynter, Dean Gaisford, President Routh of Magdalen, and the two Proctors John Foley of Wadham and W. W. Tireman of Magdalen. Hawkins offered to recommend him to the electors if he would give assurances on the vexed questions of residence and his religious views. As to the latter, he remarked, Vaughan had 'a little mistook the matter' on a former occasion, and it was no affront to call upon a candidate to subscribe to the Thirty-Nine Articles. 'The affront is only when he has subscribed and people will not

believe him.'[1] Vaughan undertook to reside in Oxford for three
months in the academic year and managed to satisfy Hawkins on
the religious question. It is possible that he sheltered behind his
previous subscription, but it may be that the publication of Tract
XC destroyed the authority of the Articles as a Shibboleth of
orthodoxy before the question was put to the test. Hawkins spoke
on his behalf to each of the electors, Liddell was optimistic of his
success, and Tireman, to whom Payne had written informing him
of Vaughan's 'taste for the science of morals', was thought likely
to support him unless a candidate from Magdalen appeared or
'the cry of heresy were raised'.[2] In a letter to Vaughan, Payne
spoke eagerly of the great things expected of him if he were
elected. 'You will', he said, 'have it in your power to do something, nay a great deal, towards imparting a different tone.
Hitherto under Sewell and Newman authority has been the
watchword and the doctrine "search all things" regarded as
deadly whether in religion or morals.'[3] Although the storm
blowing about the Newmanites made it unlikely that the cry of
heresy would be raised, the electors, who included three of the
most conservative Heads in the university, were not disposed
to choose a candidate who exposed authority to the doctrine
search all things, and elected C. W. Stocker.

Stocker held the chair for a year, but before he relinquished it
the regius professorship of modern history fell vacant by the
sudden death of Arnold. It was with some reluctance, real or
assumed, that Vaughan allowed his name to be submitted to the
Prime Minister, Sir Robert Peel. Liddell, who had himself
considered standing, withdrew, rejoicing in the prospect that
Vaughan might be established in Oxford, and Hawkins again
lent his support, while simultaneously being engaged in depriving
Vaughan of his Fellowship. Vaughan's interests were philosophical, but his candidature for the chair was not so unusual as
it would have been thirty or forty years later. To his contemporaries there was nothing remarkable about it, and already in 1839

[1] E. Hawkins to Vaughan, Feb. 1841.
[2] P. S. H. Payne to Vaughan, 19 Mar. 1841.
[3] The same to the same, 23 Mar. [1841].

Tait had suggested that he should try for the same chair when Nares became ill. For the moral philosopher, history and philosophy were not unrelated, and Hume, himself a moral philosopher and Vaughan's idol, had written a standard history of England which was shortly to find its way into the Oxford curriculum.

There were, Peel confided to the Duke of Wellington, who was Chancellor, a great number of applications.[4] Besides Vaughan, they included A. P. Stanley, Herman Merivale, who had been appointed to the chair of political economy in 1837, William Palmer of Worcester College, the learned author of *Origines Liturgicae*, C. W. Stocker, who had just been appointed to the chair of moral philosophy, Henry Wellesley, shortly to become Principal of New Inn Hall, and John Ormerod, Fellow of Brasenose College. Of all the candidates, Ormerod was the strongest. He was the son of George Ormerod, the historian of Cheshire, and had been at Rugby under Arnold, who said of him that it would be difficult to find his equal among men of his own age.[5] He was an accomplished linguist, and had contributed historical articles to the *Encyclopaedia Metropolitana*. A. T. Gilbert, who had been Principal of Brasenose before his elevation to the see of Chichester, said he knew no one so well qualified for the chair, Hallam excepted.[6] His application was supported by another distinguished historian, Dean Milman.

The regius professorship, however, was given to none of these applicants, but to John Antony Cramer, a former Student and Tutor of Christ Church, who, as Principal of New Inn Hall, sought, in the uncharitable words of G. V. Cox, to recoin the dross of other societies.[7] His appointment casts a revealing light on the exercise of crown patronage. Peel found difficulty in obtaining reliable advice from the university because many of the Heads of Houses had signed certificates in favour of men from their own colleges, and accordingly he sent the applications to Archbishop Howley.[8] The Archbishop consulted his old friend

[4] B.M. Add. MS. 40459, f. 251.   [5] Add. MS. 40510, f. 239ᵛ.
[6] Ibid., f. 243ᵛ.
[7] G. V. Cox, *Recollections of Oxford* (2nd ed. 1870), 194.
[8] Add. MS. 40459, f. 251.

and contemporary at Christ Church, Dean Gaisford, who had written to Peel in June to ask him to make the chair more effective by requiring the professor to reside at Oxford for at least five or six months in the year, instead of the three required by the regulations. Gaisford confessed he was not sanguine of success 'as long as the professor has another occupation to detain him elsewhere'.[9] The shaft was directed against Arnold, who, during his brief tenure of the chair, had shuttled to and fro between Rugby and Oxford, and had complained, not without justice, both to Hawkins and to Sir John Coleridge, who had taken the matter up with Peel, of the heavy burden of lectures which he was required to give.[10] In the circumstances, it was natural for Howley and Gaisford to recommend two men who were known to be resident, Cramer, who had not presented himself as a candidate and was abroad at this time, and Ormerod.

Peel in the meantime had hit on the excellent idea of appointing Cardwell, the Camden Professor, and was warmly supported by Philip Wynter, the Vice-Chancellor, who informed him that Cardwell had larger classes than any other professor.[11] But it was thought that Cardwell would be unwilling to make the exchange, and being a man of means the additional emoluments of the chair would not be an inducement.[12] Peel thereupon wrote to Wellington mentioning the Archbishop's recommendations and suggesting the appointment of Cramer. The Duke in his turn consulted the Vice-Chancellor, whose strong conservative convictions allowed him to support Cramer without any violation of his conscience. But of Ormerod he wrote:

In many respects I should consider his appointment as good a one perhaps as could be made. But as your Grace permits me to speak in confidence I think it right to state that his political opinions are understood to be Whig. Undoubtedly the late Dr. Arnold's appointment

[9] Add. MS. 40510, ff. 147, 151.

[10] The episode is referred to by Vaughan in his evidence to the Royal Commission, p. 271. Arnold's letters to Coleridge are in the Bodleian Library (MS. Eng. lett. d. 130, particularly ff. 208ᵛ–209, 216–18, 222–3, and Coleridge's letter to Peel is entered in the Minutes of the Hebdomadal Meetings, 1841–54, 7 (University Archives).

[11] Add. MS. 40459, f. 257.   [12] Ibid.

was a good one and his lectures showed vast powers of mind and immense knowledge. But I confess I always had some anxiety as to the effect which they might ultimately produce among our young men. Whenever he had an opportunity he availed himself of it to extenuate or set off to advantage the acts of those who are recorded in History as adverse to what I venture to believe your Grace would consider sound constitutional principles both in Church and State.[13]

On the following day, Peel offered the chair to Cramer, and on 15 August notified Vaughan that his application was not successful. Vaughan never stood much chance. Unlike many of the applicants, he had made no contribution to historical studies; his reluctance to reside would have told against him, and association with Arnold would have been as injurious to him as it was to Ormerod.

Meanwhile Stocker resigned the chair of moral philosophy on being presented to the living of Draycot, and Vaughan thought briefly of standing a second time. Hawkins went so far as to speak to Routh on his behalf,[14] but in October 1842 Vaughan decided to proceed no further and wrote to explain his reasons to Hawkins.

The inconvenience and expense of leaving the neighbourhood of town and the discharge of my occasional official duties here (which it is *possible* (not likely) may now be increased), which long periodical absences in term time would involve, and the expense of residing as an independent member in the university, coupled with the *short duration* of the professorship itself, which I must leave in a few years, lead me to feel upon the whole that it will be safer to decline the competition if the *matter* is *entirely* as it was when you wrote to me.[15]

The 'matter' in question was that of residence, and Hawkins felt obliged to tell Vaughan that he could not be elected unless he undertook to reside because of the express stipulations of the statutes.[16] The electors eventually appointed the Savilian Professor of Astronomy, G. H. S. Johnson.

[13] Add. MS. 40459, f. 257ᵛ.
[14] Magdalen College MS. D. 5. 16, no. 174. 24 Oct. 1842.
[15] Oriel Letters no. 810.
[16] E. Hawkins to Vaughan, 13 Oct. 1842.

Four years passed until in 1846 the chair of moral philosophy fell vacant yet again on the resignation of Liddell, and Vaughan made his fifth attempt to obtain a chair. On this occasion the candidates included J. M. Wilson, who was eventually elected, C. P. Eden, and Benjamin Jowett, who withdrew in favour of Vaughan, 'not liking the appearance of measuring myself against him'.[17] It was the third time that Vaughan had applied or considered applying for this particular chair, and his resolution indicated the triumph of hope over experience. The familiar obstacles reappeared. Apart from the matter of residence, there was also the question of his religious views. Jowett, whose own heterodox religious opinions made him particularly conscious of the difficulty, wrote of Vaughan,

I have no doubt that an honest and truthful mind, like his, although I could not agree with his views about religion, would do more real good than those whose highest ambition is to throw up a new dyke in defence of Church and State ... but in Oxford I do not think that his views upon any subject would be fairly received on account of a general prejudice against his tenets about religion. I may be mistaken about what these views are, but it would be surely painful to him to find not merely that he was at open war with the 'malignants', but that such men as Stanley and Liddell thought it right to stand apart from him, which might possibly be the case.[18]

Far from standing apart, Liddell energetically supported Vaughan, and as Proctor possessed a vote in the election. Wilson generously wrote to the Junior Proctor and to the President of his own college to say that he did not wish to obtain the appointment by Vaughan's exclusion. When it came to the election, both the Proctors voted for Vaughan, and there was little doubt that the Vice-Chancellor and possibly the President of St. John's would have done so too but for the violent opposition of Gaisford, 'that Siberian monster our Bear of Ch.Ch.'.[19] 'He smote upon the table', recounted Liddell, 'and (almost) swore

[17] *Letters of Benjamin Jowett*, ed. E. Abbott and L. Campbell (1899), 159. The letter is conjecturally dated 1844 but must have been written in 1846.
[18] Ibid. 160.
[19] H. G. Liddell to Vaughan, 15 July 1846.

that he would not vote for a non-resident man, and when I attempted to explain what your residence would be, he got still more angry and declared *he* would not vote for *you*.'[20]

Vaughan's unwillingness to reside at a time when residence was increasingly felt to be desirable, his religious opinions, which had offended moderate men as well as the Newmanites, the fact that he was unknown to the majority of the electors, and the cumulative effect of repeated failure, made it unlikely that he would secure a professorship by election either in Convocation or by one of the electoral boards of the university. There remained the patronage of the Crown. With the disarray of the Tractarian Movement, the small group of liberals at Oxford became a force of growing importance. Many of them were friends of Vaughan and wished to see him active in the university. Many, such as Stanley, Conington, and Congreve, were like him Rugbeians, and like him too had become interested in university reform after experiencing the religious doubts which so often seemed to be the fate of Arnold's best pupils. This still nascent party had little influence in the university, but from 1846 it had the ear of Lord Russell's government.[21] Thus, when J. A. Cramer died in 1848 and the chair of modern history fell vacant, there were many to press Vaughan's claim. Amongst them was Liddell who records that he was active on Vaughan's behalf.[22]

Vaughan did not share the view that his best hope lay with the Crown, and while his friends were lobbying the Prime Minister he was trying to muster the support of Oriel for another attempt on the professorship of logic. On 4 October 1848, Hawkins wrote to say that he would with great pleasure make Vaughan's wishes known at the audit, though he added the warning that the college had seldom if ever voted as a college and that his success would largely turn on the exertions of his friends inside and out of Oxford.[23]

[20] Ibid.

[21] W. R. Ward, *Victorian Oxford* (1965), 135.

[22] H. G. Liddell's recollections of Vaughan. Twisleton told Vaughan that it was to Liddell that 'in all probability you mainly owed your appointment' (Letter in the possession of Lord Saye and Sele).

[23] E. Hawkins to Vaughan, 4 Oct. 1848.

It was not a change of heart but of circumstances which finally impelled Vaughan towards the chair of history. Indeed he became professor of history almost by accident. 'Neither in 1848', he wrote to Twisleton many years afterwards, 'nor at an earlier or later period would I have cared to hold a Professorship of History at all. I do not say that I might not have accepted it. But I was induced in '48 to offer myself as a candidate on account of the ruin which the direction of the London and Birmingham or N. Western Railway had brought upon its proprietors, and the pecuniary liabilities in which their policy involved them.'[24] But Twisleton wrote to Lord Russell, and the indefatigable Hawkins offered to do so, and although the editor of *The Times* canvassed for G. W. Dasent[25] and there were remours that Hallam was a candidate,[26] the reluctant bride was at length brought to the altar when Russell offered the regius professorship to him on 13 November.

If his own statement is to be believed, Vaughan accepted for financial reasons a professorial chair he did not really want. Certainly all but one of his previous attempts had been directed to philosophical chairs. Apart from economic considerations, what perhaps finally persuaded him to accept Lord Russell's offer was the enthusiastic wish of his friends to bring him to Oxford. To his younger contemporaries he had become almost a symbol. A brilliant career had been cut short by his refusal to compromise his conscience and take Orders; he had been oppressed by obsolete college statutes; he had been defeated by the tyrannous ways of the Heads; he had suffered martyrdom at the hands of the Tractarians. On his head were visited all the iniquities of the old order, the removal of which would usher in the bright new day of reformation. But by accepting the chair Vaughan also accepted the political character of his appointment. All crown appointments were, and remain, to some extent political, but with notable exceptions, such as that of Hampden

[24] Vaughan to E. Twisleton, 23 Feb. 1860.
[25] *History of The Times* (1939), ii. 97. Delane wrote to Sir Charles Wood on 28 Aug. 1848 in support of Dasent (P.R.O. 30/22/7 C, f. 399).
[26] Bodleian Library MS. Pattison 47, f. 400ᵛ.

and later of Stanley, they were seldom criticized on that account. Vaughan, however, was the nominee of a Prime Minister committed to university reform and to the imposition of a Royal Commission. The fact that he was the first layman to hold the chair of history, and his appointment in a secular discipline widely expected soon to be elevated into a School of the university, served to emphasize his position. His historical attainments were considerably less than those of his three immediate predecessors, Nares, Arnold, and Cramer, and it may be supposed that Lord Russell appointed him less for these than for his intellectual powers in general and his liberal opinions. His appointment was thus an earnest of reform, particularly in the sensitive area of the professoriate, and Vaughan found himself cast into the rising tempest of university politics, in which the claims of the professoriate would in part be tested by his performance as professor.

6. Inaugural Lecture

In October 1849 Vaughan delivered his inaugural lecture in the newly completed Taylor Building.[1] It was a great university occasion. Jowett described the scene in a letter to Stanley. 'Imagine', he wrote, 'the room in the new Taylor Building crammed with hearers:— Vaughan, with cap on head, surrounded by a bevy of ladies and of Heads of Houses (Soapy Sam in a corner) ready to burst, "das zwanzigjährige Geheimniss". It reminded me of another inaugural lecture delivered about eight years since.'[2] When Vaughan was appointed Regius Professor, history was not regarded in Oxford as a subject comparable in intellectual rigour with the study of classical literature, and he grasped the occasion to enunciate in majestic and eloquent terms what he conceived to be the nature of the study, and by implication the purpose of the professor. History was presented as a severe intellectual discipline, encompassing the whole of human experience, and possessing canons of truth as exacting as any and more elusive than most. Jowett likened the first of the two lectures to 'a kind of intellectual sermon, written in the spirit of one who felt the nothingness of human knowledge'.[3] Much of what Vaughan had to say was new, in Oxford at least, and owed little to German thinkers or to the utilitarians. It was significant of the new ground he took that he made no mention of Arnold or any of his predecessors, and it was significant too of his conception of the duties of the professor that he made no mention of the School of History, which was about to come before Convocation.

[1] H. H. Vaughan, *Two General Lectures on Modern History* (1849).
[2] i.e. Arnold's. *Letters of Benjamin Jowett*, ed. E. Abbott and L. Campbell (1899), 164.
[3] Ibid.

History was defined by Vaughan in a striking phrase as 'a disclosure of the critical changes in the condition of society'. Society rather than the individual was the proper subject of history. Society was not merely an aggregate of individuals but existed in time, and it was in time that the *condition* of society existed. The condition of society was constantly changing towards increased complexity. This did not imply that early society was simple—indeed the contrary was the case. Early society was complex, but its complexity was of a different kind to that of modern society.

The latter is the complexity of division, distribution, and development; the former is the complexity of disintegration and intermixture. The latter is the complexity of different ends, and different functions assigned to separate organs; the former is the complexity of similar or identical effects accomplished by different instruments. In the earlier society three or four languages were doing the work of one. Two or three systems of law were controlling the devolution of the same kind of property upon different principles.

If society was more important than the individual, it was also more important than the nation. It was in society that Vaughan expected to find 'the operation of some uniting principle, through the varied destinies and condition of modern nations'. This distinction between the community and the state was a fertile conception for historical studies, though not original to Vaughan and present in the writings of historians such as Grote and Buckle. It enabled him to break away from the stifling tradition of political and military history. How far it broadened the spectrum of history may be seen in the following passage.

There are [he says] institutions, laws, customs, tastes, traditions, beliefs, convictions, magistracies, festivals, pastimes, and ceremonies, and other such elements of social organisation, which are both in thought and in fact, distinguishable from the conditions of a national unity. It is essential to the latter, that it should be attended by some executive or legislative power, which extends over all its parts, and which can control the collective action of the whole community. History exhibits this unity often gradually impaired and dissolved, sometimes as suddenly and violently severed; while, in many of these instances, the social unity survives the shocks, or the principal of natural decay, by which the national unity has been broken up. Indeed the whole character of Modern History is due to the fact, that, while nations perish, society lives on.

Society existed in time, but time also existed before society. Natural history existed before society and was preparatory to it. It was essential, he remarked, to the full and comprehensive view of civil history that it should take its place as a part of natural history. Vaughan's attempt to relate human to natural history not only placed the brevity of human history in perspective, but had another consequence of great significance. Drawing on his knowledge of science, and in particular of physiology, he identified the relationship between natural and human history in terms of the principle of development towards increased complexity which he had already defined in society. From confused and shapeless forms, he said, there eventually emerged spiritual and intellectual man. The implication was that the natural history of man led to the evolution of man's moral nature. This was a theory of evolution without natural selection, but in its place the critical changes in the condition of society which he had defined as the subject of history. By attempting to apply the methods and discoveries of science to the study of history, Vaughan brought new terms of reference into the discussion far removed from those of Arnold and his predecessors. Arnold, for example, believed that history expressed the divine Providence, and that Revelation provided an explanation of the difference between ancient and modern history. To Vaughan, on the other hand, there was no such distinction between ancient and modern history, for both were parts of a single unified process.

Vaughan drew a sharp distinction between science and history. Both were concerned with the discovery of truth, and therefore with universality, which was the characteristic of truth. This implied the formation of laws, but the laws of history were essentially different to the laws of science because the process of historical causation differed from the process of change in science. History was defined as the disclosure of critical change to distinguish it from other kinds of change. Chemistry, he remarked, was a science of change, but the changes were constant and recurring. The changes of history on the other hand were not recurrent nor periodic but critical. The complexity of society involved an equal complexity of change, and change acted 'collaterally, through the surrounding circumstances, as well as lineally through its own direct influence upon the general condition, which is the sum, result, and effect of all'. It followed from this analysis that history never repeated itself. 'The whole condition of one society tends to differ from that of another.... Rarely then can the same condition attend separate nations. Further, it can never revisit the same people, at different periods of its history.'

His conception of the non-recurrent nature of historical change led him to reject the claims of those historians, such as Arnold, who, following Vico, discerned an analogy between the cycles of life in the individual and in the nation.[4]

It would [he said] be dangerous to hazard any close comparison between the national and individual identity; between the national and individual life. We know that at the best the individual must pass through certain stages of infancy, adolescence, manhood, and decline, and then perish. We see this course of human life as a fact, and as a necessity. Our historical experience has not disclosed any very close analogy to this in the destinies of nations. There is no law to be collected by observation, prescribing certain periods for development, maturity, and decay.

If, as Vaughan claimed, historical change was non-recurrent, it may be asked how it was possible to formulate any historical laws at all. He met this difficulty by detecting the presence of universal principles in society which evolved through the process of change. An example was to be found in the history of institutions. They doomed themselves, he said, to alteration, for by their effect they threatened the circumstances which brought them into existence while at the same time possessing a permanency of their own 'They preserve their name, but they change their qualities, or maintaining the type of their original

4 See D. Forbes, *The Liberal Anglican Idea of History* (1952).

structure, they exercise new powers altogether. Under such conditions alone are they truly, actively, and healthily permanent.' A further example was the bequeathal of property, a concept which he traced in some detail from the practice of Roman colonization to the relationship of landlord and tenant. Jowett was unimpressed by this example, and wrote that Vaughan 'seemed to expect to find in History simple ultimate laws, analagous to the Law of Gravitation in Physical Science. The instance he gave was the Bequeathal of Property as a simple ultimate fact of the social state. These "ultimate facts", while in the physical world they have a simple beauty, are in the world of history of a very meagre and dubious character.'[5] Jowett, however, misunderstood what Vaughan meant by a historical law. Historical laws were not like scientific laws except that both expressed a universal truth: they were ideas which developed in the complex texture of society.

Any great pervading condition, any large and important fact, which visits society, loses as we have seen its form, but it preserves its active force, it propagates an influence, or is metamorphosed into other facts, which without it would never have been evolved. These again pass away in their turn, not by annihilation, but by a similar transmutation into new and active elements. The very principle of decay and change is a principle of modified vitality. Things are plied to some new purpose; they are either broken into stubborn fragments, or distintegrated into a vegetative mould on which new growths may flourish. The principle of change, which forbids them to remain as they have been, empowers and enjoins them to subsist by alteration. . . . And from this very process is necessitated the law, that no past states can ever be renewed; for could the same outward circumstances again befal society, the inward forces in society which must accept and digest them are altered.

Faced with such a complicated pattern of change, it was difficult to recognize the laws of history. Vaughan's solution owes much to Hume. To arrive at historical truth two things were needed: first, observation of the facts and second appreciation of them. For the simple act of observation, vigilance and

[5] *Letters of Benjamin Jowett*, ed. E. Abbott and L. Campbell (1899), 166.

keenness were required and 'a principle of attraction to the facts', which consisted in a familiarity with objects of a similar or identical kind. In addition, 'instincts of *expectation* more or less definite', and 'habits of rapid *recognition*' were needed. Historical truth was approached when a common principle was discovered connecting disparate facts, and 'the particulars in this case are fused into the universal, and knowledge is exalted into science'.

Vaughan's inaugural lecture, the longest ever delivered, raised important questions about the meaning and purpose of history. Indeed it raised more questions than it settled, but it is arguable that what the study of history most needed at that time was an attempt to define its scope and direction in the light of the intellectural developments of the previous fifty years, and this Vaughan sought to do. He broadened the field of historical study in Oxford by suggesting society as its proper object; he secularized its study by the application of scientific methods; his conception of historical change destroyed the old idea of cyclical history and offered a principle for connecting what would otherwise have been unconnected facts; by bringing science into history and history into philosophy he emphasized the ultimate unity of knowledge. His method was empirical, and despite his desire to find laws in historical experience he offered no doctrinal nostrums for unlocking the past. Yet in spite of the fertility of his ideas he had no appreciable effect on the development of historical studies in England, and where ideas discussed in his lecture were later assimilated by English historians it was from other sources. There were many reasons for this neglect. He was always a philosopher first and a historian second, but as a philosopher he failed to establish a reputation which would have given credence to his ideas on history. He never illustrated his ideas on history in a work of historical scholarship; as professor he never consolidated a school of history. Finally, the foundation of the School of History prevented the true development of the role of the professor as Vaughan envisaged it.

7. The Examination Statute

1850

THE 1850s saw many reforms in the university. They witnessed in rapid succession the Royal Commission which published its justly famous report in 1852, the Oxford Act which followed two years later, and the University Commission appointed by Parliament. A few months after Vaughan had delivered his inaugural lecture, the Hebdomadal Board submitted to Convocation a statute which occupies a position of great importance in the history of reform. This was the Examination Statute, and on its details Vaughan exerted much influence and through it acquired his first taste of the practical problems of reform.

The statute was the most important measure of university legislation since the reforms of 1800 and 1807, and like them it was concerned with the public examinations. It occupies a key position in the reform movement because from it were derived many of the problems and issues which dominated the debate. By reforming the structure of examinations and establishing new Schools, the statute acted directly on the teaching system of the university and raised the question, which was largely dependent on that system, of the nature of a liberal education. By its provisions, far from removing the need for action by the government, which many hoped it might avert, it increased the educational difficulties of the university to such an extent that the intervention of the legislature became unavoidable.

In 1850 the teaching system was already suffering great strain. The introduction of Class lists and the separation of the Mathematical from the Classical School caused a steady rise in the level of attainment required. Between 1845 and 1848 the average number of Firsts was ten, whereas between 1808 and 1813 it had been sixteen. Between 1845 and 1848, out of 387 candidates for examination, only 287 were successful and the rate of failure was thus considerably higher than at Cambridge or Durham.

The examinations became more and more written instead of oral exercises, requiring skill in composition rather than in construing, and in 1830 the important provision that ancient authors might be illustrated by modern was introduced. In the majority of colleges these changes placed a burden on the tutorial system for which it was not designed and to which it could not easily adapt. In origin college tutors were the guardians of their pupils, as the name implies, but as the system of public education, represented by the professors and lecturers, declined they became teachers also. College tutors became the principal source of instruction not only at a time when the public examinations were still oral and before the introduction of Classes had stimulated competition, but at a time when undergraduates often entered the university at a much lower age than was customary in the nineteenth century. Tutors were thus obliged to discharge some of the duties of schoolmasters, and it was natural for them in the circumstances to adopt the methods of schoolmasters, who not only gave oral tuition but did so to large classes. Even in the early part of the nineteenth century it was still common for schools to be divided into very large classes. In the university, classes of twenty pupils were not unknown in some disciplines. Because so much of the tuition consisted of construing ancient authors it was possible for the same tutor to teach the whole curriculum, and few tutors were required.

The combination in a tutor who was invariably a clergyman of the functions of moral guardian and academic teacher, and the oral teaching of a pre-eminently classical curriculum, significantly shaped the traditional liberal education given by the university. It was not designed to impart great knowledge but to infuse Christian principles and to train the mind through the mental discipline necessary for construing Greek and Latin authors. By raising the level of attainment required and by emphasizing the acquisition of information, the reform of the public examinations early in the nineteenth century put the tutorial system and the old idea of a liberal education under steadily increasing pressure. As the age of matriculation rose, the need for the university to discharge the functions of the grammar school declined. Although there were pressures on the educational system from outside the university in the rise of the professional middle class and the aspirations of the dissenters, a principal cause of its erosion came from within.

Tutors found themselves teaching classes of men of different abilities whose attainments were tested by competitive examination, and the same tutor was no longer able to teach the whole gamut of subjects to the standard now required. In order to give adequate tuition in these altered circumstances it was necessary for tutors to specialize. In order to preserve the character of the education provided by the university it was necessary to retain its religious basis and to subordinate to it any new disciplines that might be introduced into the university. At Oriel in 1830, Newman, Froude, and Wilberforce sought to achieve these ends by introducing private classes and the study of particular books and by strengthening the pastoral relationship between tutor and pupil,[1] but the resistance of Provost Hawkins and the divisive influence of the Tractarian Movement curtailed the experiment.

Most colleges could not provide specialized tuition because they were unable to appoint enough able tutors. Only Balliol and Oriel had accepted the logic of the competition injected into the public examinations by the introduction of Classes and had thrown their Fellowships open to competition. But even at Balliol, where a considerable measure of specialization was introduced, W. C. Lake, Senior Dean and tutor, declared that the number of tutors was insufficient and that a tutor teaching history would have to lecture in the same term on Thucydides, Herodotus, Livy, and Cicero, and in addition give lectures on divinity and even philosophy.[2] Elsewhere the

---

[1] Oriel Letters no. 1303.
[2] *Report of the Oxford University Commission* (1852), Evidence, 165.

quality of Fellows was often very low. Out of 550 Fellowships in the university, only 22 were open to general competition in 1850. Of the rest many were restricted to founder's kin or to particular localities and schools. The number of Fellows in a college available for tutorial duties was frequently small owing to the prevalence of non-residence, and in many colleges it was not possible to provide tuition in mathematics. The almost universal obligation to take Holy Orders further weakened the tutorial system by excluding able men from Fellowships, and by causing a rapid turnover of experienced tutors as college livings fell vacant. Fellows looked to a career outside the university, and a tutorship was seldom regarded as an office to be followed for life. 'No tutor', wrote John Wilkinson, 'seems to regard his office as a profession.'[3] 'Education', observed John Conington, 'is not likely, at least for some time to come, to become so definite and substantive a profession that men in general will be unwilling to combine it with orders, especially if College livings continue to exist.'[4] It is thus not remarkable that even a college so large as Christ Church found difficulty in obtaining more than half a dozen tutors. Most halls had only one.[5]

Even where these difficulties were recognized and there was a desire for reform, college statutes, and particularly the oaths exacted from Fellows to observe them, presented a formidable obstacle to change. It is the case that the impediment caused by statutes was exaggerated by the opponents of change, and the royal commission was at pains to show that for centuries colleges had departed from their statutes when it suited them to do so. There is also evidence that in some colleges statutes governing closed Fellowships were interpreted with latitude in order to improve elections, and Vaughan's experience at Oriel had demonstrated the existence of powers of amendment. Yet when all qualifications have been made, the question of the statutes prevented any universal reform of the tutorial system.

The shortcomings of college tuition were not mended by university teaching. The alleged decline of the professorial system was often attributed to the predominance of the colleges and the

3 Ibid. 75.　　　4 Ibid. 115.　　　5 Ibid. 98.

consequent withering of university institutions. But the real cause of the decline of professorial teaching, as of the tutorial system, was the development of the public examinations. The worst-attended lectures were those on subjects unconnected with the examinations. On the other hand, J. M. Wilson, the Professor of Moral Philosophy, declared that his lectures, which were directly relevant to them, averaged forty to fifty students, and Henry Wall, the Praelector in Logic, claimed to have audiences of 200.

Into the vacuum created by the inadequacy of college and university teaching stepped the private tutor. Unlike the college tutor or the professor he gave specialized tuition to small classes or individuals. Private tutors were either college tutors who gave private tuition, or recent graduates who remained resident in the university without college connection. Almost all undergraduates resorted to them, usually for a period of about three terms previous to the examinations. 'Within the last three or four years', wrote G. O. Morgan in 1850, 'there have been few instances of Undergraduates obtaining a Pass Degree, and scarcely any of their obtaining high honours, without having previously received assistance from a Private Tutor.'[6] George Rawlinson recorded that as a Fellow of Exeter no fewer than 30 out of 35 of his pupils between 1842 and 1846 had had recourse to private tutors, and that of this number 16 were candidates for honours and 14 for a pass degree. The system was approved by the majority of college tutors. Bonamy Price called it 'indestructible',[7] and Rawlinson said that it was 'the *only* means whereby rapid progress is made in the higher branches of knowledge'.[8] Gaisford attempted to forbid the undergraduates of Christ Church to read with private tutors outside the college, but he met with small success and Robert Lowe stated that half his pupils came from the House.[9] Private tutors formed a large group of learned men in the university, and a number of them served as Public Examiners. Without them the educational system at Oxford would speedily

[6] *Report of the Oxford University Commission* (1852), Evidence, 196. Sewell's description of Vaughan as his pupil (see p. 44) suggests that he acted as his private tutor.   [7] Ibid. 195.   [8] Ibid. 218.   [9] Ibid. 12.

have ground to a halt. The best of them taught a single subject to a few men, and their example influenced the direction in which college tutors, and for a time it seemed professors also, would develop. Their specialized knowledge was a corrosive force on the traditional liberal education of the university, and it is notable that many of the criticisms of them were not dissimilar to those subsequently levelled by Pusey against professors.

Far from easing the educational crisis in the university, the examination statute of 1850 made it much worse. It sought to introduce two reforms, both desirable in themselves. It sought to increase the amount of work required of undergraduates and to spread it more evenly. Since two thirds of undergraduates read for the modest requirements of a pass degree, and since the hurdle of Responsions did not take place until the second year, the temptation to idleness was often irresistible. The statute also sought to provide some elementary professional training. In short it created new and heavy burdens for the already creaking tutorial system to bear.

By the statute originally put to Convocation on 20 March 1849, the academic course was divided by three examinations taken at intervals of a year. The first of these was Responsions, which was brought forward to the end of the first year and so discharged some of the functions of a university matriculation examination. The second, or First Public Examination, was in classics and mathematics and was a new examination. For the Second Public Examination, all candidates were required to take two Schools, of which one must be Classics and the other mathematics, natural science, or 'history and cognate sciences'. The statute also proposed to insist on attendance at professorial lectures and to transfer the nomination of examiners to professorial boards. Most of the provisions of the statute were adopted, but the appointment of examiners was rejected and the School of History and Cognate Sciences lost by six votes. For procedural reasons, Convocation was obliged to throw out proposals of which it only partially disapproved, whereupon the Hebdomadal Board was enabled to bring forward what were in fact amendments, and the narrow defeat of the History School was thus interpreted as signifying doubts about the details rather than the principle. The details were indeed ill chosen. The *Morning Post* dismissed the curriculum as a collection of odds and ends swept together 'for no better reason than that there was no room for them elsewhere'.[10] For passmen, the statute prescribed the history of England, France, or Germany in the sixteenth or seventeenth centuries, with an unspecified portion of Blackstone, and for honours modern history to 1789, general jurisprudence (including civil law), the laws of England, moral philosophy in the works of English writers, and the philosophy of language.

The most strenuous opposition to the Fourth School, as it came to be known, was founded on important questions of principle as well as on objection to detail. The most vehement critic was the historian E. A. Freeman, who, in his own words, was 'more prominent than any other Member of Convocation in opposition to it in all its stages'.[11] Freeman believed that it was not possible to combine the traditional education given by the university with the specialization demanded by the statute, and he argued that the statute was calculated to promote superficial and erroneous views of history unless the course were so lengthened that the Master's degree was revived. It was, he maintained, preferable to preserve the existing system, which, by the study of Greek and Roman history, furnished the foundation on which true historical scholarship could be built. 'The end of an Undergraduate course', he said, 'was not the complete carrying out of any one branch of knowledge, but the laying a foundation on which the Student may subsequently build up a thorough knowledge of any. The old course did not profess, in three or four years, the arduous task of producing perfect historians, or perfect philosophers; but it gave the Student the best possible start for becoming whichever his taste might dictate in after-life.'[12] Fear that the traditional studies would suffer was also expressed by Provost Hawkins, who declared that history would draw men away from the more exacting study of the classics.[13]

---

[10] 22 Mar. 1849.

[11] *Report of the Oxford University Commission* (1852), Evidence, 138.

[12] Ibid.   [13] *Correspondence of A. H. Clough*, ed. F. L. Mulhauser (1957), i. 247.

Equally strong objection was taken to the statute on overtly religious grounds. Some claimed that the absence of prescribed texts and impartial books would foster political and religious controversy, and Freeman was amongst those who held that the study of sixteenth- and seventeenth-century history was particularly liable to this result. Others objected to the inclusion of moral philosophy, not from a sense of its incongruity, for in the absence of Schools of Theology or Philosophy there was a case for combining post-classical philosophy with history, but because the authors to be studied included some hostile to religion. Finally, there were complaints that the curriculum was inadequate for the training of lawyers. Law, declared the *Guardian*, was buried beneath a mass of history, and the elegant pages of Blackstone were no substitute for the rigours of Justinian.

Vaughan took no part in the initial drafting of the statute. Not only had it been drawn up in essentials when he was appointed, but the drafting of statutes was the responsibility of the Hebdomadal Board from which professors as such were excluded. He made no reference to it in his inaugural, but was nevertheless simultaneously canvassing support among the tutors for a scheme of his own. In a letter apparently written in November 1849, Jowett wrote that he

. . . has devised a very good plan for the Modern History, which he has been propounding to various Masters and C[ommon] Rooms. The plan, as nearly as I can remember, is as follows:—

Necessary. One of two portions of English History, which is to be divided at the reign of Henry VII. The first of these portions to be accompanied by the part of Blackstone relating to the (Feudal) Laws of Real Property: the second by that part which treats of the Constitution. *For Honours*. Both portions of English History, with the corresponding portions of Law.
But one of these portions may be commuted for a portion of some Foreign History, which is contemporary with the English History. In this latter case Civil Law or International Law must be taken up. And in any case for Honours the 'Blackstone' may be commuted for the 'Civil Law'.[14]

---

[14] *Letters of Benjamin Jowett*, ed. E. Abbott and L. Campbell (1899), 168.

Vaughan's own version has not survived, and Jowett's account, although apparently unreliable in omitting mention of political economy, may be accepted as presenting its main features. The scheme was an improvement on the proposed statute. The periods offered to Passmen were longer and the division between them not unreasonable; the objections to the exclusive study of sixteenth- and seventeenth-century history and to moral philosophy were removed; the legal requirements were more appropriate; foreign history was taken from the Pass School and became an option for Honours.

If the Hebdomadal Board was cognizant of Vaughan's scheme, no notice was paid of it when on 7 December 1849 the statute was sent to Convocation for a second time, for the details of the History School were identical with those of the earlier version, except that the title was changed to Jurisprudence and History. This time the principle of the School was accepted by 153 votes to 139, but on Vaughan's intervention and special plea the details were lost by 178 votes to 106.[15]

The second defeat of the statute created an unusual situation, for the controversial proposals of the Board on the content of the Fourth School could not hope to succeed having been twice rejected. Despite the leading part he had taken in Convocation, Vaughan could not introduce his own scheme directly, and the Board refused to appoint a delegacy of M.A.s.[16] At this juncture he was fortunate in finding two willing allies on the Board itself in Francis Jeune, the reforming Master of Pembroke College, and Edward Cardwell, Principal of St. Alban Hall. In January 1850 he sent his scheme to them, and on the 24th Jeune replied in the following encouraging terms:

I have communicated with Dr. Cardwell about your proposed scheme for the Modern History School.

I am happy to say that there appears to be no irreconcilable difference between us and you on the matter.

---

[15] Add. MS. 44181, f. 54.
[16] *Report of the Oxford University Commission* (1852), Evidence, 30.

We think that the statute should be as comprehensive as possible with regard to the Class men.

Doubtless they will take up what the pass-men must take up, but scope should be given to individual tastes. Moreover experience has shown that the Examiners and Examinees between them modify systems and generally speaking modify them about yearly. We would not cramp development.

As to the pass-men it occurs to us that English History should be divided into two portions indeed...precisely such as you have set down.

The former should comprehend the centuries between the Norman Conquest and the *end* of the reign of Henry VIIth.

The second from the accession of Henry VIIIth to the end of the 18th century.

As to law we think that the portion of Blackstone which treats of *real* property would be the proper accompaniment to the earlier period of history.

We would have what you suggest, 1, the law of personal property and constitutional law connected with the latter.

Political Economy we greatly desire and have often urged on the Board but have always been scornfully refused. Now even Adam Smith stinks in their nostrils. I fear he must be adjourned.

I shall be glad if you and your friends can consent to these modifications of your scheme. They are not very damaging.

It appears from this letter that Vaughan, Cardwell, and Jeune were in agreement on the curriculum for a pass degree, except on the syllabus for law, but that there was a divergence of opinion on the requirements for honours. Jeune and Cardwell wished to avoid precise definition of the curriculum and were evidently prepared to leave much in the hands of the examiners. In his reply, Vaughan, who objected strongly to the system of appointing examiners and believed that professors ought to have a measure of control over examinations, urged that the course should be laid down in the statute. Development ought not to be cramped, it was true, but, he remarked, 'The statute is absolutely creative. There is at present nothing to develop. Our first want will be order, unity and guidance.' Candidates for honours, he maintained, ought to study to a higher level the whole of the course offered to passmen with the appropriate law, and the possibility of substituting a period of foreign history was not trespassing on individual choice.

A day or two later, Jeune wrote to Vaughan that he had shown 'the paper which we jointly drew up' to Cardwell and that he intended to propose the details of the Fourth School 'in the later form' to the Hebdomadal Board on 5 February.[17] At his suggestion, Vaughan wrote to the Vice-Chancellor, F. C. Plumptre, stating that the opposition of himself and his friends to the statute had been actuated only by a feeling that the prescribed course of sixteenth- and seventeenth-century history was too narrow.[18] On 23 April 1850, the revised statute was accepted by Convocation by 127 votes to 74.

The School of History and Jurisprudence created by this statute offered passmen a choice of two periods of English history. The first extended from 1066 to 1509, with Blackstone on real property, and the second from 1509 to 1714, with Blackstone on the rights of persons and the law of personal property. Justinian's *Institutes* might be substituted for Blackstone. For classmen, the curriculum comprised English history from the birth of Christ to 1789, with the appropriate Blackstone, certain periods of European history, jurisprudence and especially the laws of England, the laws of nations, and Adam Smith's *Wealth of Nations*. The first examination in the new School was to be held in 1853. It is not possible to isolate Vaughan's contribution to the statute from that made by Jeune and Cardwell, but it would seem probable that the opening out of the curriculum beyond the narrow confines originally proposed was largely due to his efforts. In November he was advocating a scheme not dissimilar to it in essentials, while in the following month Jeune and Cardwell were presumably in agreement with the terms of the statute sent to Convocation, in which the curriculum rejected in the previous March was repeated. It would follow from this argument that the division of the pass school in 1509, the study of international and civil law, and the introduction of Adam Smith were suggested by him. To him also may perhaps be attributed

---

[17] F. Jeune to Vaughan, 31 Jan. 1850.
[18] Hebdomadal Meetings Register (1841–54), 176.

the commencement of the pass school with 'the temporary destruction of English nationality', which Freeman described as 'the strangest enactment of all'.[19] In one important point the statute departed from Vaughan's scheme, for the sections of Blackstone prescribed were less appropriate to the study of history than those recommended by him, and caused Stubbs to complain that that there was no unity about much of the required reading and that much of the law had no more real connection with history than 'a similar bulk of entomological reading'.[20]

Considered as a whole, the examination statute was in many respects an unsatisfactory measure, and even at the time was regarded with less than enthusiasm. Henry Wall said that other schemes would have been more acceptable, but 'Members of Convocation were too glad to get what they could'.[21] The university reversed the natural order of priorities by creating the new studies without first reviving the professorial system, reforming the examinations, and improving the supply of tutors, and thereby aggravated the crisis in the tutorial system. 'We have inverted the order', Wilson observed to Jowett, 'because one could be done without the assistance of Parliament, the other not.'[22] What the university had omitted to do the colleges were unable to do until their statutes were reformed.

A difficulty no less serious was created by the necessity of taking a degree in classics before proceeding to one of the new Schools. In his evidence to the royal commission, Vaughan advocated the abolition of compulsory classics and theology for all, 'nor do I think that until this be done, much will have been practically effected in physical, historical, and mathematical instruction'.[23] Compulsory classics was the price of compromise. It was designed to preserve the existing liberal education given by the university. Since it was 'the sole business of the University to train the powers of the mind',[24] the same education had been

[19] Report of the Oxford University Commission (1852), Evidence, 139.
[20] W. Stubbs, Seventeen Lectures (1886), 36.
[21] Report of the Oxford University Commission (1852), Evidence, 149.
[22] Letter from B. Jowett to A. P. Stanley, 10 Jan. 1849. Balliol College.
[23] Report of the Oxford University Commission (1852), Evidence, 86. Classics continued to be compulsory until 1865.   [24] Ibid. 70.

impartially given to all whether intended for the Church, the law, or any other profession. It was no accident that the Heads in 1850 commended the Laudian system as 'a system of study admirably arranged at a time when not only the nature and faculties of the human mind were exactly what they are still, and must of course remain, but the principles also of sound and en-larged intellectual culture were far from imperfectly understood'.[25] The new studies, however, were widely regarded by the powerful conservative element in the university as professional rather than educational. The remarkable definition of the nature of natural science which Pusey propounded in his dispute with Vaughan in 1854[26] allowed little educational value to its study, and his views were shared not only by many in the university but by the majority of the headmasters who gave evidence to the Public Schools Commission a decade later. The School of Jurisprudence and History uneasily straddled both educational and professional studies. Law might have some professional value, but history was generally considered to be a moral study. If, with the exception of history, the new studies were regarded as professional training, which involved the learning of skills and the absorption of information, it was reasonable to require that young men should undergo a course in the traditional studies of the university before undertaking them. It was not an easy matter to achieve. If the B.A. course were shortened, it would involve the creation of a new School of classical studies unless classics were to diminish in status beside the new Schools. If, on the other hand, as the statute eventually resolved, the B.A. examination remained at the end of the third year, the second final examination followed so closely on its heels that the curriculum was likely to be perfunctory and superficial.

Vaughan challenged the premises on which the statute rested and questioned the validity of the university's definition of a liberal education. He denied that the study of classics was the only or the best way of training the mind or that it was the only basis of a truly liberal education. 'I cannot', he wrote, 'assign that

[25] *Report of the Oxford University Commission* (1852), appendix A, 4.
[26] See p. 140.

very great practical effect to the actual study of languages, as a means of giving a discipline to the mind, which many claim for them'.[27] He asserted instead that the justification of the new studies lay precisely in their educational value, and strongly discounted the view that the university ought to provide professional training. 'I consider it strange', he wrote, 'that both Dr. Pusey, and the Hebdomadal Committee should regard the studies of the modern history school and physical science, as *professional* studies. They were not introduced as such, advocated as such, nor defended as such. . . . It is not to be maintained, therefore, for an instant, that devotion for a year to one of those Oxford schools of study, is an adoption of professional at the expense of general education.'[28] His views raised important questions about the nature of a liberal education. It was a subject to which he was repeatedly to return.

[27] *Oxford Reform and Oxford Professors* (1854), 29.
[28] Ibid. 31.

8. Oxford University Commission

1850

HARDLY had the Examination Statute passed through Convocation, when the Royal Commission to inquire into the state, discipline, studies, and revenues of the University of Oxford was issued on 31 August 1850. It was one of the most celebrated commissions of the century, and certainly the most important ever to concern itself with Oxford.

'The Commission', said Goldwin Smith, 'was a reforming Commission, and the Report was a reforming Report.'[1] Appointed by Lord John Russell, it was strongly liberal in temper. It was made up of a bishop, a Head, two professors, three schoolmasters or ex-schoolmasters, and a lawyer. The first members to be appointed were A. C. Tait, Dean of Carlisle and subsequently Archbishop of Canterbury, a former tutor of Balliol and Headmaster of Rugby in succession to Arnold, and leader of the tutors' protest against Tract XC; H. G. Liddell, Headmaster of Westminster and soon to succeed Gaisford as Dean of Christ Church; Francis Jeune, who had been Headmaster of King Edward's School, Birmingham, and was now Master of Pembroke College. Jeune doubted the expediency of a Head sitting on the commission, and the Hebdomadal Board so far shared his doubts as temporarily to exclude him from their sessions, but he accepted, so he claimed, out of a sense of obligation to Lord Russell.[2] The legal member was J. L. Dampier, whom Tait described to his wife as 'a jolly sort of old gentleman'.[3] He was a retired lawyer with a post in

[1] G. Smith, *Oxford University Reform* (Oxford Essays, 1858), 268.
[2] Lambeth Palace Library MS. Tait 78, f. 198ᵛ.
[3] Ibid. MS. Tait 102, f. 366ᵛ.

the Duchy of Cornwall, and specialized in the law of corporations on which he was invariably consulted by the Attorney General, Sir William Follett.

Lord Russell was anxious to appoint Vaughan as the fifth member, and on 7 August wrote to the Duke of Wellington, the Chancellor, to ask him to sound opinion in Oxford.[4] Liddell, too, actively canvassed support for Vaughan, and on the 16th wrote to Tait, 'I was and am very anxious to have Vaughan on the Commission. He is a good Constitutional Lawyer, has deeply studied some branches of Physical Science, which Lord John *particularly* said he wished to be attended to—is a Professor (and I must say I think a Professor should be in the Oxford as well as the Cambridge Commission), and has that calm philosophical temper which for a difficult work is most necessary and most profitable.'[5] In his reply, Tait maintained that the principal need was for a reform of the colleges, but, answered Liddell, '*my* mind is not so much occupied with the *misdeeds* of Colleges as with the necessity of advising some course for raising the character and reputation of the University as a seat of learning . . . for neglect of learning, in any sense befitting a university, conferring degrees in all Arts and Sciences, this will be a more delicate task [than reforming colleges], and for this purpose I desiderate such a man as Vaughan in the Commission.'[6] Whether owing to Tait's opposition or to other causes, Vaughan was not appointed.

On 20 August, Russell appointed Samuel Hinds, Bishop of Norwich, to head the commission. Hinds was a shrewd man, whom Tait once described as crafty as a fox. He was a friend of Jeune, who had first suggested him for the post of chairman, and an old acquaintance of Archbishop Whately, whose chaplain he had been. His business habits were casual, and on one memorable occasion during the sessions of the commission he is said to have placed letters addressed to the Hebdomadal Board and to the Duke of Wellington in the wrong envelopes. Some considered that he carried his liberal principles too far when in old age he married his cook. The remaining vacancies were filled by G. H. S.

---

[4] Apsley House Papers.   [5] Lambeth Palace Library MS. Tait 78, f. 207.
[6] Ibid., f. 209.

Johnson, who had held the chairs of astronomy and geometry, and was to be rewarded for his services on the commission and on the Parliamentary Commission which followed it by the Deanery of Wells, and Baden Powell, the professor of geometry. Baden Powell held strong and sensible views about the admission of dissenters and the improvement of the professoriate, but he suffered from a serious defect, which Tait diagnosed in a letter to his wife. 'Baden Powell', he wrote, '[is] the most talkative of bores—rendering business very difficult by his perpetual chatter.'[7] The secretary to the commission, strongly supported by Lord Russell, was A. P. Stanley, and the assistant secretary Goldwin Smith.

The most active and influential members of the commission were Tait, Jeune, Liddell, and Stanley. Hinds, although usually late for meetings, was otherwise regular in his attendance, and ways were found of keeping the talkative Baden Powell at bay. 'Baden Powell', wrote Tait, 'remains at home writing a long harangue on Professorships which we have assigned to him to keep him quiet.'[8] Johnson, who supported Tait and contributed greatly to the final drafting of the report, was frequently driven to despair by his overpowering brethren. 'Recollect', he once wrote petulantly to Tait, 'how I have stood by you like a man during many an ugly fight. . . . It will not take much to make me give up the whole concern which has almost ruined me and in which I find so little consideration from friends or foes.'[9] In another letter, also to Tait, he wrote with bitterness, 'I know full well how difficult it must have been to resist Liddell especially when joined to A. P. S[tanley] . . . I can now do nothing as I am virtually going over what has been sanctioned by a majority of the Commission. . . . When I object to anything A. P. S. says "what is the use of striking it out when you will have Jeune, Liddell and Tait against you?" And so it is: in short I am *betrayed*.'[10]

Johnson's lamentation is not the only evidence of discord within the commission, and Goldwin Smith once told Gladstone that there was a great danger at one time that it would be unable

[7] Lambeth Palace Library MS. Tait 102, f. 368ᵛ.   [8] Ibid., f. 376.
[9] Ibid. MS. Tait 78, f. 238.   [10] Ibid., f. 239.

to agree to a report.[11] Two groups formed in the commission. On the one side were Liddell and Jeune, who pursued a radical course designed to strengthen the professoriate, and on the other were Tait and Johnson, who favoured more moderate measures emphasizing the reform of colleges. Liddell described the divisions in a letter to Randall Davidson in 1886.

The Report [he wrote] was written almost entirely by Arthur Stanley. We met very frequently and came to Resolutions on the different matters into which the inquiry divided itself. Then Stanley drafted them and they were again discussed and modified. Some of us wrote portions of the Report in order to have our views more exactly formulated, and these portions were in some cases accepted, in others not. I remember that Dr. Jeune wrote a long paper, which Dr. Tait privately characterised as like an article in the Edinburgh Review:[12] it was not accepted. I wrote a passage on 'Standing Delegacies' (p. 15 sq.), which was adopted with some modifications . . . I cannot remember that the Archbishop [Tait] wrote any definite part. But he was very intimate with Stanley and may have assisted him more than I am aware of.

The Archbishop and Johnson acted together in what may be called the Conservative sense. I fear I was what may be called a Radical, and Dr. Jeune more or less worked with me. My chief interest was in the restoration of the *Professors* to life and action. The Archbishop was more inclined to give energy to the College system. The Bishop of Norwich took little active part except when he was in the chair. Mr. Dampier and Professor Baden Powell also took little part. Stanley was the life and soul of the Commission.[13]

With Stanley, Tait and Liddell dominated the commission, and parts of the report demonstrate clearly the different emphasis placed on various aspects of reform by one or the other. Perhaps because he was that rare animal, a reforming Head, Jeune has had a high place assigned to him in the history of university reform. Tait, however, found him mainly useful for his knowledge of Oxford. There was, he wrote, 'great difficulty in keeping Jeune to the point. He is almost as full of talk as B.P. My opinion

11 Add. MS. 44303, f. 131.
12 The paper was probably on college reform (Add. MS. 44221, f. 9).
13 Lambeth Palace Library MS. Tait 104, f. 72.

of him as a man of business is lowered though it is obvious he will be of great use to us from his knowledge of Oxford details as a Head of a house.'[14] But for Tait and Liddell the commission might have collapsed early in 1851 when the university obtained an opinion that it was illegal. Tait arrived late at a meeting on 18 March, and found the Bishop of Norwich

haranguing in favour of an immediate appeal to Lord John to know whether he meant to support the Commission or not, and magnifying the difficulties which the legal opinion had raised. Powell in the most senseless way was urging that it was better to be extinguished at once than to attempt a hopeless work. The Master of Pembroke, who had come up from Oxford to urge that without consulting Lord John we should immediately lay the matter before the Attorney General who would give us a legal opinion to quash that obtained by the University, had been quite converted by the Bishop, who for the first time since the Commission opened had arrived before the time and had talked to them as they arrived. Stanley and Johnson were silent. My belief is that the Bishop had been so discouraged by his interview with Lord John and the trouble that seemed likely to arise that he had come down with the intention of terminating the existence of the Commission unless Lord John would pledge himself to give us warm and strong support—a thing obviously out of his, Lord John's, power at this juncture, when he is very cold about everything and has no strength. I threw myself most vehemently immediately into the opposite scale, represented that if we went to the Prime Minister at this juncture to tell him that we could not go on without his aid, we were virtually throwing up the whole thing, and would expire amidst the just laughter of the world. Dampier was disposed to view the matter as the Bishop did. Liddell now arrived and viewed the matter as I did, being evidently resolved to proceed. The matter was talked over carefully, and the opinion gradually preponderated that it would be very foolish to throw upon Lord John at this time any responsibility that was unnecessary or give him the idea that we were alarmed.[15]

When the commission was issued, the question of university reform had rumbled intermittently for more than twenty years, though in Oxford it had been almost forgotten during the hectic

[14] Lambeth Palace Library MS. Tait 103, f. 19.   [15] Ibid., f. 49.

years of the Tractarian Movement. The university remained fundamentally as Laud had moulded it—an enclave of the Church of England. By its inability to change sufficiently rapidly and radically under increasing pressure from without and the threat of collapse within it stumbled towards crisis. It excluded dissenters, now able to voice their discontent in Parliament, it failed to meet the need for professional men demanded by the rapidly growing Civil Service at home and in India; it failed even to meet the needs of the Church of England which was passing through a period of unprecedented expansion. The reason that this long smouldering discontent erupted in 1850, and not earlier or later, and that the government entered upon a course so politically dangerous as interference with a corporation as powerful as the university of Oxford, was the situation created by the examination statute of the same year. 'In passing that statute', wrote Goldwin Smith, 'the University drew heavily in advance on Parliamentary assistance, and would have been unable to meet her engagements to the studies of the new schools if the draft had been dishonoured.'[16]

The unstated question which the commission was required to answer was how to make the statute work. The provision of better tuition is the matter which lies at the heart of its report, and college and constitutional reform, the revival of the professoriate, and even university extension were means to it or were dependent on it. It was not simply a question of opening Fellowships and reforming college statutes, for fundamental questions about the nature of a university were raised. Did, for example, the encouragement of merit by competitive examination, and the increase in secular studies undermine the moral and intellectual basis of the education previously given in Oxford? What was the purpose of college endowments? How far could the needs of the university as a place of education be reconciled with its development as a place of learning? Should teaching remain almost exclusively in the hands of the clergy? Could professorial and collegiate teaching be combined without the university becoming the dominant partner? Depending on the answers to these

[16] *Oxford University Reform* (Oxford Essays, 1858), 267.

questions was the further question whether the university should retain its existing institutions reformed and reinvigorated, or should be reconstituted perhaps in the manner of continental universities. Should there be reform or revolution?

Amongst those who gave evidence to the commission it was widely agreed that the one essential reform from which, as Frederick Temple expressed it, all other reforms would follow spontaneously,[17] was the opening of Fellowships to competition. Since Fellows swore to obey the statutes of their colleges at the time of election, reform could only come through the action of Parliament. The opening of Fellowships and the abolition of closed Fellowships would, it was hoped, not only produce better tutors but by creating more of them allow a measure of specialization in teaching. But although the opening of Fellowships would improve the quality, other factors tended to diminish the number. If, as was frequently suggested in evidence, the income of Fellowships were increased and Fellowships were suppressed for the endowment of professorships, the total number must be reduced. In addition, Fellows who pursued careers outside Oxford or occupied college livings were non-resident and so not available for teaching duties. At Oriel, where Fellowships had been open for many years, there were in 1850 only three tutors out of a list of eighteen Fellows. Considering this situation many were convinced that colleges would remain unable to meet the requirements of the examination statute even after opening their Fellowships. 'It is quite impossible', said R. W. Browne of St. John's, 'to expect that any individual College and Hall could supply men qualified to teach all the subjects of study introduced by the New Examination Statute.'[18] H. H. Wilson, the professor of Sanscrit, was equally pessimistic. 'Unless', he wrote, 'the students could be apportioned among the College tutors, in classes of three or four at most, which is not possible, the supplementary accession of private instruction must always be of use.'[19] Professor Daubeny believed the solution was for the smaller colleges to combine, but Hayward Cox, the former Principal of St. Mary

---

[17] *Report of the Oxford University Commission* (1852), Evidence, 129.
[18] Ibid., Evidence, 8.   [19] Ibid., Evidence, 11.

Hall, saw little prospect of colleges sending their pupils to other colleges.[20]

It was, therefore, necessary to take additional steps to increase the number of tutors, and those most often suggested signified a great change in the social and intellectual standing of college tutors. The most obvious method was to curb non-residence. Some favoured compulsion, and in 1854 Gladstone was one of these, but many felt that the best solution was to make conditions in the university such that Fellows would wish to reside and make a career in it the business of their lives. It was proposed by some that the obligation to take Holy Orders should be relaxed, if not for all Fellows at least for a greater proportion of them, and in particular for those concerned with the new studies. 'Entire devotion to lay studies,' remarked Goldwin Smith, 'such as the purposes of a University require, is scarcely consistent with the ordination vows of the ministers of the Church of England.'[21] Others, amongst them John Conington then in his brief noonday as reformer, urged the abolition of the rule of celibacy.[22] More important still, Fellows needed to be offered a prospect of advancement in the university, and such a prospect was to be found in the revival of the professoriate, which was declared to be 'the natural and appropriate reward' for those who distinguished themselves as tutors and examiners.[23]

To conservatives, the total effect of such measures, in particular the secularization of Fellowships and the substitution of preferment in the university for preferment in the Church, constituted a threat to the old educational system. Few of them gave evidence to the commission, but Arthur Haddan spoke for them when he wrote to Gladstone during the passage of the Oxford Act:

There is good ground for placing the office of moral training in the hands of the clergy: there is *no* ground for preferring a clergyman for communicating mere information in any branch of education: there is *sufficient* ground for restricting ordinarily to clerical hands such

[20] Ibid., Evidence, 98.
[21] G. Smith, *Oxford University Reform* (Oxford Essays, 1858), 278.
[22] *Report of the Oxford University Commission* (1852), Evidence, 115.
[23] Ibid., Evidence, 13.

subjects as necessarily although indirectly involve moral training as e.g. Ethics or any species of Mental Science, History, etc. But in order to secure the *first* and all important of these three things it becomes necessary that the second as well as the third should be undertaken by clergymen, so far as they enter into a general education.[24]

The professorial question became the most inflammatory issue in university reform. The main question of debate was the nature of the institution: was the principal duty of the professor the pursuit of learning or was it to teach, was he an instrument of professional training or of education? It was generally held that Oxford suffered from a lack of learned men compared with continental universities, and there was much support for measures designed to attract scholars to Oxford, such as an increase in the number and endowments of chairs and the representation of professors in university government. Had the professor been seen simply as a scholar devoted to learned pursuits it is probable that there would have been little if any controversy. But if even after the reform of Fellowships, colleges were still unable to provide adequate tuition, particularly in the new studies introduced in 1850, the professor, who was often the only source of instruction in such studies, would be required to contribute directly to the teaching of undergraduates. W. C. Lake, then a tutor at Balliol, expressed the opinion of moderate men when he remarked, 'It is indeed allowed on all sides, that there is no possibility of doing justice to the new subjects of Modern History and Physical Science, without extensive assistance from Professors.'[25] It was a view which retarded the development of the professoriate for a generation, for if professors were actively engaged in the practical work of teaching in the capacity of tutors they could not be expected also to produce 'the fruits of learned leisure and meditations'.[26]

The attempt to consider the professor as a superior tutor caused bitter opposition, and even those such as Lake who accepted it did so with reluctance. It struck at the roots of the existing system

[24] Add. MS. 44183, f. 90ᵛ.
[25] *Report of the Oxford University Commission* (1852), Evidence, 165.
[26] G. Smith, op. cit., 283.

of education and teaching. The conservatives, for whom Haddan spoke, regarded education as essentially moral in character. The new studies, with the exception of history, were concerned with the acquisition of information and were therefore not educational. Professors were men who devoted themselves to learning and to increasing the stock of information. They were, it followed from this argument, unsuitable and even dangerous instruments for the education of the young. Mark Pattison, who believed that it was the duty of the professor to advance knowledge, attacked professorial lectures, however necessary they might be in the sciences, on these grounds. 'The mischief of the Professorial system', he wrote, 'is that it implies a different idea of education; that it aims at, and is the readiest and easiest way to, a very inferior stamp of mental cultivation. . . . The Professorial and Tutorial methods represent respectively the education which consists in accomplishment and current information, and that which aims at disciplining the faculties, and basing thoughts on the permanent ideas proper to the human reason.'[27]

Such arguments were greatly influenced by professorial practices in the sciences, where there was a tendency, because of the need to demonstrate apparatus, to lecture to classes as large as those customary for many college tutors. Such lectures occurred with frequency, and Professor Daubeny, for example, began by giving 40 lectures a year, which he later reduced to the still high level of 22 or 24, and Bartholomew Price found nothing extraordinary in recommending that professors should deliver at least 30 lectures a term.[28] Not all professorial lectures, however, were of this kind. Many of those who gave evidence to the commission envisaged professors who taught by catechetical methods similar to those adopted by college tutors. 'By a professorial system', said R. W. Browne, 'I of course mean not the mere delivery of oral lectures, but catechetical lectures also, occasional examinations by the Professor, the use of text-books, and above all strictness in requiring . . . a certain preparation for the lectures on the part of the students.'[29] N. W. Senior, the professor of political

---

[27] *Report of the Oxford University Commission* (1852), Evidence, 45.
[28] Ibid., Evidence, 64.   [29] Ibid., Evidence, 6.

economy, recommended that lectures should be 'conversations with pupils', and proposed to convert the professor 'from a mere preacher into a sort of University tutor'.[30] Such lectures differed not only from those given in the sciences, but in important respects from those given by college tutors. In the small size of the classes and in the fact that the professor taught a single subject, catechetical lectures by professors resembled the tuition given by the private tutor rather than that given by the college tutor, and the private tutor was almost universally accepted as inevitable and desirable.

There were, however, reasons why what was acceptable from private tutors was strongly resented when provided by professors. The private tutor, who was often a college tutor as well, worked until 1850 in the area of classical studies which was the traditional arena of the college tutors, and was not in obvious competition with them. But if tuition in the new studies, where there was as yet very little college teaching, were to be placed predominantly in the hands of the professors, the effective control of studies would pass from the colleges to the university, and if professors were in addition to control the examinations, which would, as Bonamy Price put it, 'turn on what the Professors teach',[31] the superiority of the university over the colleges became complete.

Various schemes were put forward for combining professorial and collegiate teaching. The examination statute raised the question whether college tutors should confine themselves to the first two years of an undergraduate's career or should also teach during the third and more specialized year. Because the First Public Examination occurred at the end of the second year, it was argued that professorial teaching should take place in the third year because the professorships for the most part existed in the new studies. This was, it so happened, another point of similarity between the teaching of professors and of private tutors, whose services were also required during the third year. One school of thought, composed of scientists and those who were dissatisfied with the compromise of the statute, believed

---

[30] *Report of the Oxford University Commission* (1852), Evidence, 281.
[31] Ibid., Evidence, 193.

that instruction in the third year ought to be placed entirely in the hands of the professors. Many of this way of thinking also favoured a reduction in the time needed for a Bachelor's degree from three years to two, and the abolition of the double honours school. Such schemes would have raised the standard of the new studies, but would have eroded further the status of the college tutor.

A different scheme was put forward by two of the most influential tutors in Oxford, Jowett and Lake. Lake maintained that to place teaching exclusively in the hands of the professors during the third year would weaken the college tutorial system, which was 'the very best part of Oxford', by destroying the bond of 'interest and affection' between pupil and tutor.[32] He thought that the able and less able student would benefit from tutorial teaching throughout their academic careers. Lake and Jowett conceived tutorial and professorial teaching as supplementing one another. The tutor, said Jowett, began the work which the professor took up and completed, and to Lake the task of the professor was to investigate 'such points as Tutors are precluded from doing effectually'.[33] Neither of them envisaged a tutorial system so reformed that it would be able to provide instruction without the help of the professors: Jowett contemplated the continuance of tutors who taught many subjects, and Lake assumed that private tutors would still be needed.[34] But whether professorial teaching was separated from collegiate teaching or integrated with it, one thing was certain: the college tutors would resist any proposal to invest the professors with preponderant power in the university.

The relationship of the professors to the tutors was again raised by university extension, the need for which, according to Litton, the Vice-Principal of St. Edmund Hall, was 'the one point upon which all parties, or nearly all, are agreed'.[35] It posed the question whether a large measure of university extension was compatible with the college system. Those who thought that it was supported affiliated or independent halls, ostensibly on

[32] Ibid., Evidence, 166.   [33] Ibid.
[34] Ibid., Evidence, 37, 168.   [35] Ibid., Evidence, 176.

the grounds of lower cost or because of the difficulty of exercising moral discipline over men who did not reside within the walls of a college, but some others held that men ought to be allowed to live in private lodgings without college connection. The majority believed that residence in lodgings contained two great evils: it provided no means of religious instruction comparable with the college chapel and so was thought to prepare the way for the admission of dissenters, and the education of such men must be largely in the hands of the professors. Henry Wall, one of the advocates of residence in lodgings, defended it precisely because it would strengthen the professoriate, and Richard Congreve defined the issue as whether the university was a place of learning or of education—if the former it should be open to all, and the colleges brought into competition with the residents. Through such arguments the question of the professoriate came in the minds of many to be identified with the admission of dissenters and the overthrow of the monopoly of the colleges. Thus the constitution of the university, and the extent to which college tutors and professors should participate in it, became a vital issue, for whoever controlled the constitution controlled the university.

It has been necessary to dwell on the educational problem which confronted the royal commission and the views of those who gave evidence to it in order to place Vaughan's evidence in perspective. His ideas on university reform were revolutionary in character. That is to say he proposed measures which were subversive of the existing order and desired to make institutional changes in order to implement them. Much of the force of his argument derived from the fact that he did not so much offer remedies for particular abuses as a systematic and connected web of ideas concerning the nature and function of a university. Although many of his ideas have since passed into common currency, they struck contemporaries with the force of a convulsion.

Pusey could only account for the genesis of Vaughan's ideas by the evil example of the continental universities, and accused him of seeking to remodel Oxford on the German pattern. Some apparently Germanic influence may be discerned in Vaughan's conception of a learned professoriate invested with a position of dignity and power in the university, but the matters where he rejected the German system were fundamental and there can be little doubt that his own experience in Oxford had a much greater effect in moulding his ideas. In particular it gave them their coercive character, for his clashes with the Newmanites and the Heads convinced him that the existing system was so strongly entrenched as to be incapable of reformation from within and should be swept away. The philosophical temper of his mind reinforced experience to convince him that the religious foundation of the university in the Church of England ought to be weakened and that neither learning nor education could flourish until this was achieved. It was not enough to reform statutes and open Fellowships if there was no will inside the colleges to open the university to the new forces in society. So deeply ingrained was Vaughan's distrust of the clergy that he believed it was only through force, exerted initially through Parliament and thereafter through the university constitution, that reforms could be made. It was an attitude which provoked opposition to ideas which if urged more temperately might have earned acceptance.

Vaughan proposed a secular university governed by the professors. The professor represented the university, and in him the supremacy of the university over the colleges was made manifest. His main duty was the pursuit of learning without regard to religion or any other restriction. Learning, he believed, was pursued not for the glory of God nor for the education of the young, but for its own sake, because it was 'the purest, the deepest, and the most enduring pleasure, in comparison with which, so long as vigorous health remains, idleness is privation, and amusement a meagre pastime'.[36] Professors had a place in the educational work of the university, but their real work was elsewhere.

They will investigate, reflect, and write, even if they do not very actively lecture; they will address the world if not the students of the academy, and their words will come back to the University in some

[36] *Report of the Oxford University Commission* (1852), Evidence, 274.

form, 'after many days'. They may not irrigate the ground immediately beside them, but the abundance of their spring heads, and the larger volume of their pent-up waters must go forward to feed and cleanse the cities of the earth, or to move the vaster wheels of European literature, or to deepen the main sea of the world's knowledge.[37]

Oxford had no such body of men.

The great want of Oxford hitherto has not been merely nor chiefly that the Professors have not been sufficiently active in teaching, but that the system has disfavoured the existence, and missed the general effects of Professorial learning. Some powerful men we have had; a considerable body, or a constant succession of such we have not had; men who could give authoritative opinions on matters connected with the sciences; whose words when spoken in public or private could kindle an enthusiasm on important branches of learning, or could chill the zeal for petty or factitious erudition; men whose names and presence in the University could command respect for the place, whether attracting students of all kinds and ages to it, or directing upon it the sight and interest and thought of the whole learned world; men whose investigations could perpetually be adding to knowledge, not as mere conduits to convey it, but as fountains to augment its scantiness, and freshen its sleeping waters.[38]

Such a body of learned men would not introduce a style of teaching or a tone of opinion similar to those which pervaded foreign universities. The work of foreign professors already indirectly influenced the teaching of the university, but an indigenous professoriate would replace them by a national and independent scholarship.

Early in his evidence, Vaughan observed that it was necessary either to construct something like a university system apart from the colleges, or to identify the colleges more effectively with the university.[39] He proposed to achieve these ends by transferring power from the colleges to the university. He proposed to reform the university constitution by replacing the Hebdomadal Board with a revived and strengthened Congregation in which the professors had a permanent majority. The language in which he

[37] *Report of the Oxford University Commission* (1852), Evidence, 274.
[38] Ibid.   [39] Ibid., Evidence, 83.

advocated the change was notably more moderate than the change itself.

It would be desirable [he said] that in the seat of learning and instruction, those who have attained the highest position as cultivators of literature and science, who must be considered as intimately acquainted with the state of the several departments of knowledge, who are brought into occasional contact with students of all ages and degrees in the place, who have proved themselves to possess a considerable degree of intellectual power, and who are necessarily interested in the success and reputation of the University, should take some active part in making and administering the laws.[40]

The governing body ought to include such a learned element. What he actually proposed was a Congregation composed of the Heads, all the professors, and six representatives of the Masters, who were to be elected by Convocation. Although the majority of the Heads and of the professors had been appointed to their various positions by election, the principle on which the new Congregation was to be constructed was not elective, though representative in a general sense, and all the members except the six elected Masters sat in Congregation *ex officio*. The Heads and Masters numbered 30, but there were 34 professors if the professor of music and the Lee's Reader were included, and Vaughan proposed that new chairs should be created in Mental Philosophy, the History of Philosophy, of Morals, and in English and European History.

Congregation thus reformed was to exercise not only the powers wielded previously by the Hebdomadal Board, but was to have power to legislate in matters connected with the discipline and instruction of the members of colleges. Since it would be too large for direct administration, he suggested that there should be created out of it an executive board of about 24—the same number as the Hebdomadal Board—composed of fixed proportions of Heads and professors with the two proctors. Alternatively, Congregation might act through the existing pattern of delegacies and committees. Here again was an avenue for extending the powers of the professors.[41]

[40] Ibid., Evidence, 82.   [41] See recommendation 3 of the *Report*.

Not only were the professors dominant in Congregation and enabled to interfere in the internal affairs of colleges, but they were given decisive control of the educational system. This important step was again to be achieved by institutional means. The professors were to be divided into Faculties entitled Theological, Historical, Physical, Mathematical, and Moral or Mental, and each Faculty would consist of the appropriate professors. Although a Head and one elected Master might be associated with each Faculty, if it were deemed necessary, the creation of new chairs ensured a professorial majority in even the smallest of them. The creation of Faculties was a desirable measure in any scheme to make the professors more effective, but Vaughan was alone in making the suggestion in the evidence submitted to the commission.

The Faculties were intended to serve three purposes. First, they were to give the professors a large, and it may be assumed, decisive control of the examinations, and so, it was hoped, lead the examinations away from textbooks to wider and more general themes.

The Professors [said Vaughan] ought, I think, to exercise a constant though *not an exclusive control* over the examinations. This is to be desired, in the first place, in order to aid the introduction and maintenance of first-rate examinations; it would also serve the purpose of diffusing the results of Professorial teaching generally through the academical body. Students and teachers would wish to become acquainted with the Professor's mode of teaching the subject, so soon as they thought it probable that the knowledge thereby gained might avail somewhat in the schools.[42]

The second purpose of the Faculties was to serve as a board of appeal in the case of disputed elections to Fellowships. Without such special provision, Vaughan feared that Fellowships in the new subjects would not be awarded on a sufficient scale and that for lack of suitable rewards they would languish, as the study of mathematics had done. It is possible that he preferred a new machinery for appeals to the time-honoured visitorial system because of the large clerical element among Visitors and the

[42] *Report of the Oxford University Commission* (1852), Evidence, 87.

preference which that suggested for the traditional subjects in which Fellowships were awarded. Whatever its cause, the proposal represented a serious invasion of the independence of the colleges, and was widely interpreted as offering the means for unattached students, that is, of students without collegiate connection, to obtain Fellowships. Taken in conjunction with other of Vaughan's proposals, it threatened to admit an unlimited number of laymen, and, even worse, of dissenters, to the heart of the citadel.

The third purpose to be served by the Faculties was the election of a proportion of the professors. A third of the professors were to be elected in this manner, a second third appointed by the Crown, and the remaining third elected by Convocation. Election by Faculties, he argued, had the special advantage of knowledge of the candidates, interest in the subject, and above all a sense of responsibility.

This last ingredient it is of great importance to preserve, and it appears impossible to secure its existence except by intrusting the election to a single person [i.e. the Crown], or to a few persons who will consider themselves, and will be regarded by others, as morally accountable to public opinion and to their own consciences for the success and propriety of the election. Any method of appointment which approaches in its nature to a popular election must be objectionable from the practical irresponsibility of the individuals who vote.[43]

Any faith Vaughan may have had in the efficacy of popular election as a method of determining academic ability had long ago been destroyed by the eccentric behaviour of Convocation, and he later abandoned election of even a third of the professors by Convocation in favour of the professorially dominated Congregation. The change was significant, for Vaughan visualized a university governed by an intellectual oligarchy, which was largely self-perpetuating through faculty boards, and by a Congregation in which the professors had a permanent majority. It was not a utopia the tutors could be expected to welcome.

Control of the university, however, was to be transferred not only to professors but to lay professors. If learning was to flourish

---

43 Ibid., Evidence, 89.

and inquiry to range freely, if scholars were to be drawn to Oxford and not chosen for their religious orthodoxy, if the new studies were to flourish untrammelled by the passions and prejudices of the clergy, Vaughan believed that the historic link between the university and the Church needed to be severed, and the obligation to enter Holy Orders relaxed. Theology, he believed, ought to be deposed from its predominant position, and the final examination, which made a candidate 'in point of attainments three-fourths of a Clerk in Orders', should be emancipated from compulsory theology and classics for all. Theology would then be organized as a separate Faculty similar to those in other subjects.

It is small wonder that Vaughan's scheme to secularize the university and place its government in the hands of the professors raised the battle cry of Germanization from his opponents. But although Vaughan accepted the learned function attached to the professor in Germany, he assigned to him a very different role in educational matters.

He wanted learned not teaching professors, and rejected the German system, which many supporters of the professoriate in Oxford were taking up, that professors ought to take a direct part in education. 'The teaching of undergraduates', he said, 'is not, I conceive, the only nor indeed the chief use which Professors may answer in our Universities',[44] a sentiment twice repeated in his evidence. In particular he rejected the suggestion that teaching in the third year should be placed entirely in their hands. 'The function of Professor', he said, 'would become merged in that of Tutor-Professor, and the tendency towards this result would carry with it an undesirable change in the habits and faculties of the Professor himself.'[45] In the physical sciences, which required apparatus and laboratories, and in those 'moral sciences', such as mathematics, where it was possible to enunciate established principles, he admitted that professors might lecture frequently and effectively, but in history and in subjects where 'there is still a region and mass of phenomena which have not yet been so

[44] *Report of the Oxford University Commission* (1852), Evidence, 86, 274.
[45] Ibid., Evidence, 87.

assigned to general principles', frequent lecturing was impossible without 'second-hand learning, hand-to-mouth lectures, and the instalment of a race of men in our chairs without enthusiasm, eloquence, profundity, or venerable acquirements'.[46] Teaching duties debased and denied the proper function of the professor. In as much as professorial teaching tended towards the increase of professional training it was also bad educationally. 'It is', he remarked, 'one peculiarity of our social condition that we have too much rather than too little time to learn the specialities of the higher branches of professions; and it has been hitherto the evil of our system of education that a good foundation in general knowledge has not been laid through which these specialities can be approached effectively and in a liberal spirit.'[47] Vaughan shared with the traditionalists the belief that the basis of education was moral and that its purpose was to train the mind and discipline the faculties. Where he differed from them was in holding that its foundations ought to be broadened. The professor, he believed, should influence education indirectly through the intellectual excitement he inspired and directly through his control of the government of the university and the examinations. The most he would allow was that undergraduates should be permitted to attend professorial lectures throughout their academic careers and that a portion of each day should be left sacred to attendance on them. It was thus essential to his conception of the professoriate that professors should not assume the burden of direct teaching. In view of his unequivocal stand on this matter and in view of his definition of the nature of education, the charge that he intended to Germanize the university is difficult to sustain. But if professors were not to teach, how was tuition to be given? Unlike the continental universities, Oxford had its tutors, and they formed an integral part of Vaughan's educational structure.

The scheme which he advocated was greatly influenced by the question of university extension. The introduction of new studies, he remarked, provided opportunities for a class of students hardly seen hitherto. For this poorer class of student, he was one of the

[46] Ibid., Evidence, 274.   [47] Ibid., Evidence, 86.

keenest advocates of residence in private lodgings. Ostensibly he defended it on the ground of economy, but it was at least open to argument whether it was cheaper than residence in college or hall, and the true reason for his preference was echoed by the Royal Commission itself which declared that 'we feel it to be a matter of great importance to raise up by the side of the Colleges an independent body, which will bear witness to the distinct existence of the University, and excite the Colleges to greater exertion'.[48] The importance of university extension depended on the number of students likely to be admitted, and the evidence on this point was necessarily conjectural. Residence in lodgings allowed for a much greater degree of expansion than any other scheme conceivable in practice. Mark Pattison, for example, who favoured a modified form of residence in lodgings, thought that between 300 and 500 persons might be involved, but Pusey, who supported affiliated or independent halls, put the figure as low as 50 or 100.[49] When it is realized that the average number of matriculations between 1841 and 1850 was 400 a year, it is evident that even a moderate expansion would lead to a large proportionate increase in the undergraduate population.

The problem which faced Vaughan, therefore, was not only how to provide better tuition for the members of colleges but how to provide instruction for a large quantity of students with no college connection. The majority of unattached students would be unable to afford a private tutor, since the main object of extension was to admit a poorer class of student, and the idea that their tuition should fall on the professor was quite unacceptable to him. So far as the colleges were concerned the problem was different. His distrust of the colleges led him to doubt whether sufficient learned laymen would be appointed to Fellowships, and he believed that in any event the smaller colleges would be unable to provide tuition in all subjects.

He offered two suggestions, both of which were destructive of the college system as it then existed. He proposed that members

[48] *Report of the Oxford University Commission* (1852), Evidence, 45.

[49] *Report and Evidence . . . Presented to the Board of Heads of Houses and Proctors* (1853), Evidence, 66; *Report of the Oxford University Commission* (1852), Evidence, 44.

of colleges might resort to private tutors, and, with the reservations he had previously expressed on the subject, to the professors. In this case the duty of the university was to ensure that teaching was given on reasonable terms, 'an achievement requiring much delicacy of management'. The proposal limited college tutors to their original function of giving general superintendence to their pupils and reduced the number of tutors required. In many colleges, the Head and Dean would be sufficient. How the remaining revenues of Fellowships were to be employed he did not say, but presumably they were intended to augment professorial stipends and to pay the private tutors. Alternatively, he suggested, colleges might appoint tutors to teach one subject only and permit them to take pupils from any college, and, it may be assumed, from none at all. By this scheme the efficiency of tutors would be increased because on their success would depend the number of their pupils, particularly if, as was also suggested, undergraduates were free to select their own tutors. The strong point of both his schemes was that they envisaged a much better qualified tutorial body than then existed, but they also contained the implication that the reform of Fellowships alone would not enable colleges to recruit enough able tutors to teach the whole curriculum. Whether by converting Fellows into private tutors or by the radical redeployment of the endowments of the richer colleges to subsidize the poorer and to pay for the education of unattached students, both his schemes tended to diminish the power of the colleges.

Of those who gave evidence to the Royal Commission, Vaughan alone advocated a degree of change so violent that it swept the old order away. A learned professoriate reflecting credit on the university, a measure of laicization of Fellowships, the specialization of college tuition, were objects shared by many, but Vaughan differed from other reformers in seeking to impose them by force through Parliament and radically reformed university institutions. Two considerations drove him to such extremities. The first was his distrust of the colleges and Heads, and his belief that they would never willingly sever the link with the Church of England, which he took to be the indispensable condition of a learned university. The second was his unwavering belief in a professoriate devoted to learning, and he saw his ideal adulterated by those, many of them earnest reformers, who would have converted professors into superior tutors. Vaughan stood almost alone at this time in his belief in a learned professoriate. He spoke for no party. He was the champion of the professoriate but not of the professors, and indeed his most redoubtable opponent, Pusey, was a professor. In other respects, many of his ideas as was so often the case sprang from his own experience. His distaste for teaching professors, for example, reflected his strong aversion to residence in the university, and his scheme for the use of college endowments echoed one of the main issues involved in his deprivation at Oriel. Nevertheless, when the heat of the 1850s had evaporated, reform moved in the direction indicated by him rather than in that of his opponents: the colleges successfully developed specialized tuition without bringing the professors directly into the work of teaching on a scale that interfered with their proper function.

Vaughan's evidence offended almost the whole university—the Heads, the college tutors, the churchmen, the opponents of parliamentary intervention. Yet because he was such an isolated figure, it may be asked why his enemies did not simply ignore his evidence. Two reasons offer themselves. The first was his influence on the Royal Commission, and the second that the opponents of reform seized on his evidence as an example of the extreme consequences to which the reform movement was leading.

On the commission, Vaughan's influence was considerable. It could hardly have been otherwise. He was a professor in one of the new studies, and the one in which the tutorial problem was perhaps most acute; Lord Russell had intended to appoint him a member of the commission; he had taken a leading part in shaping the recent examination statute. His evidence was referred to or quoted, often at great length, no less than twenty-three times in the Report, and H. G. Liddell testified to its importance when he informed Vaughan that 'the manner in which . . . your evidence is quoted throughout the Report must show that we were *forced* to acknowledge the value of your services'.[50] In Liddell, Vaughan had an old and intimate friend whose avowed ambition was to revive the professoriate, and it was mainly through his advocacy that Vaughan's ideas were brought to bear on the deliberations of the commission.

The commission followed Vaughan closely in its schemes for reforming the constitution and for university extension. '*Your* answers', Liddell wrote to him, 'formed the tent for our debates, and I carried propositions *in general terms* founded on your proposal for remodelling Congregation and the Hebdomadal Board. Your arguments in favour of Lodging Houses told. Jeune is getting jealous, I think; so I must keep you in the background.'[51] The Report proposed a reformed Congregation with power to initiate legislation and 'some control over all branches of the Executive', consisting of the Heads and proctors, all the professors and lecturers, and the senior tutors of colleges and halls. The result was to create a body which numbered over 100 and in which the professors had a permanent majority. Pusey declared that there were already sufficient professors in the university to give them a majority, but the commission aimed to convert a bare into a substantial majority by including lecturers, who were to be appointed by the professors, and by a considerable increase in the number of chairs. How many chairs were to be created was not stated with precision, but the number of Schools was to be increased from four to six and when discussing professorial emoluments at least fourteen new chairs were mentioned.

Vaughan's influence may also be traced in the commission's recommendation that the professors be formed into a permanent delegacy for supervising studies, and distributed into four boards corresponding to his faculties. On the appointment of professors, the commission went even further than Vaughan, and proposed to transfer appointments made by Convocation, the Heads, and graduates in divinity to the new Congregation, and to place the patronage of all other chairs in the Crown. Such a change would have given the professors an overwhelming voice in the

[50] H. G. Liddell to Vaughan [1851].
[51] The same to the same, 5 Mar. 1851.

choice of professors, and would have increased enormously the power of the Crown, which already appointed to the regius chairs. Liddell provides direct evidence of Vaughan's influence on the commission in these matters and reveals why the election of professors by faculties was not adopted.

We have [he wrote] had two more meetings, and proceed to sketch out the general principles to be adopted in framing the Report under the heads indicated in our Questions. In general, your Answers still *imperceptibly* seem as land-marks. Jeune, on consideration, adopts most of them, and speaks strongly for them—without adverting to your name. The Election of Professors by Faculties is objected to because *at present* at all events the Theological Faculty would only choose illiberally, and it would excite much remark if we assigned a different mode to this and to other Faculties. They incline to throw the election of this class of professors into the aggregate Faculties, i.e. into the hands of the majority of all the professors, *or* into the hands of the majority of Faculties.[52]

The proposed organization of studies into faculties had far-reaching implications. Pusey observed that it had a direct tendency to destroy the distinctive system of classical study, and must 'wholly destroy the present character of Oxford'.[53] In the body of its Report, though not in its recommendations, the commission suggested a considerable extension of studies by the division of the existing Schools. In October 1851 Liddell sent Vaughan a draft of the scheme and asked for his opinion of it. It was as follows,

That in each of the Four Faculties (as agreed upon), viz.
1. Theology
2. Mental Philosophy and Philology
3. Jurisprudence and History
4. Mathematics and Physical Science

That in each Faculty, I repeat, there should be two Schools, as, for instance,

| 1. Theology | a biblical and dogmatic |
| | b historical |

[52] H. G. Liddell to Vaughan, 13 Mar. 1851.
[53] *Report and Evidence . . . Presented to the Board of Heads of Houses and Proctors* (1853), Evidence, 92.

2. Mental Philosophy and Philology   a mental science
                                                 b philological
3. Jurisprudence and History   a law
                                                 b historical
4. Mathematics and Physical Science   a mathematical
                                                 b physical

Honours to be awarded in each of these eight Schools. Any student in any Faculty to be allowed for a common degree to substitute for either of the two Schools in his own Faculty, *certain* other Schools as in Theology for Ecclesiastical History, Mental Science, or Modern History, or fundamental branches of Physical Science &c. But for honours in each faculty, students might be sent by the Professor of their own Faculty to attend lectures in some other School (if needful) as Mental Philosophy or Modern History, and the student to pass an examination in such lectures before he can be admitted to honours in his own Faculty. I wish, you see, to restrain specialities from becoming too confined.[54]

The scheme simultaneously broadened and deepened the curriculum, and it depended for its success on the discontinuance of compulsory classics and the application of the time thereby gained to the new studies. In its Report the commission proposed that there should be freedom to specialize 'in the latter part' of the course. This was never closely defined, but a letter from Liddell suggests that specialization would commence after the first year. On 4 December 1851, he wrote to Vaughan:

Many thanks for your criticisms. They are *most* valuable,—just what we want. I have endeavoured to act on them in each case. But some of your objections arise from not having read the whole. To emancipate men earlier, we propose in p. 49 [of the draft report] to allow men (if they can) to pass their Intermediate Examination at an earlier period, or in other words to make Responsions *become* the Intermediate Examination for those who wish to go into specialties. But this is a matter to be further considered.[55]

On that section of the Report dealing with the colleges, Vaughan exercised less influence. It is significant that none of

54 H. G. Liddell to Vaughan, 14 Oct. 1851.
55 The same to the same, 4 Dec. 1851.

Liddell's letters to him touched on college reform, and Vaughan's evidence was quoted with diminishing frequency. The reason is clear. Although the commission desired to strengthen the university and reduce the monopoly of the colleges, it was more sympathetic than Vaughan to the collegiate system. In part this reflected the balance within the commission between the supporters of a strong professoriate, such as Liddell, and those such as Tait who wished to strengthen the colleges by internal reform. It also reflected the different view taken by the commission of the role and duties of the professor.

The commission wished as much as Vaughan to broaden the basis of education, and was at pains to point out that the new studies were not professional but preparatory to the professions and as such educational. But the commission regarded professors historically as teachers whose function had been usurped by the tutors, and it envisaged them not only controlling studies and examinations but actively engaging in education by teaching. They were, it is true, to be assisted by Lecturers, but the emphasis placed on their duties contrasted sharply with Vaughan's conception of the professoriate. The commission interpreted the difference between professors and tutors as one of degree rather than of kind. It looked to the professors because it had little confidence that even when reformed the colleges would be able to discharge their educational duties. It assumed, for example, that college tutors would continue as in the past to teach many subjects. 'A paramount advantage', it declared, 'of the University Lecturer over the College Tutor would be, the former confining himself to some one branch of study, while the latter is obliged to teach many, would impart his knowledge in a more perfect form.'[56] The commission's attitude is again revealed in its criticisms of Mark Pattison's evidence. Pattison believed that after reform college tutors would be able to give adequate tuition without calling on the support of the professors, but the commission denied the possibility so long as Fellows were not permitted to marry—a prohibition it did not intend to remove generally—since they would continue to look upon their position

[56] *Report of the Oxford University Commission* (1852), 101.

in the university as temporary. Determined to consider the professors as adjuncts of the tutorial system, the commission held that there was no reason why many professors should not give catechetical lectures.[57] The duty of the college tutor was to prepare men for the professor's lecture, whereby 'a great part of what they now attempt ineffectually to discharge would then be performed by the Lecturers and Professors'.[58] Such a large increase in professorial teaching was envisaged by the commission that it went so far as to describe the existing requirement of attendance at two courses of lectures as 'almost nugatory'.[59] Frequent lecturing implied regular residence, and although willing to relieve the professors of limitations of all kinds, the commission insisted on strict residence. Writing in 1853 when the statute creating the Corpus Professor of Latin was under discussion, Liddell recalled that 'Stanley had strong feelings about the propriety of residence &c, and . . . argued that you [Vaughan] ought to give more lectures than Arnold.'[60] The commission placed most emphasis on the university as a place of education, whereas Vaughan believed that it was primarily a place of learning and that learning would fertilize and invigorate the education it gave.

The Report was almost completed by the end of 1851, and Liddell was urging Jeune to bring it out at once. In April he wrote optimistically to Vaughan,

I think I may say the work is now done. Johnson's labours have been brought to light and the product is ludicrously small. On the whole he has improved the College Paper, and with Stanley's aid will no doubt improve it still more. We meet again on Monday the 22nd, i.e. Monday week, and then as soon as the printers shall have finished arranging the whole Report . . . or at all events very soon after it, I think the Judgment of the Seven will be in Her Majesty's hands. The course of proceeding is this. We all sign a perfect copy. This is carried by our chairman attended by all his satellites to the Home Secretary, in whose hands it is deposited to be laid before H.M., and there is an end of the matter unless the House of Commons orders the Report to be published. The worst of it is, thanks to Johnson and the other

[57] Ibid.   [58] Ibid.   [59] Ibid. 102.
[60] H. G. Liddell to Vaughan, 2 May 1853.

precious delays which we have had for nothing at all, that *probably* the House of Commons will at that moment be floundering in its last agonies, and a new House *may* possibly disdain to take any notice of such transcendental things as Academical Reform.[61]

Liddell was premature in his anticipation, and on 20 July Tait was confiding to his wife, 'We have been working 8 or 9 hours a day and I must confess the Report is as yet in an odd mess. Liddell's part appears to me about as tedious and ill-drawn up as the Master's [Jeune's]. Goldwin Smith and I are labouring to bring the whole into shape. I have managed now that the whole is submitted to me or to Johnson for final revision and thereby I hope all will do well.'[62]

[61] H. G. Liddell to Vaughan, 13 Mar. 1852.
[62] Lambeth Palace Library MS. Tait 103, f. 72.

9. The Radicals;
The Examinership

THE Report of the University Commission, or the Blue Book as it came to be known, was published in the summer of 1852, and was received in the university with something short of rapture. Writing in 1855, Gladstone recalled that 'when it was published, while it excited universal admiration for its ability, the most violent partisans, and the persons ill-disposed to our institutions were the best pleased with it, and there were but a very few of those persons who *are* attached to our institutions that did not regard it as (in an academical sense) revolutionary'.[1] In the months that followed its publication, opinion on reform in Oxford began to crystallize and party affiliations to harden as the government declared its intention to legislate. On 16 June, the Hebdomadal Board, ever anxious to be doing but cautious of over-exertion, appointed a committee to consider, but inconceivably to commend, the proposals in the Report affecting the university, and after the lull of the long vacation the committee began its work in October by seeking evidence from members of Convocation. Stimulated by the activities of the committee, the working residents revived the Tutors' Association at a meeting in Oriel early in November, and at about the same time the core of advanced liberals began to hold frequent meetings. All sought to demonstrate the strength of their support by presenting evidence to the committee.

The Report of the Royal Commission was notably more extreme in character than the bulk of the evidence which accompanied it, and it is probable that the commission, confident in the support of Lord Russell, preferred to depend on the intervention of Parliament, which was in any case necessary, for the

[1] Bodleian Library MS. Acland d. 68, f. 9ᵛ.

implementation of its recommendations rather than compromise in order to win the support of the university, which, by attempting to have the commission declared illegal, had forfeited the opportunity of influencing its decisions. But Lord Russell fell from office in February 1852, and the state of opinion in the university became a more important factor than before. At this juncture there were signs of a split in the ranks of the reformers whose programme was represented by the Blue Book. It reflected the division which had already appeared within the commission. Round Francis Jeune, the Master of Pembroke, gathered a group of reformers whose main interest was in college reform and whose concern for the revival of the professoriate was mainly educational in emphasis. Opposed to them was a smaller group, the existence of which has not been sufficiently noticed by historians. It was less conciliatory, more anti-clerical than the Pembroke reformers, passionately committed to the revival of the professoriate, and its dominating spirit was Vaughan. His influence on the Blue Book pointed to him as a natural instrument for its propagation in Oxford, but as a missionary he was not well equipped. He was a prophet rather than a preacher, and like most experienced prophets, he tended having delivered his revelation to retire to a discreet distance and wait upon events. This he did at this crucial time, living in Hampstead and encouraging the faithful by occasional visits and sometimes by post. He was by temperament unsuited to the hot work of conversion; he was too independent to be conciliatory; he spoke to those who already shared his opinions rather than to the unconverted. Congreve said of him, 'he never seems led away by the tone of criticism on any subject that is dominant in society. He has thought his opinions over for himself.'[2] His intransigence delighted his friends, but irritated others by its suggestion of moral and intellectual rectitude. Pattison, who was not averse to a malicious anecdote, records that when asked why Maskelyne was the most unpopular man in Oxford, Jeune replied, 'It is because he gets with Vaughan and thus comes away saying "How we apples swim."'[3]

[2] Bodleian Library MS. Eng. lett. c. 181, f. 39.
[3] MS. Pattison 129, f. 165ᵛ.

Vaughan and his friends, henceforth called the radicals, decided to keep aloof from the Tutors' Association. On 10 November, two days after their first meeting, Pattison resolved after discussions with Vaughan, Jowett, Goldwin Smith, and Conington, not to give evidence to the Association.[4] This was an important decision because it deprived the radicals of the opportunity of influencing the tutors, some sixty of whom attended the meetings of the Association with frequency, and it demonstrated their reluctance to compromise the essential principles of the Blue Book. Having thus decided to proceed independently, Vaughan, Conington, Jowett, and Pattison met in Jowett's lodgings on 12 November to consider the Report,[5] and on the 15th a further meeting was held also in his lodgings to draw up a scheme for the professors, a subject which was simultaneously being debated by the tutors.[6] On the following day, the constitution and university extension came up for discussion.[7] Liddell, who remained in London discharging his duties as Headmaster of Westminster, was conscious of the need for unity among reformers, and was anxious for moderation. He wrote to Vaughan counselling restraint.

The first question seems to me to be, are the Heads in earnest or not? Do they intend to do anything effectual, or only to propose a few bye-reforms for the sake of throwing dust in people's eyes? I suppose the *latter* to be the case, i.e. they intend to do nothing effectual.

In that case, seeing that any division of opinion among reformers will be eagerly laid hold of, I should recommend your body not to send in any *definite* statement of opinions, but to say *generally* that you have all, or nearly all of you, given in evidence to the commission, from which evidence it may be seen that you concur substantially in all the important measures of reform recommended by the commission; that if you are asked to specify what you call 'important measures' you would particularise as essential:—

1. Such an alteration in the constitution of the university as to place the right of initiating measures in the hands of those who are the public trustees of the university.

2. An extension &c. of the professoriate.

---

4 Ibid., f. 81ᵛ.   5 Ibid., f. 82.
6 Ibid., f. 82ᵛ.   7 Ibid.

3. An adjustment of the course of study, such as to call the professors more directly into action.

4. Licence to allow students to become members of the university without being members of colleges (if this can be carried).

And I would add that you are all ready to express more definite opinions on these subjects, one or all, if the Hebdomadal Board think fit to propose definite queries.

In this way, I think you would avoid at once committing yourselves to an approval of the actual *form* in which the commissioners have recommended that these reforms shall be made, and you will yet be able to indicate strongly and clearly those measures without which any reform would be nugatory.

This on the supposition that the Heads are swallowing reform, as Derby swallows Free-trade. If, which is inconceivable, they really mean work, there can be no fear of your stating fully how far you adopt the express recommendations of the commission, and how far you dissent. You know very well that all the more important recommendations were compromises and that perhaps not one, certainly not myself, of the commissioners would wish to see them adopted exactly as they stand. But the Spirit and Tendency of them is (I think) approved by all, and (if I were you) I would take this course, and confine myself to approving of the Spirit and Tendency without entering upon details.[8]

On the 23rd, Liddell's letter was discussed for three hours at a meeting in Vaughan's lodgings. Pattison reported that they 'got through a good deal of the Heads with very satisfactory unanimity . . . V[aughan] wanting to go to town tomorrow, we met again at Donkin's at $8\frac{1}{2}$ but only small assemblage and tired'.[9] But in a letter written on the same day, Congreve complained to his wife that 'the extreme reform party with one or two exceptions is under the curse of timidity, that though it is or should be clear that do what you will they cannot conciliate the non-reforming party, but that the only way is to intimidate them by bold action, they still go on calculating every expression with the object of securing some few names more'.[10] In fact a serious rift threatened to split the radicals. It occurred not over the content of the reform

---

[8] H. G. Liddell to Vaughan, 21 Nov. 1852.   [9] MS. Pattison 129, f. 83.
[10] Bodleian Library MS. Eng. lett. c. 181, f. 11.

programme but rather over the rate at which measures ought to be introduced, and it indicated a division between the moderates amongst them, who believed it necessary to win further support in the university, and the extremists who refused to compromise and, as Congreve had said, believed that the opponents of reform could not be won round. The sensitive issue, as Liddell had fore-seen, was university extension, and in particular the question of admitting unattached students. The radicals can hardly have been unaware that the Tutors' Association, which was then preparing its first report, was about to condemn this method of extension in unequivocal terms, and it was Vaughan who now forced the issue by insisting that the immediate introduction of unattached students should be recommended to the Hebdomadal Board. On 30 November Pattison wrote, 'To Vaughan's on the ad-journment—but V. not there—sent verbosa et grandis epistola from Hampstead refusing to be a party to the thing unless lodging out of Coll. was affirmed in a certain set of terms, so after some discussion, seeing disunion impending, we separated.'[11] In an undated letter, apparently written very shortly after this meeting, Congreve wrote to Vaughan:

We met yesterday. Wilson, Jowett, Conington, Maskelyne, Chretien, G. Smith, Donkin, Pattison. And the old resolution as agreed to last time was adopted by the majority, but at the same time it was agreed that there would be no objection to your adding as a separate thing, and I would be glad to join you, a statement that on that particular resolution you disagreed with the rest of the signatories, and the reason why or the degree on which, such as this: whilst agreeing in all the rest, the undersigned wish to express their feeling that the particular means of University Extension which a body of resident students unconnected with any college under due moral superintendence would offer is desirable more immediately than the others who have signed think. This clumsy statement might be thrown into shape. The essential is to know whether you will sign the paper then. I will sign with you as I greatly prefer the freer air of your resolution to the confining one of Jowett's. I think Conington and Maskelyne might join us.[12]

Vaughan accepted Congreve's suggestion, and on 3 December a revised paper was circulated. A few days later, Congreve reported that 'Wilson wants another meeting, but I hold it to be a useless waste of time. We cannot get over our disagreement. Pattison will sign with you and me, and I believe Wilson, but he thinks the wording rather bellicose.'[13]

In the paper[14] which was eventually submitted to the committee of the Hebdomadal Board in February 1853, the radicals expressed their concurrence with the recommendations of the Royal Commission except on a few points concerning the constitution, the professoriate, and university extension. The tendency of the alterations proposed was to strengthen the power of the university. On the constitution, the most important change was to invest Congregation with the sole power of initiating measures, whereas the Blue Book left the legislative powers of the Hebdomadal Board intact. On the professoriate, it was proposed that appointments which the Report suggested should be made by Congregation should be made by curators appointed by Congregation. On university extension, six of the signatories stated their hope that the university would 'ultimately' carry out all the proposals of the Report, but the minority, consisting of Vaughan, Congreve, Pattison, Maskelyne, and Conington, declared their acceptance of them 'without qualification or indefinite postponement'.

The signatories of this document were a roll-call of the party of radical reform, and what they lacked in numbers they made up for in distinction. They were C. P. Chretien, Fellow and Tutor of Oriel; Richard Congreve, Fellow and Tutor of Wadham; John Conington, Fellow of University; W. F. Donkin, Savilian Professor of astronomy; T. F. Henney, Fellow and Tutor of Pembroke; N. S. Maskelyne, Deputy Reader in mineralogy; Mark Pattison, Fellow and Tutor of Lincoln; Bartholomew Price, Reader in natural philosophy and Fellow and Tutor of Pembroke; Goldwin Smith, Fellow and Tutor of University; J. M. Wilson,

---

[13] R. Congreve to Vaughan, 12 Dec. 1852.

[14] *Report and Evidence . . . Presented to the Board of Heads of Houses and Proctors* (1853), Evidence, 341–4.

Professor of moral philosophy and Fellow and Tutor of Corpus; and of course Vaughan. A few names were conspicuously absent, amongst them Stanley who was in Egypt. A more interesting omission was the name of Benjamin Jowett. On the day after the paper had been dispatched, Congreve received what he described as 'a species of appeal for more time from Wilson and Jowett'.[15] Precisely why Jowett was dissatisfied with the paper is not entirely clear, but Congreve did not conceal his satisfaction that further discussion was prevented, and it may be presumed therefore that, as might be expected, Jowett was not among the extremists. The decision to proceed without him was probably made quite deliberately, for there was no urgency about the submission of the document, since on 12 February the Hebdomadal committee issued a notice that evidence could be submitted up to 18 April.[16] The absence of Jowett's signature did not, however, signify his dissent, for on 11 February Congreve reported that 'now that the document has gone in Jowett has sent in his adhesion'.[17] The truth may well be that, not for the first time in his life, Jowett was tormented by doubt and indecision. As a university reformer, he did not fit easily into any of the main parties then in existence. He wished to do more than the Tutors' Association for the professors and for university extension, but on the other hand he was not a whole-hearted supporter of the Blue Book. In a letter to Stanley he had written, 'I feel that I do not agree either with Vaughan's intellectual aristocracy as the idea of a university, nor with the "Gentlemen heresy" that appears to be partially entertained by Jeune and by G. Smith.'[18] For the moment he remained with the radicals, but took the precaution of ensuring that the fact was not publicly known. As a body, with or without Jowett's support, the radicals were an impressive group, though much smaller than the Tutors' Association. Their evidence to the Hebdomadal committee had, predictably,

---

[15] R. Congreve to Vaughan, 7 Feb. 1853.

[16] *Report and Evidence . . . Presented to the Board of Heads of Houses and Proctors* (1853), 3.

[17] R. Congreve to Vaughan, 11 Feb. [1853].

[18] Balliol College. Jowett letters, 9 Sept. [1850].

no influence on its Report, but as a demonstration of support in the university for the principles of the Blue Book it could not be ignored.

During the preparation of this document, Vaughan had emerged as one of the most uncompromising and unyielding leaders of the radicals. Hardly was it completed, when he became involved in a dispute with the Hebdomadal Board which raised an important principle of reform and one which the document itself had implicitly endorsed. When the names of the examiners in the new School of Jurisprudence and History were announced in February 1853, Vaughan's was not amongst them. Traditionally, examiners were appointed by the Vice-Chancellor and Proctors, and although the system came under strong criticism during the debate on the examination statute in 1850, a proposal to vest appointments in the new subjects in the hands of the professors was defeated. The Blue Book returned to the attack and proposed to deprive the Proctors of their right and to place all appointments in a standing delegacy of professors, thereby extending professorial control of examinations to the whole examination system. The omission of the Regius Professor of History from the list of examiners appointed for the first examination to be held for the new School confirmed the suspicion of the reformers that the Hebdomadal Board was not in earnest on reform. Certainly the fact was sufficiently remarkable to require an explanation, and Vaughan was not slow to provide one. He had never, he informed J. M. Wilson, received 'any definite offer of the Modern History Examinership'.[19]

From the assertions, protestations, and denials which followed it is possible to piece together the main facts in the dispute, though both sides preferred to leave some aspects in decent obscurity. Wilson repeated Vaughan's statement to Mark Pattison, who immediately confronted the Senior Proctor, W. C. Lake, in his rooms in Balliol. Lake was not only Proctor, but a prominent member of the Tutors' Association, and had been appointed or had even conceivably appointed himself an examiner. 'I told him', said Pattison 'that Vaughan had said that he had

[19] J. Conington to Vaughan, 22 Feb 1853.

never had the offer of the Modern History School.'[20] Lake, was incensed, and there took place what Pattison succinctly described as a 'scene'. Not only, declared Lake, had he offered the examinership to Vaughan, but he had pressed him more than once to accept it. There was, it appeared, a small difference in the recollection or interpretation of the evidence.

Vaughan did not say that the examinership had never been offered to him, as was reported to Lake, but that he had never received a *definite* offer. Humpty Dumpty, that master of semantics, would have appreciated the distinction. At the request of the Vice-Chancellor, Vaughan had submitted a list of books on law and English history on which candidates should be examined. At the same time he accepted the examinership which he understood Lake to have offered to him. Subsequently, Lake produced a revised book-list, which omitted some of the books recommended by Vaughan and included an additional thirty or forty books, many of which by his own testimony were unfamiliar to Vaughan. A meeting, of which Vaughan has left an account, took place between him and Lake to discuss the situation. Vaughan complained that time was short and that no man in Europe could be found capable of examining well on the list without some preparation. 'It has', he wrote, 'for years been my opinion frequently expressed that an examiner should be well acquainted with every book which candidates are invited to bring up.'[21] Lake replied that he was likely to be an examiner himself, and since he happened to be lecturing on the books in question, he would relieve Vaughan of the main part of the examination. But, answered Vaughan, as many of the candidates would come from Balliol, it would not be possible for Lake to examine them. 'I must be prepared to examine in everything.'[22] Moreover, a division of labour according to subjects was desirable among the examiners, and would be impossible since tutors could not examine their own pupils, and neither of the other examiners, both of whom were clergymen, was familiar with the law. Vaughan took his complaint to the Vice-Chancellor, and the

[20] MS. Pattison 129, f. 97ᵛ. [21] Vaughan to W. C. Lake, [1853].
[22] Ibid.

book-list was altered once again, but when the curriculum was finally settled no further offer of the examinership was made to him, though, as he told Conington, he fully expected that one would.[23]

Lake communicated his version of the dispute to Conington, who repeated it to Vaughan.

> He declares [wrote Conington] that he made the offer to you, as he thought, quite explicitly, just as he offered the Lit. Hum. and Physics Examinerships to Jowett and Acland, and that more than once he endeavoured to combat your objections in detail and press the appointment upon you. He seems to have thought it impossible that he should be misunderstood, both because the offer when made in similar terms to the other two was regarded as final, and also because the conversation between you appeared to show that you had asked yourself whether you should accept it or not.[24]

That Lake firmly believed Vaughan to have refused the offer is confirmed by a passage in a letter he wrote to Gladstone in which he stated that Vaughan 'unfortunately feels himself unable to undertake the office [of examiner]'.[25] Putting the two accounts together, it seems that a definite offer of the examinership was at one time made, and that Vaughan accepted it. It is probable that he subsequently declined to act unless the book-list was altered, and that Lake interpreted this as a refusal and did not renew the offer when the book-list was finally altered.

It is difficult to resist the conclusion that the dispute would have been settled amicably and the offer of the examinership renewed if the book-list had been its sole cause. It was far from unknown, and may well have been common practice, for the Hebdomadal Board to consult the professors on the choice of books, and Vaughan's complaint on this head seems to have been settled to the satisfaction of all parties. In fact, more important issues were involved, and Conington hinted at them when he wrote that Lake was anxious for there to be no misconception about the offer because 'he would not willingly have it

---

[23] Vaughan to J. Conington, [1853].
[24] J. Conington to Vaughan, 22 Feb. 1853.
[25] Add. MS. 44230, f. 246.

said that you had been passed over in the arrangement whatever may be your opinion of the course which the Hebdomadal Committee ought to have pursued towards you as Professor'.[26] What this course ought to be Vaughan had stated explicitly in his evidence to the royal commission and had reaffirmed in his statement to the Hebdomadal Board only a few days before the dispute with Lake. The professors, he had written, ought to be officially charged with the choice of examiners and super-intendance of the examinations.[27] There was nothing upon which the success of the 'university system' more materially depended, for only good examiners would produce good examinations.[28] It is evident from Vaughan's account of the dispute that he not only wished to alter the book-list but to influence the choice of examiners. The Hebdomadal Board was willing to consult the professors about the curriculum and to appoint them examiners, but it would not, and in the absence of an express statute could not, accept that control of the examina-tions should be in their hands to the extent that Vaughan wished, and its view was shared by the university in general.

That Vaughan deliberately manipulated a technical withdrawal of the offer made to him is not impossible, for to do so might seem to demonstrate the Board's resistance to reform. For his part, Lake, who was not known as 'Serpent' for nothing, may equally have been unwilling to introduce so voracious a cuckoo into the nest. Interpreting Vaughan's objections as a refusal, he proceeded to offer the examinership to Hallam, by whom it was accepted. Here the dispute ended, but it is worthy of note that Vaughan was never again invited to be an examiner and was thus never able to exert a direct influence on the development of the study of history through the public examinations.

[26] J. Conington to Vaughan, 22 Feb. 1853.
[27] *Report of the Oxford University Commission* (1852), Evidence, 277.
[28] Ibid. 87.

10. *Oxford Reform and Oxford Professors*

1854

WHEN Lord Russell fell from office in 1852, the radicals lost a valuable ally, and when Gladstone, the member for the university, actively took up reform in the following year it was not they but the moderate and Anglican Tutors' Association which had ready access to government. In 1853 and 1854 the Association published reports on the main issues of reform designed to modify those proposals in the Blue Book which, in Lake's words, 'give it such a *revolutionary* and anti-theological aspect'.[1] It had considerable success in influencing opinion within the university, and also in influencing Gladstone, who now began to occupy the centre of the stage.

In its reports, the Association allotted to the colleges and to college tutors the central place which the royal commission had given to the university and the professors. On university extension, for example, it defended the college system and condemned the residence of unattached students in lodgings. On the constitution it rejected the dominant position of the professors and introduced a considerable measure of representation of the working tutors. The third report, which dealt with the tutorial system, cut deeply into the commissioners' scheme and relegated the professors to a comparatively minor role. 'The influence of the Professors', it stated, 'should be rather indirect and moral than direct and legal.'[2] It took the view that by introducing a greater degree of specialization among tutors and by encouraging them to remain

---

[1] Add. MS. 44230, f. 239.

[2] *Third Report of the Oxford Tutors' Association* (1853), 76.

in the university, adequate tuition could be given by the colleges without the assistance of the professors or the assistant professors, who were not inaccurately described by Pusey as 'a new class of Tutors in different subjects',[3] except in the new studies where it was somewhat grudgingly admitted to be necessary. If the tutorial system could be improved in the manner described by the report the case for giving the professors decisive power in the university was seriously eroded.

The third report was adopted on 18 November 1853, and a few days later on 1 December the long-awaited report of the Heads appeared. It was a disappointing document, but was accompanied by a large body of evidence in which Pusey's contribution of 173 pages was in extent and importance outstanding. Together the two documents constituted a formidable challenge to the Royal Commission's conception of a university controlled by the professoriate. Pusey's essay was a brilliant piece of polemical writing, passionate, penetrating, and argued with sturdy common sense and an abundance of telling details. It was the work of a practised controversialist. That he should appear as the champion of the Heads was an irony not lost on the radicals, and Vaughan caustically remarked that, 'lips silenced without a hearing by Oxford for unsound doctrine, are still at Oxford welcome monitors against dangerous instruction'.[4]

Pusey's arguments have been skilfully summarized by Liddon.[5] He believed that the two great questions which pervaded the Blue Book were whether education should be professorial or collegiate, and whether it should be secular or clerical. In this he was defending the tradition of Oxford education, which had been weakened, so he believed, by the statute of 1850 and dangerously breached by the Royal Commission. The professorial

---

[3] *Report and Evidence . . . Presented to the Board of Heads of Houses and Proctors* (1853), Evidence, 112.

[4] *Oxford Reform and Oxford Professors* (1854), 25. Liddon (*Life of Pusey* (1894), iii. 380) states that Pusey appears to have had no opportunity of giving evidence to the commission, and Pusey himself appears to have been of the same opinion (ibid. 391). In fact, he was invited to contribute evidence but declined to do so (*Report of the Oxford University Commission* (1852), appendix B, 14).

[5] H. P. Liddon, *Life of Pusey* (1894), iii. 381–6.

system was central to his argument because it seemed to undermine education and religion. He identified it with the dissemination of facts, and therefore condemned it, much as Mark Pattison had done, as a means of education. The same reasoning led him to approve of professorial teaching in the sciences, which he regarded as professional rather than educational studies. The object of education was not the inculcation of facts but the formation of the mind by reasoning and study, and it was better secured by the catechetical methods of college tutors than by the lectures of professors. That professors also might give catechetical lectures was an inconvenient fact, damaging but not destructive of his argument, which Pusey chose to ignore. It is significant that so much of Pusey's argument was directed against Vaughan, for although he was prepared to admit professorial teaching in the sciences, history was not a scientific but a moral and educational study. If history were to be taught by professors, the way was open for professorial teaching in other moral and educational studies, including those which lay at the heart of the existing system of education. It mattered not that Vaughan himself was bitterly opposed to teaching professors in history.

An equally fundamental objection to professorial teaching lay in Pusey's conviction that it led to religious infidelity. His studies in German universities between 1825 and 1827 had persuaded him that the professorial system had engendered doubt of the certainty of knowledge in religion and philosophy, and in his evidence he developed this proposition with a wealth of illustration drawn from his own experience. It was perhaps the most powerful, certainly the most emotive, part of his indictment, and its effect in discrediting the professorial system at Oxford was incalculable. 'We have', he said, 'abundance of theories about the Professorial system. We have no facts of its having produced any but evil fruits. The training of our youth, the intellectual, moral, religious formation of their minds, their future well-being in this world and the world to come, are not matters upon which to try experiments.'[6]

[6] *Report and Evidence . . . Presented to the Board of Heads of Houses and Proctors* (1853), Evidence, 64.

These evils would be brought to Oxford if professors were given charge of instruction and students were allowed to live in lodgings. On such a scheme depended 'whether our Universities shall, more or less, in whatever degree the plan prevails, be assimilated to the Continental'.[7] Young men would be subjected to the evils of professorial teaching, they would be denied the benefits of religious instruction, and the superintendence of their morals would be neglected. 'Any weakening of the college system', he declared, 'would, I believe, be one of the greatest evils which could befall our country.'[8]

Stern condemnation was reserved for the commission's proposal to make the professors dominant in the university. Pusey attacked the reformed Congregation because it gave the professors a permanent majority, and the extension of Crown patronage because it would place control of the university indirectly in the hands of the state. He attacked boards of studies because, if they consisted of all professors, men who were expert in their own field would be required to regulate those of which they knew little, and if faculty boards were created they would in many cases be too small. Both systems destroyed the position of classical studies because a mere handful of such studies was represented among thirty-eight professors. He deplored the discontinuance of religious studies after the second year, and declared that the final year was too valuable for training the mind to be given over to professional pursuits. The religious requirements of the university were too modest to interfere with other studies, and the creation of a separate School of Theology would eventually lead to control by the professoriate of the recruitment of the clergy.

Providing that the religious basis of education was assured, Pusey was not averse to a wide range of reforms for improving the collegiate system. On the reform of Fellowships, he did not echo the moral objection to interference with foundations voiced by many conservatives, but he protested strongly against their secularization, which, he declared, raised the great question 'in whose hands the education of the future laity and Clergy of the country is to be'.[9] There were, he said, enough posts in the

7 Ibid. 73.   8 Ibid.   9 Ibid. 127.

university for laymen, and since it was the lay Fellows who were mainly absentee, an increase in laymen would increase non-residence. If Fellows were properly appointed, there was no reason for men to take Orders for the wrong reasons. He approved of more specialization among tutors, and believed that more would remain in the university if there was work for them to do; he approved of the revision of college statutes in order to provide better tutors; he opposed the drain of Fellows into the Church because of its injurious effect on the study of theology. By such reforms, the colleges would be able to offer adequate instruction without the employment of the professors, except in the sciences.

To the revolutionary solution of the Royal Commission, Pusey opposed radical conservative reform. To the idea of a secular university, he opposed the ideal of a Christian and moral university. To the idea of a national university regulated and to a large extent controlled by the state, he opposed a self-governing community within the Church of England.

Pusey's evidence and the reports of the Tutors' Association strengthened immeasurably the tide which was already running against a large part of the programme of the Blue Book, and in particular the proposals for the professoriate. To the commission party it seemed essential that an answer should be prepared, as much to provide ammunition for the government in the battle which was about to open in Parliament as to influence opinion in the university. 'Since reading the announcement that the Government have a Bill ready,' Liddell wrote to Vaughan, 'I am more than ever of opinion that the Report and Evidence must be answered. No doubt the opponents of the Bill will draw upon these documents, and we ought to furnish them [i.e. the government] with a brief on our side.'[10] It is a reflection of the extent to which the reformers were out of touch with the intentions of the government that at this time they supposed the Bill was favourable to the principles of the Blue Book. On 18 December 1853 Liddell again wrote to Vaughan:

I should be sorry to see Gladstone and Co. ejected—partly because I have more confidence in his financial abilities than those of other

[10] H. G. Liddell to Vaughan, 18 Dec. 1853.

persons, partly because I trust him for University Reform while *in* the Ministry, whereas *out* he might strike some side-blow of an awkward nature. But it is a great thing to have them committed as they now are to a Bill, which the *Times* affirms to be in accordance with our Report, and to have a fresh allusion to the subject in the Queen's Speech. Altogether I feel tolerably hopeful.[11]

Several members of the commission party, including some of the commissioners, contemplated writing an answer. Goldwin Smith considered entering the lists;[12] Liddell at one time thought of making a general reply to Pusey;[13] Jeune proposed to leave Pusey to him and to Stanley, and to write himself a reply to the evidence of Provost Hawkins.[14] But time was short, and it was agreed that Vaughan should undertake the task, not only because he was the acknowledged champion of the professoriate, but because, as he informed Liddell, he was the only one of the reformers ready.[15] He insisted on writing independently of other reformers, but when Liddell urged the practical advantages of having all the arguments in one place he agreed to accept documentary evidence. On 28 December Liddell wrote to him:

The very points which you have unfortunately taken so much pains to establish, viz. that if Stanley or G. Smith write a *general* argument against Pusey, they must write independently, or if they write in conjunction with you they must furnish mere *documentary evidence* on matters of fact, is precisely what I laid before Stanley at length on Christmas Day. He assented altogether. . . . Nothing could be further from any wish, nothing more contrary to any wish of mine, than that your Reply should be coupled with another of the same pretensions, tho' I doubt not infinitely weaker even where it agreed, and likely to jar in many points.[16]

Vaughan's insistence on writing independently and Liddell's hint of a diversity of opinion emphasize that the Blue Book was

11 The same to the same, 18 Dec. 1853.
12 Ibid.
13 Ibid. [1854].
14 F. Jeune to A. P. Stanley, 14 Dec. 1853.
15 H. G. Liddell to Vaughan, [Dec. 1853].
16 The same to the same, 28 Dec. 1853.

not a rigid programme of reform on which all were agreed but a compromise often between quite different points of view.

In *Oxford Reform and Oxford Professors*, Vaughan eventually made use of information supplied by his friends not only in the appendices but in the text also. He was particularly indebted to Stanley, notably in the passages where he dealt with the question of immorality among students in German universities, and, to a less extent, in his defence of German scholarship. It was through Stanley that information on the current state of German universities was obtained from Bunsen.[17] The first intention had been to consult Max Müller, whose appointment as professor had been warmly supported by Vaughan, but it was abandoned on the grounds that he was opposed to many reforms.[18] Stanley went to see Bunsen, who, 'when Stanley stated the main points aimed at by Pusey, expressed his great surprise. "No books from professors," he said, "then there are no books in Germany." "The only exceptions are", he said, "Niebuhr, Savigny and Humboldt —of which the two first are only *apparent* exceptions, and for the last of these see his famous answer to the King of Hanover", which, adds Stanley, should be quoted.'[19] Bunsen also complained to Stanley that some of the sources and facts used by Pusey to illustrate the behaviour of German students were out-of-date or inaccurate, and he pointed to the fact, which Lachmann the rector of Berlin university had mentioned to him, that out of 1400 students only 48 were in any way concerned in the revolutionary proceedings of 1848.[20] In addition to transmitting the results of his correspondence with Bunsen to Vaughan, Stanley himself contributed papers on the German geographers and on Pusey's own lectures, which he had attended in 1845 and had found 'strictly Professorial, not catechetical, thoroughly German, and very useful', but neither of them was used by Vaughan.[21]

[17] Bunsen read and approved the proofs of the passage (pp. 93–4) on the moral character of student clubs in German universities.

[18] H. G. Liddell to Vaughan, 18 Dec. 1853.

[19] The same to the same [1853]. The anecdote is printed in *Oxford Reform and Oxford Professors*, appendix B, 103.

[20] The same to the same, 8 Jan. 1854.

[21] Ibid. 18 Dec. 1853. See appendix A.

Conington supplied a paper on German classical scholarship, which Vaughan printed in full as an appendix. Of this paper Conington wrote:

I have done the best I could in this short time, which has not been free from other occupations. The list is by no means a complete one. I cannot speak for *all* the books mentioned from my own knowledge, so I may occasionally have singled out an edition when there are others better. Still I believe it is substantially correct, and it will afford a tolerable muster roll of names for any of our friends who wants to pelt the other side. I have had no time to ascertain how many of my worthies are Professors, but it does not signify. The point is that continental education is in the hands of Professors, and that all these good books are produced notwithstanding. I have confined myself almost entirely to the matter in hand, which I presume was what you wished ... G. Smith presumes that you have gone through the list of Historical and Legal text-books used here, so as to see to what extent we are indebted to foreigners. He also thinks that if you have time it would be worth while to send proofs down here that we might see if we have any facts to adduce in support of what you say.[22]

Although Conington's essay was a striking testimony to the extent of German scholarship, it was less impressive evidence of his own, as he modestly admitted, 'If', he wrote to Vaughan, 'you and Liddell will be good enough to correct my proofs, there will certainly be no occasion to risk delay by sending them to me. I only thought my writing of names, many of which I scarcely know myself, might lead printers wrong, and that you might not be able to discover what was meant. One error I have myself committed, I have talked of an edition of Varro de Lingua Latina by Sprengel, when I ought (I believe) to have said Spengel.'[23]

Liddell was active in assisting with the correction of proofs, and he also sent Vaughan a memorandum of what seemed to him 'actual misrepresentations in Pusey's evidence',[24] and

[22] J. Conington to Vaughan, 25 Jan. 1854.
[23] The same to the same, 29 Jan. 1854.
[24] H. G. Liddell to the same, [1853].

8223773   K

indicated lines of argument which Vaughan certainly followed in his pamphlet.

On looking over Pusey's evidence a second time [he wrote] I am struck more than ever by the 'nihil ad rem' style of argumentation. I am sure it may be answered very conclusively. But it would add to the weight of an answer if, besides shewing how little all his facts (being conceded) would prove, we could also destroy his facts. Stanley tells me that in his Hebrew Lectures he referred at every turn to German writers, no doubt professors. What have we—*in his line*— to put by the side of Gesenius, Feitag, Ewald? What in Geography to compare with Ritter, Professor at Berlin? What in Roman History but investigations raised by Niebuhr? What in Roman Antiquities to compare with Becker, Mommsen, Grotefend, Nitzsch, Marqwhart, Madvig? &c. &c. The thing is too monstrous.[25]

In another letter, he proposed

a brief notice to the effect that your argument was independent of the truth of Pusey's statement with regard to Germany. It was, however, satisfactory to know that there was reason to believe those statements to be greatly overcharged in most points and in others quite mistaken; so that, even if the recommendations of the Report did tend Germany- ward, the consequences need not be such as he apprehends.[26]

From one quarter, Vaughan received no help. Benjamin Jowett, that convinced but cautious reformer who had avoided signing the evidence submitted to the Hebdomadal Board until it was too late, declined to contribute documentary evidence. To Vaughan's invitation, Jowett, who happened at that moment to be pressing a scheme of his own on Gladstone, replied:

I have been very negligent in not answering your kind proposal that I should contribute a few pages to your pamphlet. I can only offer the contradictory excuses, which are nevertheless both true, that I have been very ill and also very much occupied for the last fortnight. I am afraid that I have nothing ready that would serve the purpose. I do not know the present state of Germany with sufficient accuracy. The true answer seems to me (to what Pusey has alleged) to draw a corresponding

[25] H. G. Liddell to Vaughan, 18 Dec. 1853.
[26] The same to the same, 8 Jan. 1854.

picture of England with its conservative scepticism in religion and the utter separation that has been allowed to grow up between Theology and every sort of criticism and science. The greatest sceptics are Pusey and his friends who not only doubt but refuse to inquire into any fact relating to the origin of Christianity. They are absolutely reckless about truth of fact and ignorant of the very meaning of such an idea. I fear I must decline to take a part in your pamphlet.[27]

In *Oxford Reform and Oxford Professors*, Vaughan wrote not simply on his own behalf but with the approval of the professorial wing of the commission party, and he was actively assisted by at least two members of the commission, Liddell and Stanley. He was, it may therefore be assumed, writing at least a semi-official answer to Pusey, if not something more. Nothing, he remarked at the outset, 'has occupied so much attention, or occasioned so much hostile remark'[28] as the recommendations of the Royal Commission concerning the professoriate. He declared his intention to defend against the charges levelled by Pusey and the tutors the principles advocated by the Blue Book, which, by its impartiality, 'still occupies a position . . . which no other reporting body has yet intitled itself to claim'. It was his avowed object to confine himself to those 'reflexions and criticisms', which sought to reverse its recommendations or to invalidate the evidence on which they rested.

The main quarry was Pusey, and Vaughan devoted less than a fifth of his pamphlet to the tutors' report, which, he observed, 'seems to accept the general plan of developing the professorial system'. Having bestowed this vague accolade of approval, he proceeded to demolish the tutors' arguments on professorial control of examinations and the regulation of professorial lectures. These were important issues, but for Vaughan they had a particular and personal importance. His dispute with Lake about the examinership was still fresh in his mind, and his non-residence and the alleged insufficiency of his lectures had been the object of comment even by members of the Royal Commission. The opportunity of taking his revenge on Lake and

---

[27] B. Jowett to Vaughan, 3 Feb. [1854].
[28] *Oxford Reform and Oxford Professors* (1854), 2.

defending his own conduct was too good to be missed. The manner of appointing examiners, he remarked, was a bad one, not only because it placed appointments in the hands of 'the undistinguished tutor of a single college', but because 'it sometimes happens that, circuitously and by agreement with his brother-proctor, he selects himself',[29] an undisguised reference to the fact that Lake had in the previous year combined in his own person the offices of proctor and examiner. It was not enough, Vaughan went on, for the professors to have that 'moral influence' which the tutors wished to bestow on them. Without constitutional rights, their personal eminence would expose them to jealousies, and their devotion to their studies would cut them off 'from that cultivation of indirect relations which astute and busy men, while truants from their appointed tasks, can find time to establish'.[30] Lake, so Pattison relates, was 'much nettled' by the reference to astute and busy men.[31]

The tutors' proposals for regulating professorial lectures raised for Vaughan an important issue on which he differed strongly from them and from the commission also. The tutors held that the commission's scheme to combine collegiate and professorial teaching would reduce them to 'mere subordinate channels for the diffussion of Professorial lessons',[32] but they admitted that, although in general the colleges could be so reformed as to dispense with the need for teaching professors, such assistance might be necessary in the new studies. One such study was history. 'It appears very doubtful', they remarked, 'whether the Colleges have means at their command to answer the requirements of a numerous class of students in so extensive a subject'. In these subjects the professor was conceived as a specialized tutor, and constant residence and the delivery of terminal lectures were expected of him. Teaching professors, however, ran contrary to Vaughan's whole idea of the professoriate.

It is clear [he said] that a Professor of History, capable of the highest things in his department, would thus write, or be expected to write,

---

[29] *Oxford Reform and Oxford Professors* (1854), 9.
[30] Ibid. 11.   [31] MS. Pattison 129, f. 131.
[32] *Third Report of the Oxford Tutors' Association* (1853), 67.

six octavo volumes in each year. 'The Decline and Fall of the Roman Empire', which occupied its able, secluded, and indefatigable and fluent author during twenty years, assisted as he was by very many grand works of research recently prepared to his hand, would at this rate of work have flowed from his pen in the course of twenty months: and left him at leisure to write with similar speed on the same scale the history of every modern nation in the world during a short academical career.[33]

The tutors, he continued, wanted professors capable of the highest achievements yet bound by rigid rules to give a large number of lectures. Their teaching was to be subordinate to that of the tutors, they were to have no fixed place in the constitution or any control of examinations and studies, and they were to be rewarded with a meagre pittance of £500 a year. Men of great attainments and of riper years than the majority of tutors could not be obtained on such terms.

Vaughan then turned his artillery on Pusey, his main antagonist. Many of the arguments used on both sides in this controversy may seem so self-evident as not to need assertion, but the fact that they were stated in 1854, and at great length, suggests that they needed to be debated because they were new to Oxford. Men were discussing the nature of the professoriate, and its function in learning and education. At a deeper level they were discussing the nature of a university, the meaning of a liberal education, the conflict between a religious and a secular idea of society. For the light they cast on these great questions the arguments of Pusey and Vaughan still merit attention.

Vaughan's principal object was to define the nature and importance of the professoriate in education and learning, and to refute Pusey's claim that in the one case it had no value and in the other it was the cause of irreligion. He began by exposing the fallacy in Pusey's acceptance of professorial teaching in the sciences. It is remarkable that Pusey, standing on the brink of the great controversy between religion and science, which dominated the the intellectual history of the second half of the nineteenth century, should have feared the intrusion of professorial studies in theology

[33] *Oxford Reform and Oxford Professors* (1854), 14.

as dangerous to faith, but have welcomed them in science. His instinct that the new studies threatened religion was not unfounded, but he misunderstood the causes because of his view that science was concerned only with information as to matters of fact—an opinion which Vaughan scornfully dismissed as worthy of 'some historical museum which shall preserve the history of prejudice or pretext'.[34] The study of science, Vaughan declared, involved 'acts of memory, comprehension, comparison, imagination, deduction', and the use of many faculties the exercise of which was a discipline truly noble. Its exclusion from general study was due less to a belief that it was concerned with matters of fact, however, than to the development in the sixteenth century of the traditional character of education at a time when science did not exist, and the system had been preserved by the jealousy of teachers fearful lest accepted traditions be upset by new knowledge. As a means of disciplining the mind, science was in no way inferior to the study of dead languages, which in practice often led to the abeyance and destruction of the intellectual powers and the paralysis of the mind.

The relative merits of the tutorial and professorial systems did not turn solely on the content of the studies themselves: Pusey made no special claim for the educational value of classics, and Vaughan none for that of history. It turned on the question whether professorial lectures, as a method of instruction, provided mental discipline comparable to that provided by the tutors. This was a central educational point at issue between Pusey and Vaughan. The tutorial system was based on the textbook, and Pusey had no doubt that books were a better foundation for teaching than lectures because they could be reread and considered at leisure by the reader, while the substance of the professorial lecture was liable to be lost by inattention. In listening to a lecture the mind was simply the passive recipient of information, and the faculties were employed mainly in listening to and writing down what was said. It could not pause and survey the arguments or consider minute points before passing on. At most it was stored. It was not sharpened or enlarged.

[34] *Oxford Reform and Oxford Professors* (1854), 27.

If books were to be compared with lectures, replied Vaughan, it should be on an equal footing. The book read several times should be compared with the lecture heard several times, and the book read for an hour with the lecture heard for an hour. It would then be found that the human voice had a special advantage over the book. 'The Professor is the science or subject vitalised and humanised in the student's presence. He sees him kindle into his subject; he sees reflected and exhibited in him his manner and his earnestness—the general power of the science to engage, delight, and absorb a human intelligence.'[35] It was true, as Pusey claimed, that successful professorial lectures attracted large audiences, and since these must be composed of persons of various attainments they could not be equally useful to all. But was not this an objection equally levelled against tutorial lectures, which Pusey sought to defend? Moreover, the same problem faced the writer of a book, 'yet he does not sit mute on that account, nor does he write twenty books, as he might, for the five times twenty classes of intellect and knowledge amongst the readers of the world'.[36] The truth was that in good lectures as in good books, 'though all is only for the highest, there is much for the many, and somewhat for the least'.[37] The great professor was rare, but so was the great book, for the same process produced both, and between the great peaks the ordinary learned and able professor harmonized existing knowledge and modified the achievements of the past.

In listening to a lecture, Vaughan continued, the student was not the passive recipient of information described by Pusey. The mind was no quart pot into which things could be thrust without any action of its own. It could not receive except by understanding, and by the exercise of memory, imagination, and reason what was read or heard was received into it. As a form of mental discipline, the lecture was in fact superior to the book. It was true that the book could be read and reread, taken up and put down, until at last it was mastered, and this gave the book an advantage over the lecture as a source of information. But the lecture was delivered without a pause, and 'must therefore be

[35] Ibid. 33.   [36] Ibid. 34.   [37] Ibid. 35.

comprehended and retained by one sustained action of the comprehensive faculties. . . . The mind must be held in command, the attention vigilantly pointed, the comprehensive faculties sustained in action, during the whole lecture, without any grave "fault" in the continuity of effort. The student will feel after this, if he have made the attempt, that his mind has been put to an athletic exercise.'[38] Neither the reader of a book nor the listener to a lecture could reflect while he received and comprehended, since these were different functions of the mind. The listener to a lecture must delay reflection until the lecture was complete, and judgement was therefore suspended until the whole material was absorbed, and premature conclusions were thereby avoided. The reader, on the other hand, was constantly tempted to reach premature conclusions which he was later obliged to revise. Thus, although the lecture was inferior to the book as a means of absorbing information, it was superior as a means of strengthening the mind by enforcing attention and training judgement.

The dispute between Pusey and Vaughan had so far concerned the educational value of oral lectures in general rather than professorial lectures in particular. Pusey maintained that time devoted by professors to lecturing was time wasted. 'The office of teaching is one thing, the office of advancing a science or study is another.'[39] The proper workshop of the professor was the study, not the lecture room. Vaughan, on the other hand, while welcoming Pusey's assertion that a professoriate 'would answer a noble purpose, even if it did not lecture at all',[40] which was a point of view not dissimilar to his own, believed that the professorial lecture had a place in education. If freedom were given in the manner and number of lectures, it was not necessary for professors to exclude learned or profound investigations. Faraday, for example, lectured for a great many years of his life but also contrived to advance knowledge, and it was beneficial for a student to be taught by such a man, for there was a freshness in

---

[38] *Oxford Reform and Oxford Professors* (1854), 38.
[39] *Report and Evidence . . . Presented to the Board of Heads of Houses and Proctors* (1853), Evidence, 18.
[40] *Oxford Reform and Oxford Professors* (1854), 43.

his views, an insight, accuracy, and caution in his statement of principles denied to others. A rigorous exaction of frequent lectures must, it was true, impede the higher researches of the professor, but at Oxford the whole burden of teaching would not, as in the case of Germany, fall on the shoulders of the professors because of the existence of the tutorial system. Vaughan thus managed to defend professorial lectures without defending teaching professors.

His retention of the tutorial system, suitably reformed, was an effective rebuttal of the charge of Germanizing, which was a charge he always strenuously rejected. The implication of Pusey's argument throughout was that the Royal Commission, following the German model, intended to replace the collegiate system of teaching by the professorial. It was a valid argument applied to unattached students, whose education would presumably have been entrusted to the professors and their assistants, but the intention clearly expressed was to combine the two methods of instruction. Vaughan's position differed from that taken both by Pusey and by the commission: he allowed the professor a greater role in teaching than Pusey, but less involvement than envisaged by the commission.

The religious issues raised by Pusey exposed the wide gulf which divided him from Vaughan. Pusey asked not only whether the education given by the university should be Christian or secular, but whether learning itself ought to be confined within the framework of religion. For him there could be only one answer. He accused professors of subverting religion and morality by seeking novelty rather than truth. 'The problem has been, what they should discover ... they have really perverted the judgement by investing with undue importance what has cost them labour, or what others, rightly, have neglected.'[41] In Germany, rivalry among professors had produced a raging conflict of opinions and a succession of opposing schools of philosophy. Instead of the firm rock of faith there was the shifting foundation of controversy and scepticism. Like religion itself, knowledge was

[41] *Report and Evidence ... Presented to the Board of Heads of Houses and Proctors* (1853), Evidence, 23.

founded on revelation. It was the gradual unfolding of the Divine Providence, and, like faith, when vouchsafed at last through great labour, was unchangeable. In moral studies, there was little place for new truth to be discovered, except on matters of fact, though in science, which was not a moral study, a vast area of knowledge remained to be discovered. It was for Pusey a telling criticism that in Germany no books were studied in religion and philosophy except those published in the previous twenty-five years, or so he claimed, whereas in England the great divines of the sixteenth and seventeenth centuries continued to be studied.

To Vaughan, on the other hand, truth was not static. Neither in morals nor in science was it revealed by the hand of God, but was constantly growing and changing out of observation and conflict. Even if Pusey were right, he said, and professors sought novelty, the consequences would be less dangerous than he feared, for erroneous knowledge was either neglected, in which case it did no harm, or it was destroyed by the same cause which produced it. 'If the "solid" and established doctrine fall below the new and hollow, much more does the hollow established doctrine rush down before the new and solid truth.'[42] The same process was at work where error was more dangerous because more plausible. Progress towards truth was not a sustained advance but rather an ebb and flow in which error was gradually eliminated. 'It required even some admixture of error to eliminate the unquestionable truth that fossil shells were originally parts of organized life, and not bivalve and turbinated stones. The discovery of oxygen gas was awhile attended by numberless theories and incorrect conceptions, which, after vanishing away from the context of truth only after fluctuations and struggles, left it in its purity.'[43]

For Pusey moral and philosophical truth was fixed and change was novelty; for Vaughan change was an aspect of truth and truth was a limitless horizon of inquiry.

Is it not true [he wrote] that the fields of discovery ray out and lengthen out on every side of us as we stand in this very moment of

---

[42] *Oxford Reform and Oxford Professors* (1854), 55.   [43] Ibid. 58.

time? Move on as time must, and as civilisation may, as genius or industry can, the mind will for ever continue to look on the same scene, of a world unknown yet inviting knowledge to the utmost horizon of its vision. . . . It will need no morbid love of novelty, but a simple and pure love of knowledge and inquiry. . . . New truths may be expected, not because the newness is desired, but because the truth not yet in our possession will be longed for, and earnestly sought.[44]

The professor was the instrument through which such truth was sought. In moral sciences, in ancient history, even in classical studies, Oxford had produced almost nothing, and what there was had been the work of professors such as Elmsley and Gaisford. It was untrue that professors did not produce good books and the evidence was plainly to the contrary. But Pusey had added a special element to the definition of a good book, which was that it should last for centuries. Yet the oblivion which Pusey complained overtook German scholarship could be accounted for without ascribing it to the quest for novelty. Each age produced a literature peculiar to itself, and thus unsuited to subsequent generations and so likely to be forgotten. In religion the causes of change were not to be found in the professoriate.

Causes far less minute—the general and natural reaction, one while on a dialectic slavery, another while on feelings overstrained or long excited, or methods exhausted—the influences of social habits, foreign literature, political power, and, of course, occasionally of some great thinker, who could affect his own age or the next—operated to produce new modes of feeling, discipline, and thought, and developed in their course new branches of learning, and modes of treatment. It was no peculiarity in professorial work which has ever been said to make the literature perishable; nor was it peculiarly a professorial feeling which obliterated and undervalued all which had gone before. These things are imputed to the Professoriate, at this particular crisis of Oxford, for the first time; the existence of active, learned men, whether Professors or others, must, of course, be one power of movement, of progress, or of change, and beneficially so often. But it is the spirit of learning and inquiry, rather than any peculiar Professorial spirit of innovation, which constitutes the main element in this particular influence.[45]

[44] Ibid. 61.   [45] Ibid. 67.

The same power of movement accounted for the fact that books seldom endured, for new discoveries caused new and better books to be written, and so learning advanced on the shoulders of the past. If books written centuries ago continued to be read, it was often merely proof that better ones had not been written since, and conversely the disuse of earlier books indicated that better had supplanted them. The proper deduction from the fact that German books did not endure was that the German professoriate had constantly produced better. If rationalism prevailed in Germany, the cause was not to be found in professors of theology. In any case, Pusey could not have it both ways. If they were mischievous, they were as mischievous in Oxford as elsewhere. But if it was asserted that the Crown made good theological appointments in England when dangerous appointments were made in Germany, it only proved that Crown appointments would not be dangerous in England, and if the past was no sufficient guarantee for the future the logical course was to abolish chairs of theology.

Finally, Vaughan addressed himself to Pusey's proposition that professors were the cause of immorality in universities. No evidence, he declared, was offered from the Scottish universities, where the professorial system was well established, or even from contemporary Germany. 'We are carried back into remote centuries of modern history.'[46] The truth was surely that the moral condition of students was neither above nor below that of the age. He concluded his argument and his pamphlet with these words:

If the professorial system, including the intellectual labours and the academical teaching of Professors, will be an incentive to industry— if it tend to the cultivation of great and noble sciences, to the know-ledge of grand and wise authors, to the understanding of a marvellous and boundless world, and to the appreciation of all social and moral laws,—it tends also to displace base sensual pleasures, frivolous, expensive occupations, false tastes, strenuous trifling, ignorant judgments, foolish words, and that mere idleness which is ever the prelude to active evil. If this, in its direction at least, be not a high moral

[46] *Oxford Reform and Oxford Professors* (1854), 82.

tendency, my conception of morals and moral instruments must be moulded anew.[47]

Vaughan's eloquent and impassioned defence of learning, which has no parallel in the writings of other contemporary reformers, did little to allay Pusey's suspicions that the professors would Germanize the university, even though his own lectures contained so many of the characteristics which he condemned that Stanley observed 'Of all the Professors in Oxford, there is none who has more frequently recurred to me as the example of what a German Professor is, and of what an English Professor might be, than the present Regius Professor of Hebrew.'[48] He and Vaughan were stating opposed conceptions of the nature of a university, and there was little common ground between them. To Pusey a university was a place of religious education and learning, identified with the Church of England, devoted to the training of Christian citizens, and bearing witness to the unfolding of the Divine Providence. To Vaughan it was primarily a place for the discovery of truth, where learning was unimpeded by religion and education was liberated by knowledge. Pusey stood for a religious university, Vaughan for a secular.

When *Oxford Reform and Oxford Professors* was published in February 1854, Conington and Jeune at once wrote to express their approval. Thomas Carlyle 'read it straight way, with steady attention, to the end, and really with great pleasure and approval'.[49] Jowett gave it qualified praise: 'I write to thank you for your pamphlet, which I read with the greatest interest. Though I do not go so far as yourself in what relates to the Professorial system, I am heartily glad you have made so bold and able defence of yourself against Pusey. The question of Professors v. Tutors is with me very much a question of what is practicable and likely to work in this place.'[50]

In the university at large it hardened resistance to the professorial system. Although Vaughan had written with the approval of several members of the Royal Commission, his earnest defence

---

[47] Ibid. 95.   [48] See appendix B.
[49] T. Carlyle to Vaughan, 17 Feb. 1854.
[50] B. Jowett to the same, 14 Feb. [1854].

of the professoriate identified the Report with the professorial question more than its generally tentative proposals merited. Far from removing the anxieties of the tutors, the pamphlet increased their animus against the professors. George Rawlinson informed Gladstone that there was 'a very strong anti-Professorial feeling among the Fellow of Colleges. This feeling has been constantly on the increase, and latterly has been specially intensified by Dr. Pusey's Evidence, and (I think I must add) by Mr. Vaughan's pamphlet.'[51]

The university was not ready for a professoriate of the kind to which Vaughan aspired. The reform movement of the 1850s was concerned principally with education, and the extension of the professoriate was considered and condemned by the majority in this context. While professors were regarded primarily as instruments for the education of undergraduates there was small prospect of a vigorous professoriate devoted to learning, and possibly inimical to religion.

It was not until the second university commission that Vaughan's ideas gained much acceptance, and by then he had been almost forgotten in Oxford. At a public meeting in 1872, Mark Pattison spoke of the application of university and college funds to learned purposes, and he was reported as saying that these ideas had never been put forward previously. Vaughan wrote to him from his home in South Wales to say that he had himself advocated precisely the same objects twenty years previously.

Such a doctrine as that the great need of Oxford was rather learning than teaching, and that there would be no learning without endowment and leisure, and that the opportunity and the means if only bestowed on the men who had the power and the spirit to be worthy Professors would not and could not be misused, were met with derision by the common herd at Oxford, utter indifference by the utilitarian improvers, incredulity by the many men of industrious habits, rejection by well nigh all. I never have doubted of the truth of what I then more than once and with some emphasis said, but such certainly was the state of opinion when I left Oxford so I understood it. After twenty years it is satisfactory to see that a powerful gathering of men can put forth almost unanimously the very same doctrines as I then broached.[52]

Pattison replied generously acknowledging his debt to Vaughan. 'I held in my hand, at the very time of speaking an extract from the blue book of the commission in which they lay down the principle we are trying to work and refer to your evidence for its further development, but time did not admit of my reading the extract I had prepared. And if you ever looked at my book on Academical Organisation you would see that I refer to your pamphlet Oxford Reform &c on the point.'[53] Pattison's tribute was echoed in the following year, when Sir Charles Newton wrote to Vaughan's mother-in-law, 'It is wonderful how exhaustively he has treated the question of the professoriate and how far in advance of his time he was when that pamphlet was written eighteen years ago.'[54]

Professor Ward has written that Vaughan's controversy with Pusey was left behind by the tide of events before it was published.[55] But not only was it charged with significance for the future, it was about to fulfil one of the functions for which it was initially written, namely to substantiate the case for the professoriate when it came to be debated in Parliament. It was, however, destined to provide ammunition for the opposition to the Oxford Bill and not, as was first intended, for the government.

[52] Vaughan to M. Pattison, 20 Dec. 1872.
[53] M. Pattison to Vaughan, 23 Dec. 1872.
[54] C. T. Newton to Mrs. Jackson, 16 Jan. 1873.
[55] W. R. Ward, *Victorian Oxford*, 1965, 187.

11. The Oxford Act
1854

WHEN *Oxford Reform and Oxford Professors* was published the radicals were still confident that Gladstone would produce a Bill embodying the main recommendations of the Blue Book. It was an ill-founded confidence which rested on nothing more substantial then his known disapproval of the plans of the Heads, which he had confided to Stanley,[1] and on the uninspired gossip of *The Times*,[2] and as late as 18 February, Johnson, who had sat on the Royal Commission, was convinced that Gladstone would quietly overthrow his friends in the Tutors' Association 'and give the Commissioners' scheme or something like it'.[3] How mistaken the radicals were became immediately apparent when the Bill was published in the spring of 1854.

Gladstone had been persuaded slowly of the need for parliamentary intervention, but the obstructiveness of the Heads had eventually convinced him that there was no likelihood of a substantial measure of reform from that quarter, and the possibility that some colleges eager for reform might seek a discordant variety of enabling acts while others sheltered passively behind oaths of obedience to their statutes pointed to the need for a single and, it was hoped, final act of the legislature, based, as he informed Lord Russell, on 'a few leading enactments, prohibitory, enabling, and positive'.[4] The principal objects of the Bill were constitutional reform directed to secure the representation of the main elements in the university on the governing body; the opening of Fellowships and the abolition of undergraduate

---

[1] H. G. Liddell to Vaughan, [1854].
[2] The same to the same, 18 Dec. 1853.
[3] MS. Pattison 129, f. 131. [4] Add. MS. 44291 f., 70ᵛ.

Fellowships; and an increase in the number of students by permission to open new halls. It was a measure, he told Bonamy Price, framed on 'the principle of working with the materials which we possess, endeavouring to improve our institutions through the agency they themselves supply, and giving to reform in all cases where there is a choice the character of return and restoration'.[5] It was, in short, a great measure of conservative reform.

The difficulty of piloting such a Bill through Parliament was formidable with an unstable ministry, in the face of expected opposition in the Lords from Derby, and, in due course, the problems created by the outbreak of war in the Crimea. Political necessity and common prudence alike indicated the need to obtain as wide a measure of support as possible within the university. Unable to count on the Heads, Gladstone looked for it to the tutors who formed the largest body of opinion in Oxford. He was much impressed by the reports of the Tutors' Association, which he described as a body intermediate between the commission and the Heads,[6] and in particular by its recommendations on the constitution, extension, and the professoriate. The Association embraced many shades of opinion, but even the conservatives, so Lake informed Gladstone, were ready to accept 'a really liberal reform if it does but respect the religious character of Oxford'.[7] The need to carry parliament and the university with him confirmed Gladstone's conviction that compromises with the proposals of the commission were necessary. To Lord Russell, who was the father of the commission and remained throughout more favourable to its proposals than any of his colleagues, he remarked that the whole cabinet believed it madness to bring in a Bill framed in the 'sense and spirit' of the Blue Book.[8]

Many recommendations of the commission, especially those relating to the colleges, had been absorbed since 1852 into the general movement for reform. But on the burning issue of the professoriate Gladstone and the tutors were in agreement that although professors ought to have some place in the constitution

---

[5] Add. MS. 44378, f. 234. [6] Add. MS. 44291, f. 70.
[7] Add. MS. 44230, f. 267. [8] MS. Acland d. 68, f. 10.

of the university and to be awarded a position of dignity, they ought not to be given predominant power.

The Government [Gladstone wrote to Provost Hawkins] have not adopted, and are not likely to adopt, those recommendations of the Commissioners which would place the commanding power over the University and the Colleges in the hands of the Professors and their Assistant Teachers. But they believe that it is essential in order to enable Oxford to discharge her full duty, let me add to vindicate her full influence, in this country, that a sensible and a considerable weight should be assigned in the Governing body to the Class, upon which it depends to represent the University as apart from the Colleges, and that an effort should be made for rearing up by the side of the Colleges an University or extra-collegiate system.[9]

The Bill preserved the collegiate and Anglican character of the university, and such measures as were designed for strengthening the professoriate were contained within this framework. For Vaughan and his friends, who desired to supplant the existing system by one in which the university, represented by a largely secular professoriate, became the dominant force, the Bill was fundamentally unacceptable.

The constitutional question was therefore crucial. Several schemes had at various times been put forward, most of them designed to keep power where it was or to shift it towards one or other section of the university. The Royal Commission wanted a reformed Congregation composed *ex officio* of the Heads, the professors and assistant professors, and the senior tutors of all colleges and halls, who were appointed by the Heads, and proposed to retain the old Hebdomadal Board with reduced powers. The plan contained no element of election and gave the professors a permanent majority. The Heads had proposed two schemes. By the first, which was the one they favoured, the existing Board was to be augmented by eight elected members of Convocation, and by the second, which was invented by Pusey, an intermediate Board was to be created between the Hebdomadal Board and Convocation consisting of the Vice-Chancellor,

[9] Add. MS. 44206, f. 118.

proctors, and twelve elected members of Convocation. To this intermediate Board all legislation was to be submitted. Both schemes of the Heads left power in the hands of the existing caucus, and neither allowed for any representation of the professors as such. The Tutors' Association rejected all these schemes in favour of the principle of representation. The conservative wing proposed a Hebdomadal Council composed of twelve Heads and twelve elected members of Convocation. The scheme made no concession to the professors and gave the power of electing half the Council to the undifferentiated and tutor-dominated Convocation. The moderates proposed a Council of twenty-seven members, of which the Heads, the professors and examiners, and the tutors and other resident members of Convocation each elected a third. This became known as sectional representation. A variation, which assumed considerable importance, was to make the whole Council, still divided into three sections, elected by all the resident members of Convocation. Both schemes of the moderates recognized the professors as a distinct element in the Council, and one of them gave the professors the power of electing their own representatives. Sectional representation protected the interests of minorities, but in the case of the Heads and the professors rested on a very narrow franchise and was believed by some to foster party strife. Election by the resident members of Convocation placed power in the hands of the tutors, and to its opponents seemed to consolidate the triumph of the collegiate system at the expense of the professorial.

The Bill which Gladstone circulated in Oxford in February 1854 adopted sectional representation, and Liddell, in sending him a copy of *Oxford Reform and Oxford Professors*, took the opportunity to remonstrate against it and its variant. The prospect of a Council elected in whole or in part by resident members of Convocation, he said, was greeted with alarm by those who wished to see an independent and learned professoriate in Oxford. What the wishes even of the liberal section of the tutors were in respect to the professors was plain to see in the report of the Association. They desired to bind them by stringent rules from which they were themselves exempt, and to fix their salaries at a level hardly greater than the average income of a tutor.

Such a deliberate expression of opinion leads many persons to fear that if by the new Constitution, the Tutors and Heads are able to command a majority in the Council, the whole Collegiate Body will be found in opposition to the professorial members, if it is intended that there should be any such. Men of age and acquirements fit to be Professors will not submit to have severe rules prescribed and niggardly salaries doled out by those who must (on the whole) be their juniors and ought to be their subordinates.[10]

Although Gladstone was far from unsympathetic to the revival of the professoriate, he considered it best achieved through the spontaneous action of the university expressed through the constitution rather than imposed by Act of Parliament. But the likelihood of such action depended on the willingness of the university to promote it, and in an atmosphere clouded with suspicion there was little chance that the university would take the initiative. Gladstone himself noted that the temper of Convocation was 'strongly anti-professorial',[11] and Lake spoke of the 'suspicion (which a pamphlet like Vaughan's does very little to disarm) of the spirit of the Liberal Party'.[12]

There were two courses open to the commission party. They could either seek to amend the Bill in Parliament, with or without Gladstone's help, or they could join the moderate tutors in supporting it in the hope that something could thereby be saved for the professors, that having accepted the constitutional arrangements concessions would be obtained elsewhere. The dilemma divided the reformers. Vaughan, Liddell, and a handful of others, who considered that direct legislation was the main protection against the tutors, opted for the first course. For Vaughan, the decision was not difficult. The ink was scarcely dry on his pamphlet defending the commission, and he was so closely identified personally with the professorial question that it was not possible for him to throw in his hand with Gladstone in support of a quite different scheme. The Pembroke party,

10 Add. MS. 44236, f. 263.   11 Add. MS. 44230, f. 281.
12 Ibid., f. 282.

on the other hand, decided on alliance with the tutors and co-operation with Gladstone. On 15 February a petition signed by forty-one liberals was sent to Lord Russell in support of a constitution which was similar to that proposed by the Tutors' Association. In place of sectional representation it incorporated an electoral body composed of all university and college officers. Amongst the signatories were all the radicals who in the previous December had supported the very different scheme of the Royal Commission in their evidence to the Hebdomadal Board's committee, with the notable exception of Vaughan. In the same letter in which he congratulated Vaughan on the publication of his pamphlet, Jeune defended the petition.

I hear that you and Liddell dislike the constitution framed by the 35[13] liberals as likely to extinguish the professorial body. I cannot think so. A third of Professors must surely lead the whole Board as they please, if they are such men as we desire. Nor can I think that Congregation would not elect the best men. Doubtless I should prefer a smaller Congregation, but have yielded because otherwise no union was possible between reformers here. We are told that government was to adopt the Tutors' scheme. So at least Lake boasted. This I think much worse than ours.[14] On the other hand the Heads had assented to Pusey's which would be destructive . . . I deeply, very deeply, regret anything like difference from you and Liddell, but I think that our common object must be attained by even such men as Lake when seated in the governing body.[15]

Liddell told Gladstone that not one of the members of the commission approved the scheme. Many, he said, had signed it on being informed that Gladstone had written to the Junior Proctor that ministers approved the scheme of the tutors, and because Lake had boasted that 'the Tutors' Association would have it all their own way with Mr. Gladstone'.[16] Privately he complained to Henry Acland that the actions of Jeune and his friends gave him 'a very strong and decided feeling that I have

[13] The letter was written five days before the petition was closed.
[14] Lake wanted an electoral body consisting not of university and college officers only but of *all* residents.
[15] F. Jeune to Vaughan, 10 Feb. 1854.   [16] Add. MS. 44236, f. 267.

been treated in a manner that I can only designate as treacherous and *politically* dishonest'.[17] Jeune, he said, had excused his conduct on the grounds that Lake had boasted that Gladstone was with the tutors. 'The excuse is as absurd as the boast was vain-glorious. But if Gladstone had not tampered so much with the Tutors, no such boast *could* have been uttered, as it *certainly was*.' The stand by Liddell and Vaughan increased the uneasiness of some of those who had signed Jeune's petition, and their reservations about the constitution were reflected in a letter which J. M. Wilson, professor of moral philosophy, wrote to Gladstone only a few days after adding his signature. The constitution, he observed, ought to contain two elements—the colleges and the university. The Heads, who were 'very often merely the Bursars of the College selected to look after the college estates', were not a separate element, and to grant them an equal share in the constitution with the tutors caused the college interest to predominate. The Board should therefore consist of professors and of representatives of the Heads and tutors. The Pembroke movement, he continued, had originated in the belief that the government had abandoned the idea of establishing a professorial and university system, and the scheme he advocated would enable the voice of the university to be heard.[18] But Gladstone had already rejected a similar scheme from Liddell, and he approved of the Pembroke scheme, which went a long way to meet the tutors, and it was this scheme which was eventually incorporated in the Bill.

The Bill was introduced in Parliament by Lord Russell on 17 March. It was destined to have a stormy passage. It provided for a Hebdomadal Council composed of the Vice-Chancellor and Proctors, seven Heads, of whom six were to be elected by Congregation and one nominated by the Chancellor, eight professors, of whom six were elected by Congregation, one nominated by the Chancellor, and one a professor of divinity, and six elected members of Congregation, which was to consist of university officers, the senior tutor of each college, and such other residents as were habitually engaged in study. Oaths,

[17] MS. Acland d. 69, f. 30.   [18] Add. MS. 44377, f. 254.

which the Royal Commission had wished to abolish, were restricted but not removed. On university extension, private halls might be opened under licence from the Vice-Chancellor, and colleges were permitted to apply their revenues to the erection of new buildings or to the establishment of affiliated halls. Half the Fellowships were to be opened and undergraduate Fellowships abolished, but certain preferences on behalf of schools were retained. The obligation to take Orders remained, but colleges were allowed to allot up to a quarter of their Fellowships to laymen. Fellows were required to reside, and must be tutors, office holders, incumbents of parishes within three miles of Carfax, or hold a certificate of study. The income of Fellows was to be raised to a sum not exceeding £250 by the suppression of Fellowships, and a maximum of one-fifth of college income might be devoted to the support of professorial chairs. This last was the only provision, apart from the constitutional arrangements, directly to affect the professoriate. Finally, colleges were to produce ordinances revising their statutes for the approval of commissioners to be appointed by Parliament.

'The Bill', Jeune wrote to Gladstone, 'generally finds great favour in the eyes of Reformers here, the clauses respecting residence excepted.'[19] H. B. Barry wrote to him, 'The proposed constitution of the University has been received with general satisfaction. It is remarkable that controversy on the subject which was so rife before the introduction of the Bill has ceased altogether.'[20] But dissenting voices were soon heard, particularly amongst those who had signed Jeune's petition in the hope that the settlement of the constitutional question would pave the way for measures to strengthen the professoriate. Bonamy Price unburdened himself to Gladstone. Nothing, he declared, was gained by the new constitution if it was animated by the same spirit as the old. The Bill aggravated existing evils because its effect was to place the collegiate monopoly in a position of more absolute ascendancy. The tutors would be all-powerful in Congregation, most of the Heads, and even some of the professors would side with them. If the new disciplines were to prosper

---

[19] Add. MS. 44221, f. 34. [20] Add. MS. 44379, f. 144.

and if tutors were to be encouraged to cultivate them, it was necessary for the professors to be given a real hold on the studies of the university, but the Bill did nothing for them. 'It says nothing about Public Professors, or their mode of appointment, or their incorporation into the academical system; it leaves them just where they are. It does indeed propose to create professorships in the colleges . . . but that alone will give them no value or importance in the university.'[21] These were matters which ought to be settled in the Bill: they could not safely be left to Council. What was wanted, he concluded, was a proper system of appointment, the assignment of defined spheres of teaching, positive influence on the examinations, and detailed machinery for the appointment of assistant professors. To this Gladstone answered that there was not the remotest chance of inducing Parliament to adopt such proposals. The changes in the Bill, he said, were based on the principle of working with existing materials, and the rate of change was as much as the English temperament would bear.[22]

Convinced that Gladstone would not alter the Bill to meet their wishes, the malcontents turned to Liddell and Vaughan, who had remained throughout true to the principles of the commission. Having failed to move Gladstone, they hoped for more success with Lord Russell, who was known to favour the views of the commission, and they sought to create an effective lobby in Parliament itself. In Parliament they discovered three willing allies in James Heywood, Edward Horsman, and J. F. B. Blackett. Heywood was an old campaigner, and through him the radicals hoped to gain access to the dissenter vote. He was a Lancashire banker, and, as befitted the founder of the Manchester Athenaeum and an original trustee of Owen's College, a keen advocate of educational reform. Edward Horsman, who was educated at Rugby under Arnold, was strongly anticlerical and a frequent critic of the government's ecclesiastical policy. Blackett was the youngest of the three. He was educated at Christ Church during Liddell's time as tutor, and became a Fellow of Merton and a lawyer by profession. His premature death cut short a promising career.

[21] Add. MS. 44378, f. 196.   [22] Ibid., f. 235.

The radicals had much in common with the dissenters. Both, for example, wished to see a large measure of university extension, and a widening of the curriculum. Above all, both, if for different reasons, wanted to reduce clerical influence in the university, and many of the reforms advocated by the Oxford radicals, such as residence in lodgings and the abolition of compulsory Orders, would have removed serious impediments to the admission of dissenters to the university as undergraduates and to Fellowships, and the constitutional proposals promised to consolidate this effect. But there were divisive points of difference and indifference. The dissenters cared little for the reform of the professoriate, and there were many who saw no advantage in reforming the university if dissenters remained excluded from it. The alliance with the radicals was useful to the dissenters mainly as a weapon for obstructing the Bill, and when the possibility of gaining admission to the university arose they did not scruple to abandon their temporary friends. The alliance with the dissenters thoroughly alarmed the university, and confirmed suspicions that the radicals were determined to impose their will if necessary by force.

Meetings between the Oxford radicals and their new-found friends in Parliament began shortly after the first reading of the Bill, and Vaughan's residence in London, which had previously been a handicap, now became a positive advantage. On 24 March Bonamy Price informed Gladstone that he, Liddell, and a few friends were about to consider the amendments which they desired to introduce.[23] On the 27th, Liddell, who made little effort to conceal his satisfaction at the discomfiture of his newly restored allies, wrote to Vaughan,

Nemesis has done her work with our friends Wilson, Pattison, and Co. They have become sensible of the treachery of Jeune, G. Smith &c., and are ready to burst with vexation. I had a visit from Wilson yesterday and quite pitied him. Of course I refrained from all allusion to the past. We are to have a meeting at my house on Thursday at 10 a.m. to draw up a memorandum for the government. At our last meeting it was resolved to adopt all that you suggested and some other

[23] Add. MS. 44378, f. 271ᵛ.

things. But I fear Gladstone is impenetrable and has full power. You cannot come to our meetings, I suppose, though it would be well if you could. B. Price, Wilson, Brodie, Farrar, perhaps Jeune, with several M.P.s will be there. If not, send anything you wish to say by return of post.[24]

It was perhaps at this meeting or at a meeting held at about this time that a petition to Russell was drawn up deploring the tendency of the Bill to increase the exclusive and ecclesiastical character of the university, and the inadequate provision it made for the professoriate. The forty-two signatories included many shades of opinion. The Oxford radicals were well represented by Liddell, Vaughan, Wilson, Brodie, Congreve, Maskelyne, and J. E. Walker. Baden Powell, who had sat with Liddell on the commission, and Stanley, who had served as its secretary, signed, and also Professor Daubeny, who had been considered for membership of it. It was also signed by Frederick Temple, R. W. Browne, and Clough, all of whom had given evidence to the commission, and by such men of literary eminence as George Grote and Francis Palgrave. Two members of Parliament added their names, one of whom was James Heywood. Gladstone was unusually vexed by the petition, and condemned it with asperity. 'These gentlemen', he wrote, 'whatever they may be as irrigators are as respects Parliament merely dreamers. An English Legislature would not, even if we were to ask it, force their "spick and span" Professoriate upon Oxford any more than they would adopt a constitution out of the pigeon holes of Abbé Sièyes.'[25]

Although Gladstone was predictably unyielding, there were reasonable hopes that Lord Russell would be more sympathetic. In his speech introducing the Bill he had spoken with enthusiasm of the prospect of reviving the professoriate, and during the second reading on 7 April he declared that in its main provisions the Bill complied with the objects which the commission had in view, namely, university extension, the improvement of the governing body, and the removal of restrictions which gave

[24] H. G. Liddell to Vaughan, 27 Mar. [1854].
[25] Add. MS. 44379, f. 141ᵛ.

preference to particular studies. The government, he declared, was bound to take into consideration all the suggestions made by the commission.[26]

Such statements encouraged the radicals to renew their overtures to him. The first move was made by J. M. Wilson, who described his plans to Liddell.

I have had a meeting chiefly of Professors. My object was chiefly to induce them to ask Lord John to appoint a commission in whom the liberal party confided.

Daubeny, Wall, Maskelyne, Price, Donkin were at the meeting. They concurred heartily in the scheme and deputed one of the number to write to Lord John to ask him to receive two or three of the Professorial body who would offer suggestions on parts of the Bill. Lord John has fixed Saturday at one o'clock, (Wall, Price, Daubeny and Walker will wait on him) and has asked Gladstone to be present.

Now will you write to Vaughan and ask him to come up? We may get something for the Professors if he will come. Most anxiously do I wish he could be present. Surely he could get his work done by a deputy for a day and on the following Monday could be at his place again. If he will come, I will come up to town on Friday night and meet him on the Saturday morning.

We shall ask for the appointment of the two professors by the Professors, see that the Commission have powers to deal with existing Professorships. All is obscure respecting the Professors. Shall we say more? Give me your ideas on the subject. I am just going to study the Bill diligently as far as it touches the Professors.

We are baulked in one of our aims, i.e. in getting you for our Commissioner. You have seen the names. Do you think we should complain? There are two Puseyites and Johnson.[27]

The meeting with Russell and Gladstone duly took place on 1 April, but it is doubtful whether Vaughan was present. It is probable that he was occupied at this time with others in drawing up an address to Lord Russell. It is undated, but if, as seems likely, it was the document to which Blackett referred in the debate on the second reading, it would appear to have been composed prior to 7 April, and the fact that he was able to refer to it was indicative

---

[26] *Hansard's Parliamentary Debates*, cxxxii (1854), 779.
[27] J. M. Wilson to H. G. Liddell, [Mar. 1854].

of its real purpose of briefing the parliamentary opposition.[28] It is the most complete statement of the objections of the radicals to the Bill.

The address dealt with the three interrelated subjects of the constitution, the ecclesiastical character of the university, and the position of the professors. It began by claiming that the election by Congregation of 19 out of 24 members of Council, not including the Proctors, gave the collegiate interest overwhelming influence, for Congregation would consist of 196 Heads, tutors, and ex-tutors, but a mere 30 professors. Although the professors were intended to constitute a third of the Council, the manner of their election ensured that they represented, not the professorial body, but the majority of Congregation.

On the endowment of professorships, it was maintained, the Bill was quite inadequate. The Bill provided that no college should be obliged to contribute for the purpose unless it had at least twenty Fellowships. But, the address argued, if Fellowships were to be suppressed in order to raise the value of the remainder, few colleges would be left with as many as twenty Fellowships and so few would be liable to contribute to the endowment of chairs. A more effective method, it was suggested, was for each college to contribute a proportion of its revenues.

The address then reverted to the familiar theme of the excessively ecclesiastical character of the university, which, it was claimed, the Bill increased by retaining the obligation to take Orders and enforcing residence. The requirement of residence would increase the number of clerical Fellows, and would not only add to the clerical bias in Congregation, but, by providing more tutors, injure the prospects of an increase in the professoriate. The argument was stated elsewhere in an extreme form by Lake.

The Commission plan for Colleges [he wrote] was based upon this notion—they diminished the Fellows to little more than the number just sufficient for the practical educational purposes of the Colleges. It seems to me to have been one of their prime mistakes in principle. But they and their friends have no idea of Oxford as a place of study, specially of any Theological study, except so far as that would be

[28] *Hansard's Parliamentary Debates*, cxxxii (1854), 701.

represented by *Professors*; and now as they cannot get rid of Fellows by unduly limiting their number, they seek to attain the same end by *unduly* allowing their absence.[29]

The address ended with a powerful plea for increasing the power of the professors.

A very important omission in the Bill is the absence of all provision for so constituting Professors and Sub-professors as to incorporate them into the practical working of the University. The mere appointment, and even the endowment, of Professors, unless security is taken that their teaching may be brought to bear on the Examinations of the University, will not found a real and living Professoriate. The Bill makes no provision for assigning to the Professors a share in the instruction of the University, and it suggests no scheme for giving them authority independent of the Colleges; and many persons are of opinion that Sub-professors should be created, who shall impart catechetical instruction, in connection with the more general teaching of the Professors. It is highly desirable to encourage the residence of men at Oxford who shall devote themselves to the pursuit of special departments of knowledge, and acquire high eminence in learning.[30]

Gladstone described the address as 'drawn by the hand of some one desirous to find objections'.[31] The phrase suggests that he already entertained the opinion, which soon became a conviction, that the radical opposition was interested in obstruction rather than in the improvement of the Bill.

The Bill passed its second reading without a division, but the debate gave ample warning of trouble to come in committee. The radical case was ably stated by Blackett. He accused Russell of betraying the principles of the Blue Book, and agreed with Pusey that the main question was whether education ought to be in the hands of the clergy or not. In his view it ought to be taken out of the hands of the clergy and placed in those of the professors.

As the Bill moved into committee, a strong effort was made to persuade Russell to promote fundamental changes. On 15 April a deputation waited on him and was kindly received and

---

[29] Add. MS. 44230, f. 313[v]. [30] Add. MS. 44236, f. 277[v].
[31] Ibid., f. 278.

concessions were promised. The fruits of the meeting were seen in a letter which he wrote to Gladstone afterwards.

When [he wrote] we first considered the scheme the Professors in the Council were to be named by Professors. Now they are to be chosen by Congregation. It is objected that the resident Tutors having a great majority in the Congregation, having a rival element to the Professors, having the Heads and College Fellows in their favour, will be able to exclude the Professors as much as now from any efficient share in the teaching of the University. This appears to me to be true. The remedy suggested is that the Professors shall have a voice in the appointment of Examiners and the rules for examinations. This appears to me true likewise.[32]

A week later he wrote, 'This question of the studies of the University requires further consideration. I told Professor Vaughan who came to see me as one of the voices of a deputation, that it was not enough to increase a professor's salary.'[33] Professorial lectures, he remarked, were useless in Greek and Latin, but not so in the sciences, and though he would be sorry to regulate such matters by Act of Parliament, he would be even sorrier not to open the way for a more perfect education.

The moment was ripe for a final effort to persuade Gladstone to make concessions. Liddell undertook the task, but in a spirit of pessimism. In a long letter he repeated the arguments for removing clerical restrictions and strengthening the professoriate. 'You will think', he said, 'I do not know when I am beaten. I confess that I do not.'[34] There was nothing in the Bill, he declared, to make certain provision for higher instruction in the university, and although salaries might be raised no endowments would avail against the disadvantage of the collegiate majority in Congregation and Council. He denied that he was motivated by hostility to the clergy, but the fact was that the Bill would reduce the number of laymen[35] in the university and thereby increase the clerical element in both bodies. Some colleges already actively

---

[32] Add. MS. 44291, f. 160ᵛ.   [33] Ibid., f. 165.
[34] Add. MS. 44236, f. 273.
[35] Liddell believed that compulsory residence would reduce the number of lay Fellows, who formed the majority of non-resident Fellows.

dissuaded, if they did not positively prohibit, their men from attending professorial lectures, and college lectures were so altered as to prevent attendance on the professors. In addition the tutors ruled the examinations. It would be a safeguard if the collegiate majority in Congregation were diminished and the professors elected to Council by their own body and not by the tutors, 'But the best security would be a clause such as we have framed (at Lord John Russell's desire) by which Professors may be invested with a place in the university beyond the reach of Council or Congregation.'

Gladstone was immovable. The practical objections to a clause on examinations, he informed Lord Russell, were unanswerable.[36] To Liddell he wrote that an attempt to abolish compulsory Orders could not be carried and might defeat the whole Bill.[37] The purpose of the residence clause, he explained, was to remove permanent sinecure Fellowships, and the effect of the Bill would be to encourage 'Fellow Students'. Turning to the question of the professoriate he remarked 'It is not less difficult than important and whatever can safely be done to make this part of the Bill efficacious undoubtedly should be done. I think, however, that this part of the case is decidedly unpopular with the mass of the House of Commons and offers boundless facilities for attack.' As for sectional representation, he reminded Liddell, this had been the government's original plan but it was given up in deference to a strong representation from decided reformers in Oxford. Thus on both the issues which the radicals regarded as essential, Gladstone refused to make concessions and took his stand on what was politically feasible.

When the Bill reached its committee stage on 27 April, Heywood proposed that it be referred to a Select Committee. The effect of such a move, as Gladstone pointed out, would have been to destroy the Bill by causing irreparable delay, and he implored the dissenters, who favoured it as a means of ventilating the question of religious tests, not to deprive the university of a useful measure because it did not provide for their admission to the university. Russell, who was anxious to deal with the question of

[36] Add. MS. 44291, f. 171.   [37] Add. MS. 44236, f. 278ᵛ.

tests, felt that it was a matter better left to a separate Bill and declared that there was no possibility of finding a Select Committee favourable to Heywood's proposal.

The debate itself afforded abundant evidence that the opponents of the Bill had studied the Blue Book with considerable diligence. Several speakers objected to the increase in clerical influence foreshadowed, and Heywood spoke contemptuously of the 'monkish custom' of celibacy. The professoriate found an eloquent champion in Horsman. The university, he said, lacked learned men, and would continue to do so while college tutors looked upon their position as temporary and had no incentive to improvement. He painted a distressing picture of the tutor, worn out in middle age, descending the vale of life with no higher ambition than a college living, feasting his eyes on this distant Paradise 'with perhaps a venerable Eve waiting for him in the garden'. The professors had no recognized place in the university, and there was no demand for their services; they were subordinate to the smallest functionary of the smallest college. As for the cry of Germanizing, the fact was that already German scholarship prevailed even in the classics, and there was no theological scholarship except that produced in Germany. With none of these problems did the Bill concern itself. The solution, he declared, was to raise up the professors, to place instruction in the third year in their hands as the Blue Book proposed, and to give them influence in the examinations.

Despite the vigour of his attack, Horsman did not support Heywood's amendment on the grounds that the appointment of a Select Committee would prevent legislation during the session. His decision reflected the instability of Liddell's parliamentary alliance: Heywood was prepared to see the Bill lost, but Horsman was not. Horsman was in closer touch than Heywood with Liddell, who was actively briefing him with amendments to the Bill at this time, and his stand on the question of a Select Committee suggests that Liddell and Vaughan still hoped to alter the Bill by removing its obnoxious clauses rather than to destroy it. Liddell was certainly delighted with his speech. 'I wish you had heard Horsman last night', he wrote to Vaughan, 'It was very *good*. Badly reported. He wished not to offend the ministry and put some things too strongly. But taken in comparison with other speeches it was very good. Bright hit very hard. Disraeli was as bad as could be. Gladstone not much. Could you come to Horsman's tomorrow at 12 or a little after? He is taking our amendments in hand *well*.'[38]

What these amendments were became apparent towards the end of May. The first of them concerned the commission which the Bill proposed to appoint. Gladstone regarded it as more vitally important than almost anything in the Bill.[39] By the choice of members, the government hoped to convince the university of its good intentions and to create the confidence on which the implementation of reform depended for success. To the radicals the commission was also of great importance, not least because by its power to approve, or if necessary to draw up, college statutes it was able to create and endow professorships which the colleges might be unwilling to do if left to their own devices. In March, Lord Russell had suggested the appointment of Liddell, and thereby seemed to indicate his intention that the Bill should, as he claimed it would when introducing it to Parliament, carry out the programme of the Royal Commission, of which Liddell had been a member. But in Gladstone's eyes, Liddell was unacceptable to the university at large precisely because of his identification with the commission party, and he proposed instead the appointment of G. H. S. Johnson. Johnson too had been on the Royal Commission, but he had taken no active part in propagating its views after the publication of the Blue Book. Gladstone defended his choice on the grounds that Liddell's youth would make him less influential than Johnson with the older commissioners, though in reality only three years separated the two men, but what attracted him to Johnson was that he could be depended on not to make difficulties. Johnson regretted his earlier radicalism and told Bishop Hinds that he had lost the headship of Queen's through being on the commission.[40] Blackett was not far short of the mark when he described him as

[38] H. G. Liddell to Vaughan, [28 Apr. 1854].
[39] Add. MS. 44251, f. 432.   [40] MS. Pattison 129, f. 133.

M

'the least likely, from his peculiar turn of mind, to stand up against an adverse majority'.[41] The same point was made more colourfully by J. M. Wilson, who, reporting a conversation at Liddell's, observed to Jowett that 'Johnson would go down Judge Coleridge's throat like a fly down a whale'.[42]

The announcement of the commission caused anger and alarm in the radical camp. Lord Ellesmere, the chairman, was said to be an invalid. C. T. Longley, Bishop of Ripon, and Johnson were described by Liddell as 'nobodies'. But the strongest objection of all was taken to Sir John Coleridge and Sir John Awdry, who were regarded as friends of the Tractarians and the latter as having a particular animus against professors. Blackett wrote to Richard Congreve that he intended to make the House understand how thoroughly Coleridge represented the Puseyite tutors, 'and how mischievous the latter element is, and how antagonistic to reform. Now I want you to send me, 1st a sketch of the way and the methods by which the Puseyites have worked against Reform as Tutors, and 2nd a list as full as you can recollect of the men who have gone over to Rome in our time.'[43] When on 1 May Horsman proposed that the appointments be postponed, ostensibly because they would be unable to attend to the laborious work of the commission, he was supported by Blackett who claimed that Coleridge and Awdry would control the commission. He could not, he said, vote for strengthening the Tractarians in the university. Although supported from other parts of the House, the amendment was defeated, but the struggle for the commission was far from over.[44]

The second amendment to come out of the discussions with Horsman was for the restoration of sectional election, but before it could be put a similar motion was made by Spencer Walpole. Although Gladstone claimed that an undifferentiated franchise

---

[41] *Hansard's Parliamentary Debates*, cxxxii (1854), 1113.

[42] B. Jowett to A. P. Stanley [1855]. Letter in Balliol College.

[43] MS. Eng. lett. c. 185, f. 160.

[44] After the commission had begun its work, Heywood wrote to Mark Pattison, 'We imagine that Judge Coleridge is really the governing spirit of the proceedings of the Oxford Commission, and that Sir John Awdry acts with him, and probably the Earl of Harrowby.' MS. Pattison 51, f. 207.

was what the university wished and that it was necessary to display confidence in the ability of the voters not to be swayed by party differences, sectional election was restored to the Bill by a majority of thirteen. It was to some extent a victory for the radicals, but they owed it less to their dissenter friends than to the conservatives who wished to transfer the election of Masters to Convocation.

By 11 May the House had considered only nineteen out of fifty-eight clauses, and the contentious sections of the Bill which concerned the colleges directly had yet to come. It was clear that a hot campaign lay ahead and that the Bill was in serious difficulties. Liddell asked Vaughan to look over the remaining clauses and brief him on any questions that might arise.[45] Gladstone was in low spirits, and remarked that he had never known a Bill more foolishly discussed in committee.[46] 'I am low about the Bill', he confided to Jeune. 'The House is demoralised (you will understand me) with respect to it, and every man his own master. A small section of those who would call themselves your friends acting as unlike you as possible, and a party of perhaps 100 being ready to vote for anything that will best us no matter what effect it has on Oxford.'[47] To Jacobson he wrote that the so-called reformers resident in London, or rather a fraction of them headed by Liddell, were working keenly against the Bill 'and producing small secessions that break us down'.[48] The radical opposition particularly angered him because he believed that since it could not hope to achieve its object it was directed to the destruction of the Bill by provoking delay. 'There is', he told Jeune, 'no chance that Mr. Liddell and his friends will obtain their object. They are unconsciously playing the game of the anti-reform men.'[49] Evidently struck by the truth of this remark, he returned to it the next day. 'I said', he wrote, 'the London so-called Reformers were playing the game of the Obstruction Party. That is true on the supposition that the Bill passes, for if it is only mutilated it will be mutilated in the obstructive sense. But

45 H. G. Liddell to Vaughan, [11 May 1854].
46 Add. MS. 44282, f. 297.   47 Add. MS. 44221, f. 109.
48 Add. MS. 44218, f. 95.   49 Add. MS. 44221, f. 109ᵛ.

on the other hand if it is abandoned, then the obstructives will very likely have played the game of the others.'[50]

Although Liddell told Gladstone that the reform intended by the Bill was worse than no reform at all,[51] and his intervention put the Bill in serious jeopardy by provoking delay, the Oxford radicals still cherished the hope that sufficient improvements might be made to render it, if not welcome, at least acceptable. With a powerful voice in the constitution now that sectional representation had been restored, and with a favourable commission it was reasonable for them to suppose that something substantial might be done for the professors.

Gladstone resolved that the only way to save the Bill was by removing the clauses relating to the colleges and by increasing the powers of the commission. 'Our weakness in the House of Commons on the Oxford Bill', he wrote to Lord Russell, 'the determination of Mr. Liddell's friends to oppose it, and the prospect of Lord Derby's opposition in the Peers, lead me to doubt whether it might not be wise on the whole to recast all that part of it which refers to Colleges in a simpler form.'[52] To this proposal Russell agreed, and a week later Gladstone informed Jowett of his decision. 'Various causes', he wrote, 'among which stand most prominently forward the strength of private interests, the infusion of religious jealousies into our debates, the indifference of most of the Dissenters to the mere improvement of the University, and the actual opposition offered by the *London* portion of the Oxford Reformers, have given obstruction such a power that to pass the Bill in its present form would require nearly the whole Session even if all other public business were abandoned by the Government.'[53] The threat that the Bill might be lost disrupted the cohesion of the university supporters of the Blue Book in Oxford and London, and Conington and others joined Lake, Haddan, and reformers of many shades of opinion in a petition which Sir William

[50] Add. MS. 44221, f. 114.
[51] Add. MS. 44206, f. 140ᵛ. This phrase of Liddell's evidently stuck in Gladstone's mind and he quoted it in a letter to Henry Acland on 21 July 1855 (MS. Acland d. 68, f. 10ᵛ).
[52] Add. MS. 44291, f. 181.   [53] Add. MS. 44381, f. 69.

Heathcote presented for the House to pass the Bill since from the nature of the opposition to it the character of any future measure could not be foreseen.[54]

Although isolated, Liddell and Vaughan showed no disposition to abandon the struggle, and on 2 June Evelyn Denison wrote to Vaughan proposing a conference on the new Bill. The alteration in the measure changed its character in an important respect. Instead of being an enacting it had become largely a permissive Bill and its main power now turned on the names of the Commissioners.[55] Liddell expressed his feelings on the subject in a letter to Vaughan after he had attended a long and meandering debate.

Last night I went to the House and sat for 5 dreary hours, during which the relative merits of 'according to' and 'with due regard to' were copiously discussed, and much other laborious trifling. . . . The Bill now in the hands of a good commission and good secretaries might do very well. . . . There will probably be some warm work on the third reading. It is not quite certain whether the Tories will vote *for* it or no. But with a bad commission we are done—done regularly—and I fear the odds are against us.[56]

Liddell regarded as a bad commission one which included Coleridge and Awdry, and as early as 23 May Jeune had warned Gladstone that a desperate effort was to be made to remove them. He suggested that the appointment of N. W. Senior and Sir Charles Lyell as additional commissioners would probably be accepted by the radicals as a compromise.[57] Gladstone, anxious to get the Bill through before the end of the session, was willing to compromise, and, if Liddell's suspicions were well founded, commissioned Earl Granville to sound him out and to suggest the names of Edward Twisleton and Sir G. C. Lewis in addition to Senior and Lyell.[58] Eventually Lewis and the evangelical Earl of Harrowby were added to the commission, and Goldwin

54 Ibid., f. 42.
55 J. E. Denison to Vaughan, 2 June [1854]. *Hansard's Parliamentary Debates,* cxxxiv (1854), 181.
56 H. G. Liddell to Vaughan, 16 June 1854.   57 Add. MS. 44221, f. 131.
58 H. G. Liddell to Vaughan. Dated 25 May [1854].

Smith, who as a reformer identified himself with Jeune rather than with Liddell, was appointed one of the secretaries. In place of Goldwin Smith, Russell had desired to appoint Stanley, who had been secretary to the Royal Commission, but Gladstone objected that to do so would be regarded by many as 'a declaration of war'.[59] The campaign to unseat Coleridge and Awdry never gained much steam in the face of Gladstone's conciliatory gestures, though a half-hearted motion was made by R. D. Mangles and seconded by Horsman.

Any hope that Liddell and his friends entertained of obtaining further concessions was abruptly dashed by the defection of their dissenting allies in parliament. The enthusiasm of the dissenters for the reform of a university from which they were excluded had always fallen short of ecstasy. 'What', said George Hadfield, the member for Sheffield, 'was this Bill to him, or to those who, for 150 years and more, had been excluded from the Universities?'[60] During the passage of the Bill, a strong movement for the admission of dissenters swept through the country and Parliament, and culminated in the motion put by James Heywood on 22 June for the removal of subscription.[61] With victory in their grasp, the dissenters had no further use for Liddell and his friends. The truth of the situation was forcefully brought home to Liddell when the House of Lords threw out sectional election, and on 14 July he wrote to Vaughan,

I fear the game is up. Denison entered fully into our views, and had entered into communication with Walpole, who was equally eager to refuse the amendment. I saw Heywood who said he was aware that Sectional Election was the only method of introducing a really liberal element into the Hebdomadal Council, and that he would write to the Dissenters and try to get some of them to come and help in restoring the clause as the Commons framed it. All seemed well. Denison thought they were certain of success. On Wednesday that nincompoop Heywood finds himself in a Division with Lord John, who enters into conversation with him, and the end of it was that

[59] P.R.O. 30/22 11d, f. 60ᵛ.
[60] *Hansard's Parliamentary Debates*, cxxxii (1854), 959.
[61] W. R. Ward, *Victorian Oxford*, 1965, 197–9.

Heywood agreed that as the Lords had so graciously accepted the Dissenting clauses it would be ungracious in the Dissenters to throw the Lords over. Denison thinks there is now no chance of doing anything. But he is still seeing if there is a chance. People are leaving town. The government still keep an official phalanx together. But there is little chance of beating them on a subject of so little interest *without* the Dissenters. So I fear we are done.[62]

Vaughan took the blow badly, and on his return in September from his legal duties on the south-western circuit wrote to Edward Twisleton, 'All the while, I bore about with me the sense of that heavy blow which the Bishop of Oxford, in conspiracy with Gladstone, dealt to Oxford Reform—by an utter subversion of the Constitution as given and settled by the House of Commons, and by the establishment of a clerical democracy, in its place.'[63] So far as the professoriate was concerned, the constitution given to the university was for Liddell 'an act which banishes hope'.[64]

The incursion of Liddell and Vaughan into politics was an act of reckless desperation. Blinded by the bright horizon they stumbled into one pit after another. They were deceived by their allies, they misinterpreted Lord Russell's sympathy for their cause, they were outmanoeuvred by Gladstone. They had no weapons in their arsenal except words, and they were no more successful in persuading Parliament than they had been in persuading the university. On their two main objectives, the reform of the constitution and the strengthening of the professoriate, they were defeated. Their temporary success in restoring sectional representation was due to the vote of the conservative opposition, and their influence on the composition of the commission was more illusory than real, for Sir G. C. Lewis proved an inattentive member. They succeeded beyond expectation in obstruction and greatly added to the difficulties experienced by Gladstone, who complained that he had never encountered such difficulty with a Bill.[65] Out of their obstruction came the only

---

[62] H. G. Liddell to Vaughan, 14 July 1854.
[63] *Letters of the Hon. Mrs. Edward Twisleton* (1925), 248.
[64] MS. Acland d. 69, f. 31ᵛ.   [65] MS. Acland d. 68, f. 11.

positive, if entirely unexpected, benefit of the campaign: the extension of the powers of the commission, which ensured a more sensitive instrument of reform than direct legislation.

It was in the university itself that the most serious and enduring consequences of their actions were felt, for by their arrogance and extreme views they caused bitterness and resentment, and fomented an antagonism between tutors and professors of which traces lingered for a century. The responsibility for these unhappy developments must rest as much with Vaughan as with Liddell, for although Liddell occupied the foreground Vaughan was constantly at his elbow urging him on. 'I have', wrote Jacobson, 'once and again heard friends of the Measure speak deploringly of Liddell's wilfulness and of the effect which his idolatry of Vaughan has upon him.'[66]

[66] Add. MS. 44218, f. 97.

12. Professor of Modern History

IN their inaugural lectures, neither Goldwin Smith, nor Stubbs, nor Freeman, who in turn followed Vaughan in the chair of modern history, made any mention of his achievements as professor, yet it was during his term of office that the School of Jurisprudence and History was created and the foundations of its study laid. It was not until he delivered his farewell lecture in 1884 that Stubbs made amends, and he then did so in characteristically generous fashion, commending Vaughan's lectures for 'the soundness and learning displayed in them and the stimulus which they supplied to the study of Modern History at the moment that it was taking its place among the recognised subjects of the Schools'.[1] Vaughan left no monument of historical scholarship, nor does he appear to have contemplated one. The only work of a purely historical nature to come from his pen was a slight paper on a medieval effigy at Upton Castle, his Pembrokeshire home, which he delivered to the British Archaeological Association in 1884.[2] The chair of modern history offered him an

[1] W. Stubbs, *Seventeen Lectures* (1886), 384. In his inaugural Stubbs excused himself from paying tribute to Vaughan 'because I cannot'. Vaughan complained of the imagined slight, and on the eve of Stubbs's retirement wrote to him on the subject and obtained the following reply, dated 28 Feb. 1884. 'I was very sorry at the time that the words which were certainly uttered without the slightest intention of hurting your feelings or your reputation, seemed to you to give just grounds for offence. The lecture had been printed and the impression was exhausted long before you wrote to me on the subject; as you may remember, it was because I could find no copy that I sent you the manuscript to read.

I have not reprinted it, nor have I any intention of doing so. If it ever is done, I will take care that the passage is so treated that no mistake can be made as to my true meaning, which was that during your tenure of office I was not resident in Oxford and could not say anything about your lectures. I have never hesitated whenever I have had occasion, in private conversation, to mention the matter, to express my sorrow, that you had misunderstood me.'

[2] H. H. Vaughan, Effigy at Upton Castle, Pembrokeshire', *British Archaeological Association* (1885), 124–8.

opportunity of realizing the claims he had made for the professoriate, but this he failed to do. The reasons are many, but amongst them must be numbered the immense personal hostility which his advocacy of extreme measures of university reform had incurred and the fact that he found the nature of his professorial duties in practice to be precisely those against which he had consistently protested.

When he was appointed to the chair in 1848 it possessed no convincing traditions of scholarship or utility, nor indeed was the study of history highly regarded in Oxford. 'We are not', Arnold observed in his inaugural, 'inclined to rate very highly the qualifications required either in the student or in the writer of it.'[3] It had long ceased to discharge its original function of preparing men for the diplomatic service, if it had ever fulfilled it, and the study of modern history had no place in the curriculum. The duties of the office were sufficiently great and the stipend sufficiently small to deter historians of eminence from occupying it, and the leading historians of the day, Hallam, Macaulay, Grote, Carlyle, never held a chair at Oxford, or for that matter elsewhere. Edward Nares, the author of an imposing work, to which Stubbs applied the epithet weighty as a term of praise and Macaulay as one of contempt, was appointed to the professorship in 1813. Reflecting gloomily on the difficulties he had to contend with, he wrote to the Vice-Chancellor in 1832, 'For some time I complied with all the rules, and at so great expense, by the removal of my family, hire of expensive lodgings, and payment of a curate at home, as to exceed the income, and certainly without any material benefit to any member of the University, being sometimes unable to procure any class, and at best so uncertain a one that long before I could get through 20 lectures, many were called away to college collections, public examinations, or to attend upon private tutors.'[4] In 1841 he was succeeded by Arnold, 'the great name, never to be pronounced without reverence'.[5] Arnold gave a single course of eight lectures

---

[3] T. Arnold, *Introductory Lectures on Modern History* (1843), 1.
[4] University Archives WPβ 11 (3).
[5] W. Stubbs, *Seventeen Lectures* (1886), 6.

on general problems of historical study, but before he could begin his promised lectures on the history of English civilization from the fifteenth century, doing for England, as he put it, what Guizot had done for France, he was dead.[6] Had he lived, he would almost certainly have experienced many of the problems of which Nares complained. He seems to have recognized that he could not hope to retain an audience of any size composed of undergraduates, and declared his intention of directing his lectures to those who had recently taken their degree.[7] J. A. Cramer, who followed him and was Vaughan's immediate predecessor, adopted the tutorial style of lecturing, taking a Latin text or modern work, such as Commines or Guicciardini, on which he commented to classes which averaged eight students.

But within little more than a year after Vaughan's appointment, the School of Jurisprudence and History was created, and his first course of lectures was delivered after the passage of the statute. The nature and duties of the chair became vastly different. By connecting the study of history with the public examinations a permanent audience was created for the professor, but at the same time a burden was laid on his shoulders which no single man could discharge. The Royal Commission recommended that new chairs should be created and assistant professors appointed. Vaughan himself proposed to the commission that there should be two new professors of European history, a proposal which he later amended in favour of a professor of English and French history and a professor of other European history.[8] But none of these proposals was acted on during Vaughan's tenure of office, and in 1856 Travers Twiss complained that 'the University itself has not in any way come to the aid of the candidates who elect to proceed in the School of Law and History.'[9] Nor was much assistance provided by the colleges. In 1852 only Balliol and Corpus appear to have provided lectures in history,[10] and

[6] MS. Eng. lett. d. 130, f. 208ᵛ.
[7] T. Arnold, *Introductory Lectures on Modern History* (1843), 63.
[8] Evidence submitted to the University Commissioners, Jan. 1856.
[9] T. Twiss, *Letter on the Law Studies of the University* (1856), 16.
[10] *Report of the Oxford University Commission* (1852), Evidence IV (111).

at University College the delivery of historical lectures was discontinued after 'the direct connexion of the Lectures of the Professor of Modern History with the studies of the place'. By 1856 only four or five colleges had established lectureships in law and history since the creation of the School.[11] It could hardly have been otherwise until the university commissioners appointed by the Oxford Act had completed their work of statute revision. For the rest, college tutors added history to the Latin, Greek, logic, mathematics, and theology they already taught, and looked to the professor of modern history for anything more required.

Circumstances thus combined to emphasize the professor's role as a teacher of undergraduates, and the reality of Vaughan's position was in sharp contrast with his conception of the professoriate. He admitted that professorial lectures were valuable and in his controversy with Pusey had stated what he conceived their benefits to be, but if the professor was expected to act as a substitute for the tutor his lectures would reproduce the defects of the large classes which were the subject of general complaint in the tutorial system. Moreover, he was not able to examine his pupils in the same way as the college tutor, and was denied the discipline of collections and control of the public examinations.[12]

In order to teach it was essential for the professor to lecture frequently, and here again circumstances clashed with convictions.

It seems impossible [he wrote] to exhaust the history of any one country; and in respect to each country, the work of the Professor must vary in harmony with the different character of the facts, the different richness and number of the documents, the more or less perfect state of the historical literature. If lectures are carefully composed by judicious selections from a great number of existing authors,

[11] T. Twiss, op. cit., 16.

[12] It is of interest that on one occasion Vaughan attempted to examine those who attended his lectures, and he relates that after his second course he offered to examine any who wished. 'I had', he said, 'for this purpose a private interview with each examinee, and pointed out to him his errors.' (*Report of the Oxford University Commission* (1852), Evidence, 274.)

they may be well fewer in number than if they were more directly compiled from some one or two trusted authorities; and if, further, they are drawn from no modern author, but are the result of the original and contemporary authorities, sifted, compared, contrasted, and harmonised, so many can not be expected as if they were put together from many modern writers. But if, in addition to professed historians and chroniclers, and memoir writers, &c., all the other floating and detached monuments of the time are scrutinised for the collection of such scattered rays of light as may illustrate the period in laws, letters, charters, treaties, homilies, poets, &c., the actual amount of writing and composition which is the visible fruit of so much labour may reasonably be still further diminished in quantity as the toil required is greater.[13]

The regulations of the chair required the delivery of twenty lectures a year, but Vaughan objected that so many were not possible unless they were 'hand-to-mouth' lectures, and he quoted with approval on several occasions Arnold's complaint about frequent lecturing. His conception of the lecture differed in scope and intention from the textbook-based lecture of the college tutor.

In order to lecture frequently it was necessary to reside in the university. The regulations of the chair required the professor to reside for ninety days in each year, but the requirement had in the past seldom been observed and Arnold had sought without success to have it amended. Residence became a more important issue with the creation of the School of Jurisprudence and History, but Vaughan refused to reside at all. All his lectures, except for the first course, were given in the summer term, and he came up from London specially to deliver them. His rooted objection to residence, which was to be an important factor in his decision to resign the chair, made it difficult for him to take a significant part in moulding the infant school of history.

It was against this background of conflict about the true function of the professor that Vaughan gave his lectures, many of which survive in manuscript. The period he chose was medieval history, and all his lectures were concerned with English or European

13 Ibid. 273.

history from pre-Conquest times to the reign of King John. Yet he was a medievalist more for reasons of logic than of inclination. 'I have', he wrote, 'commenced with the most remote, the most cold and the most obscure times simply because I deemed it well to begin fundamentally.' His first course of lectures was on Anglo-Saxon history, and was followed in 1850 and 1851 by a course on Anglo-Norman history. In the following year he gave two lectures on the Danish Invasions and four on Magna Carta, and in the same term began a course on the life of William the Conqueror, which he completed in the summer of 1853. In that term he also lectured on the civil war in England in the reign of Stephen. His last course of lectures was delivered in 1854 on the history of the foundation of the church establishment in England. He gave no lectures in 1855, but prepared, though he did not deliver, a course on the Northmen in Western Europe from the eighth to the eleventh centuries, in 1856.

The first Public Examination in history held in 1853 was based on Hume and Smollett for passmen, and on Lingard, Hallam, Gibbon, and Guizot for classmen. Vaughan, true to his principles, rapidly discarded the tutelage of the textbook and sought to push forward into new fields of knowledge. Speaking of his lectures on the Anglo-Normans he wrote, 'in the commencement these lectures were intended as a kind of commentary on the text of Hume, but after the first three lectures, Hume was altogether thrown aside'.[14] The only direct reference to Hume in his surviving lectures occurs when he discusses the question, which Hume had asked, why Anglo-Saxon resistance to the Conqueror collapsed with Hastings. Yet it was as much to Hume and his philosophical heirs as to his study of science that Vaughan owed his belief in the nature and importance of historical facts. The facts of history were to him what the facts of natural science were to the scientist, and he sought to discover them by returning so far as his inadequate training would permit to the original sources rather than to the writings of other historians. 'I have', he wrote, 'hardly committed a single fact to paper which was not drawn directly and

---

[14] *Report of the Oxford University Commission* (1852), Evidence, 275.

exclusively from the original documents of History, not by the verification of references originally made by others, but by a first hand perusal of the documents themselves, and as I have most rarely drawn my facts from any intermediate author so in the same way have all my constructions, reasonings and general views been caught by my own mind from the effect of the facts thus freshly and originally ascertained.' His claim is supported by the contents of his library, which was rich in chronicles and source books such as Michel's *Chronique de Normandie, Danicarum Rerum Scriptores*, and *Byzantinae Historiae Scriptores*, but comparatively weak in monographs.

In his handling of historical sources, Vaughan combined his classical training with the methods of science. He constantly compared different accounts of the same event, he was aware of the difficulties of medieval chronology, and he was conscious of the complex motives and concealed bias of the chroniclers and the often fortuitous sources of their information. He sought to understand the past rather than to judge it. He used not only the methods of science, but science itself, particularly his knowledge, rudimentary though it was, of psychology and geography. To geography he paid constant attention, and at his lectures displayed large maps visible to all parts of his audience.[15] His account of the Danish invasions revolved on the distribution of rivers and waterways, and his lectures on the Conqueror contained a careful and detailed account of the topography of Normandy, based no doubt on his travels there during the autumn of 1852.[16]

Turning to the lectures themselves, they fall into two categories. Most of them are interpretative and discursive rather than narrative, and often presuppose considerable familiarity with the subject on the part of the audience. Three of his lectures on William I consist of a compact narrative of the Conqueror's early career in Normandy, and the whole of the course on the civil war of the twelfth century is narrative in character. On both these subjects there was a lack of adequate textbooks, and to some extent Vaughan's lectures supplied this deficiency. In his

---

[15] Evidence submitted to the University Commissioners, Jan. 1856.
[16] E. Twisleton to Vaughan, 22 Oct. 1852.

first lecture on Stephen and Matilda he explicitly justified his omission of Rufus and Henry I, which by the chronological system he usually followed ought to have come after his course on William I, on the grounds that a history of the period 'by one of our most learned historians' was to be published. An immense amount of labour went into the preparation of these lectures, but despite interesting digressions, such as his view of the significance of hunting in enabling a medieval army to keep the field, or his account of the importance attached to verbal insults in a society largely illiterate, the narrative is at times impenetrable rather then imperishable.

It is through the interpretative lectures that a glimpse may be caught of those qualities in Vaughan which so captivated his contemporaries. They have the eloquence, imagination, and fertility of ideas of the good conversationalist. They were invigorating by their freshness and originality, by the impression they conveyed, whether true or false, that Vaughan's ideas were his own. They were free from religious and economic dogma. With the possible exception of William I, no Carlylian heroes represented or directed the pattern of history. Vaughan detected no continuous impulse of constitutional progress. His remaining lectures on Magna Carta, for example, contain no reference to its constitutional or parliamentary importance, and are concerned solely with the incidence and abuse of wardship. These omissions, if omissions they are, were no accident. In his inaugural lecture Vaughan had declared that while nations perished, society lived on, and that society was greater than the individuals who composed it. The subject of history was not, therefore, the actions of great men, nor the battles and dynasties which formed the substance of political history. The purpose of historical study was the discovery of the laws which lay concealed within the infinitely complex state of society.

The nearest Vaughan came to the practical formulation of historical laws, as he defined them, was in his lectures on the Church establishment. 'The great parent fact' of European history, he said, was the mingling of Teutonic and Roman. The fall of the Roman Empire was accompanied by a Teutonic invasion out of which emerged a new Roman civilization in the south and west of Europe. In the north the process was reversed when under Charlemagne the new Roman civilization in turn invaded the Teutonic lands in Germany. This invasion was only partially successful in extending the boundaries of Roman civilization, and drove before it the unsubdued and independent peoples of the north. It thereby generated, Vaughan argued, a series of invasions of England and northern France by the Danes and their neighbours. Regarding the Danish invasions as part of a European movement, he explained their spasmodic character by what he called the law of oscillation, by which he meant that when the tide of war in France ran in their favour the Danes withdrew from England, only to return when it moved against them. From the mingling of Saxon and Dane a new English nation was eventually created, but in the meantime the empire of Charlemagne fell and in its place rose up the ecclesiastical empire of the papacy.

In England, the conflict between Roman and Teutonic came with the introduction and settlement of Christianity. It was, in Vaughan's view, a clash of civilizations rather than of religions. His account of the reasons for the spread of Christianity would not have brought a righteous glow to the cheeks of the missionary. Since Christianity was not imposed initially by conquest but accepted by conversion, it was necessary to explain the reasons for its adoption. He rejected the idea that Christianity was intrinsically a superior religion to those it replaced, nor did he subscribe to the view that the Dark Ages were a period of pagan barbarism. 'The glimpses of the courts of heathen England', he observed, 'disclose scenes which though not without traits of evil do honour to humanity.' Having himself found Revelation an unsatisfactory explanation of religious behaviour, he declined to admit its efficacy for others. Moreover, political and dynastic considerations might contribute to the conversion of kings, but clearly did not operate on the multitude. He therefore put forward what can best be described as a psychological explanation. Conversion was caused, particularly where no common language allowed the missionary to communicate with the convert, by 'the great acts publicly performed, the great ceremonies openly and frequently repeated.' It was due to the recognition of such Christian practices as the sign of the cross, which the heathen identified with the warding-off of demons, and to the symbolic and purifying ceremony of baptism—'the convert was led down to a stream in itself perhaps long an object of veneration or worship, he was immersed for a moment in its waters. . . . He stood up henceforth, his nervous system braced by a salutary shock, his imagination fully and freely following the supposed doctrines of his new Church.' A similar style of explanation applied to a belief in miracles. Vaughan neither followed the well-worn rationalist argument that miracles were explicable in scientific terms, nor did he brush them aside on the grounds that they violated the laws of nature. Miracles, he declared, were 'the rhetoric of action' directed to the eye, as the 'rhetoric of words' was directed to the ear. They were displays of power in harmony with the ideas of the time and of a people disposed to believe in prodigies. 'The understanding was appealed to according to its condition in that age.' His treatment of miracles was an example of the theory he had advanced many years before in his Chancellor's Prize that each age developed its own pattern of thought which made it receptive of certain ideas while rejecting others.

The object of the Roman missionaries, he said, was less purely religious than the creation of 'a great and visible church system'. It was the organization of the Roman Church which enabled it to defeat the Celtic Church and to consolidate its hold on the country. The system which the missionaries brought with them embodied the fusion of Church and state. 'What the Roman missionaries desired to introduce was not simply a religious faith, nor was it even simply a Christian society teaching a religious faith. It was that Christian society which union with the Roman empire had produced at once or developed in the course of the years.' At the conversion of England, this highly developed system came into conflict with another system, for the Anglo-Saxon kingdoms had their own sovereigns and institutions. 'The problem before them was that a religious system itself in part the result of a connexion with one state and its institutions should be united with another state and its institutions.' The collision of the two systems modified both of them, and from it developed those features of the English constitutional and legal arrangements, such as the position of the lay element in the councils of the realm and the rights of the secular arm in ecclesiastical tribunals, which distinguished them from the continental. To this collision the main principles of the Church establishment were traceable. The original dioceses were almost coterminous with the Anglo-Saxon kingdoms, and there were almost as many bishops as there were kings. During the vacancy of a see, the king was at hand and exercised control of the succession. When the kingdoms coalesced into a single kingdom the same relationship continued, and the king 'virtually and practically' nominated every bishop. 'Thus did the very number of the English kings at the introduction of the Christian Church, acting on an ancient principle of church and state union during the Roman Empire vitally change and modify the nature of a constitutional provision while it accepted its letter and even carried out its spirit, and thus a change of deepest consequences to the monarchy and nation was effected by practical and easy adherence in England to a right which in the Roman Empire was asserted in theory alone.'

In such passages, Vaughan sought for historical laws, for the connection between the critical changes in society which were the subject of history. Despite evidence of wide reading, his lectures display the philosophical bias of his mind rather than the depth of his learning. Sir Charles Firth remarked that Vaughan was not a great historian but a very eloquent lecturer, and it was to his eloquence that the impact of his lectures on his contemporaries was mainly due.[17] Even at this distance of time it is possible to detect a distant echo of the enthusiasm they inspired. Richard Congreve wrote of them, 'My energy will be kindled at the lamp of Vaughan's compressed enthusiasm. . . . He produces the impression of such great power, and of his viewing his subject with all the freshness given by a very superior mind, who

[17] C. Firth, *Modern History in Oxford* (1920), 5.

approaches it from higher ground, not from lower.'[18] Of his lecture on the death of the Conqueror, George Butler wrote, 'The lecture was a powerful, poetical, and sometimes sublime oration. Six hundred people were looking fixedly at him, holding their breath, while he described the death and burial of William the Conqueror. He confessed that William was a selfish being, but a great instrument in God's hands—an instrument fearfully and wonderfully made. Vaughan is almost too brilliant, both in conversation and in lecturing. He dazzles one.'[19]

The impact of the lectures on the university was astonishing. Oxford had never heard anything like them, reported Trithen the professor of modern languages.[20] The inaugural was attended by vast audiences, and many came up specially from London to hear it. 'All seem struck with the great beauty of the language,' Conybeare told Liddell, 'with the imagination and wide illustration as well as the philosophical power of mind shewn in them.'[21] Its success is said to have frightened some members of the Hebdomadal Board, and was even used by Greswell as an argument against the History School, which, he declared, 'will beat Natural Science out of the field'.[22] Vaughan's course on the Normans in 1850 was attended by an average of 160 persons, and he recorded that 'many stood, and some went away as unable to find accommodation'.[23] The next course, being designed expressly for undergraduates, was not so well attended by senior members of the university, but the audience was still large. Some 74 names were put down, but reduced to 57 owing to the incompatability of the time at which they were given with college lectures. In 1852 the numbers were again so great that Vaughan was obliged to transfer his audience to the Sheldonian where additional benches had to be provided.[24] So popular were his lectures that 105 members of the university signed an address begging him

[18] MS. Eng. lett. c. 181, f. 50.
[19] J. E. Butler, *Recollections of George Butler*, n.d., 88.
[20] Vaughan to Liddell, n.d.
[21] H. G. Liddell to Vaughan, 17 Nov. 1849.
[22] Ibid.
[23] *Report of the Oxford University Commission* (1852), Evidence, 275.
[24] F. C. Plumptre to Vaughan, 17 May 1852.

to publish the courses of 1852 and 1853. Surely a tribute unique in the annals of the chair!

Part of Vaughan's success was due to his manner and appearance, and caused Frederick Meyrick to remark spitefully that his lectures were more appreciated by the ladies than by the undergraduates.[25] He had an impressive presence suggestive of great intellectual energy. His musical voice and melodious, often poetical, prose held his audiences spellbound. Liddell wrote of him, 'Vaughan's personal appearance was striking. His features were large, well-defined, and mobile, especially his eyes. They revealed at one time bright enjoyment of some humorous thought or word, and admiration of some strong and vigorous sentiment; at another time they were fixed on you with an intensity of expression that seemed to pierce to your very soul. He had an immense "fell" of rough hair . . . [which] gave a sort of wild Olympian character to his head.'[26]

Despite the undoubted success of his lectures, however, Vaughan exercised remarkably little influence on historical studies in Oxford. His lectures were intended for classmen rather than for passmen, for most of them related to periods of history excluded from the curriculum of the latter, but the majority of those who attended took either a pass degree or honours in classics. His lectures in 1850, for example, were attended by 47 undergraduates, excluding those who fell out before the end of the course, but of these only 9 took honours in law and history. Of the remaining 38, over half took a pass degree and the rest a degree in classics or in a few instances mathematics. Of the 105 signatories of the address to publish his lectures, only 17 took honours in the School. It is evident from such statistics that many of those who were sufficiently interested in history to attend lectures refused the double hurdle imposed by the examination statute, and took only a degree in classics.

Vaughan cannot be blamed for the effects of the statute, but perhaps a more significant indication of his lack of influence is

---

25 F. Meyrick, *Memories of Life at Oxford* (1905), 101.
26 Quoted in H. L. Thompson's *Henry George Liddell* (1899), 124–5. Liddell's original manuscript is in Christ Church archives.

the small proportion of those who actually took honours in law and history to attend his lectures. The evidence is not entirely satisfactory, but seems to point to an established trend. Nine undergraduates attended his lectures in 1850 and later took a class in 1853 and 1854. During the same two years a further forty-four men took honours in the School, but none of them appears in Vaughan's register of attendance. A similar situation is revealed by his register of testamurs in other years. Attendance on professorial lectures has seldom been interpreted at Oxford as a measure of the professor's or of the student's ability and industry, and even Stubbs complained that on occasion he lectured to 'two or three listless men',[27] but in the 1850s there was little instruction in history except that provided by the professor.

Although, according to Liddell, some colleges actively dissuaded undergraduates from attending professorial lectures, and although from 1852 Vaughan evoked an increasing amount of hostility from the tutors, there is no evidence to suggest that undergraduates were deliberately discouraged from attending his lectures, though there is some evidence that the largest numbers came from colleges, such as Wadham and Lincoln, where there were tutors on terms of friendship with him. There were more cogent reasons than prejudice for the small attendances. The reformers had hoped that an active professoriate would reduce cramming, but the extent of the curriculum in history, the increased content of the School of Literae Humaniores, and the shortness of the time allowed for the second School tended to make cramming more necessary than before. Vaughan's lectures were stimulating but they were also a luxury the student anxious for a good class could ill afford, and they were not tied to the textbooks which formed the basis of the curriculum. The relevancy of his lectures was further diminished by the absence of professorial control of the examinations. In 1852 Vaughan lectured on William the Conqueror, the Danish Invasions, and Magna Carta, but the assiduous frequenter of his lectures would have found few questions he was thereby enabled to answer in the paper set for the first examination in Law and History in

[27] W. Stubbs, *Seventeen Lectures* (1886), 32.

Easter Term 1853. There was no question on pre-Conquest history.[28] The paper set for honours in period I, which ended at the death of Henry VII, contained twelve compulsory questions, of which two related to the Conquest and the Charter, but neither to aspects dealt with by Vaughan.[29] In 1853 he lectured on the reign of Stephen, but the paper set in the following Easter contained no question on the subject. The task which faced Vaughan was indeed a hopeless one, for no professor could hope to range over the whole period.

During Vaughan's term of office, the anticipated benefits of the professoriate were not realized in the study of history, and in its formative years the new School owed little to its only professor. The nature of the examination system, the lack of professorial control of examinations, the absence of a faculty board, the extent of the burden placed on the professor's shoulders all contributed to this result. The Oxford Act determined that education should be in the hands of a reformed and invigorated staff of college tutors and not in those of the professors, and as history tutors came gradually to be appointed it was to them that the development of the study of history was largely due. The bitter controversy on reform and the enmity of the tutors to the professoriate isolated Vaughan. His non-residence denied him the opportunity of joining with others in measures concerning the School, and it is notable as an instance of his exclusion that he was not consulted when special subjects were introduced in 1855. The enthusiasm with which his lectures were received was no doubt beneficial in its effects, and was in his own estimation the proper purpose of professorial lectures, but otherwise it was only in peripheral activities, such as the award of prizes and

[28] Although the statute prescribed 'modern history to the year 1789' for classmen, the examiners interpreted this as commencing at the Conquest, though in subsequent years it was gradually extended to include the earlier period.

[29] They were 'Mention the principal changes in the political and social state of England which the Norman Conquest produced. Give an account of Domesday Book', and 'Trace the steps which gradually led to the introduction of the Commons into Parliament, and give the most probable date of their final admission. Mention facts which have been thought to warrant our carrying this considerably higher.'

scholarships, that he was able to exert influence. It was during his tenure of the chair that the Arnold and Stanhope prizes were established, and for both he was an examiner.

In 1856 Vaughan was a disappointed man. The Oxford Act had frustrated his dream of a university governed by an active and energetic professoriate; his experience in the lecture room had demonstrated the impotence of the professor and his dependence on the tutors; the demands of teaching interfered with the production of those works of scholarship in his case philosophical rather than historical, which he believed to be the main objects of the professorial system. Final disillusion came as the effects of the Oxford Act penetrated the university.

13. Progress of Reform
1854–1858

THE Oxford Act ushered in a period of reform which centred on the colleges. It was a time when statutes were revised and the measures which Gladstone had been compelled to abandon when the Bill was altered in mid-stream were introduced by the parliamentary commission. The professorial question ceased to agitate the public mind, and the radicals, who as a party had been almost annihilated during the passage of the Act, were subdued and ineffective. Vaughan cut himself off from Oxford even more completely than before, giving no lectures in 1855, and his continual non-residence excluded him from university politics by making him ineligible for election to the Hebdomadal Council. The radical cause was upheld by Liddell and J. M. Wilson. But Liddell became Dean of Christ Church in 1855, and ill health, the problems of his own college, and the experience of practical politics which he gained as a member of Council, steadily tempered his radical zeal, and Wilson was not the man to inspire others. 'There is no depth in him either of character or thought', Jowett wrote. 'He is a different man in the neighbourhood of Vaughan and Liddell and of you and me.'[1]

The elections to the new Council took place in October 1854. Vaughan was filled with dismay. The representatives of the Heads were Williams (New College), Scott (Balliol), Hawkins (Oriel), Gaisford (Christ Church), Jeune (Pembroke), and Symons (Wadham); of the professors, Hussey, Pusey, Cardwell, Daubeny, J. M. Wilson, and Donkin, and of the Masters H. L. Mansel, J. B. Mozley, Lightfoot of Exeter, R. Michell, and Osborne Gordon. For the last place there was a tie between

[1] B. Jowett to A. P. Stanley, [1855]. Balliol College.

Charles Marriott and Pattison, resolved on a second poll in favour of the former. Liddell wrote to Vaughan,

Your feelings about the election I fully share. The Heads are well chosen, the Professors badly, the Masters shamefully. I have no doubt that the last especially was a declaration against anything like a real professoriate. How could Mansel secure so large a number of votes except as being *your* most active antagonist? I observe that Hussey had 146 votes, whereas Mansel had only 82. Did fewer people vote for the Masters' batch or were the votes more divided? It is certainly a scandal that Pusey should have been chosen and you *not*. For Pusey's only claim is *as* a professor. In every other point he is objectionable and ought not to have been returned. Mais ils ont peur. I do not understand how on the general election Mansel, Michell, Gordon and Co. came in atop, while Marriott was doubtful, and at the election between Pattison and Marriott, the Puseyite won the day. Is it that Pattison is unpopular, or that the Puseyites did not exert themselves in the first election? Or what secret and tortuous motives altered the relative position? Altogether it is disgusting, and one can only hope that Gladstone is a little disgusted at seeing none of *his* pets returned.[2]

The balance of the Council remained substantially unchanged for the rest of the decade. In 1855 Bartholomew Price succeeded to the seat vacated by the moderate reformer Donkin, and Liddell was elected on a chance vacancy, but Mark Pattison was again unsuccessful in contesting the seat resigned by his old opponent Marriott. In 1857 the whiggish Principal of Brasenose, Cradock, defeated Plumptre, but later in the same year Cotton of Worcester and Provost Hawkins routed the liberals, Thomson of Queen's and Jowett. Within the Council, the leading figure was Pusey, who developed an unexpected capacity for business. 'Pusey', wrote Liddell, 'appears to be dominant in the Council, supporting Jeune where he can and receiving Jeune's support in other cases.'[3]

[2] H. G. Liddell to Vaughan, 30 Oct. 1854.
[3] The same to the same, 28 Oct. 1855. Jowett wrote to Tait of his contact with Pusey, 'I cannot say I quite like him; he is very shrewd for a "saint" and has more than any man I ever came across the gift of concealing his thoughts and intentions. In the Hebdomadal Council he appears to have great influence.' Lambeth Palace Library MS. Tait 78, f. 270ᵛ.

Although the radicals had little support in Council, they had more sanguine hopes of the University Commission, to which they looked for measures to strengthen the professoriate. In July 1855 Liddell complained that Cornewall Lewis never went near the Commission, 'so whether his professorial views are sound or not, they are of no avail'.[4] There was a suggestion that Liddell himself might join it, but he was unwilling to commence his reign at Christ Church with such arduous duties and favoured the appointment of Edward Twisleton, who duly joined the Commission in the autumn when Cornewall Lewis resigned.

Twisleton was a liberal reformer of radical persuasion, and, next to Liddell, Vaughan's closest friend. Their acquaintance dated from the 1830s, and ripened under the beneficent influence of common interests and attitudes. Both were lawyers, both held generally similar views on university reform, and Twisleton's religious faith, like Vaughan's, had been permanently shaken by doubts about Revelation.[5] Twisleton lived in London and Vaughan was a frequent guest at his house. His American wife described the relationship as 'a thoroughgoing heart and soul friendship'.[6] Twisleton rapidly became one of the most active members of the commission, and poor Johnson found all the troubles he had experienced with the Royal Commission repeated. Twisleton, he complained, 'hurries on the business without any consideration for me . . . and he acts too without any consultation with me, and I must either act with him (blindly) or against him. It is most difficult for me, as Lords H. and E. are always absent at the critical moment, and the other Commissioners . . . are wholly without judgment.'[7] But as Twisleton faced the practical problems of reform his radical views were modified by experience, and on an issue of reform his friendship with Vaughan eventually foundered.

A question which could not long be deferred was the endowment of professorships and the creation of new. In Council

[4] The same to the same, 12 July 1855.
[5] R. Palmer, *Memorials Family and Personal* (1889), i. 144.
[6] *Letters of the Hon. Mrs. Edward Twisleton* (1925), 104.
[7] H. G. Liddell to Vaughan, 15 Apr. 1856.

Jeune took the initiative and went out of his way to reconcile Liddell and Wilson. In December Liddell wrote to Vaughan, 'Something is begun about Professors. Jeune joined Wilson and me in a walk and propounded many things, liberal for him. But certain words he let drop to Wilson before induce suspicions. He has now sent in a memorial to the Commissioners without shewing his paper to us though he professes it contains nothing but what is agreed to.'[8] In the following February the commission formally raised the matter, and on the 11th Council appointed a committee consisting of Liddell, Pusey, Jeune, Daubeny, the Warden of Wadham, and the Principal of St. Alban Hall to consider it.

The Commissioners [wrote Liddell] have applied to us to know what professors of the university we think need to be established or endowed, and a committee has been appointed to give an answer, of which I am one. We meet to-day for the first time. It is a great loss that Wilson continues to be absent, as he would certainly have been on this committee. Since I entered the Council, I think Jeune has materially altered his course. I hold him to our Report in private conversation and he has hitherto stuck to it. But he wants to be a Bishop and fears to offend.[9]

The committee's report was ready by the beginning of March, but a procedural difficulty prevented Council from communicating its views to the commission until the following November. The difficulty illustrated the uncertainty which surrounded the new constitution.

Michell, Gordon and others [wrote Liddell] raised the previous question, whether *Council* was entitled to answer an application from the Commissioners on a subject so important without reference to Convocation. It was argued that we were merely called upon to submit an opinion, and that to refer such a matter to Convocation was either to adjourn it sine die or to refuse all answer whatsoever. At length Goldwin Smith's letter was called for, and when it appeared in terms that it was desired to know the mind of the 'University' with respect to a scheme of professorial teaching, the right of Council to reply

[8] H. G. Liddell to Vaughan, 3 Dec. 1855.
[9] The same to the same, 13 Feb. 1856.

was at once given up by Cardwell and it was useless to fight any more. Jeune then moved to adjourn the question to next term, and the only course to take will be to prevent any answer being sent, and to write individually to every commissioner. I shall do so.[10]

When Council eventually reported the mind of the university to the commission, the scheme proposed for the professoriate was cautious and unimaginative. Its principal recommendations were that a chair of physiology be established at Merton and chairs of English history and international law at All Souls; the stipends of existing chairs were to be increased; and the university was to be represented on boards of electors. It was better, said Council, to improve existing chairs than to found new.[11] 'Without method—crude, sporadic', was the way Mark Pattison described the commission's work in extending the professoriate.[12]

Meanwhile Council had also appointed a committee to consider the examination system. Liddell was again a member together with Jeune, Cardwell, Hussey, Wilson, Price, Michell, Osborne Gordon, Daubeny, and Scott. The examination statute had been in force for only three years, but the need for amendment was becoming abundantly plain. Compulsory classics was hampering the development of the new studies, and many students who did well in the first School were plucked or fared ill in the second. It was sometimes thought that the work of the two Schools compelled men to reside longer and that this discouraged some from coming up at all. Certainly the number of matriculations fell steadily in the 1850s. Although the study of classics maintained its ascendancy, there were grave misgivings about the way it was developing. Pattison described it as in transition from literature and language to philosophy,[13] and complained that Moderations had become an examination in language without Literae Humaniores becoming one in philosophy. Rhetoric, poetry, a good deal of logic, and ultimately ancient history, he said, ought to be removed from the curriculum, and transferred either to an earlier examination or to other Schools. Doubts were entertained

---

[10] The same to the same, 12 Mar. 1856.   [11] P.R.O. H.O. 73/44 pt. 1.
[12] M. Pattison, *Memoirs* (1885), 304.
[13] *Essays by Mark Pattison*, ed. H. Nettleship (1889), i. 469.

by others about the suitability of the examinations to the Indian Civil Service, and J. M. Wilson informed Vaughan 'I see that the papers on Mental and Moral Philosophy are such as no one could answer who confined his reading on these subjects within the limits which the university examinations define. Unless higher instruction in these subjects is given in Oxford than the college tutors give and the examinations, which are in the hands of the tutors, require, our young men will get but few marks for their performances in this part of the examination.'[14] Pattison's remedy for the ailing state of classical studies was the abolition of honours in all other subjects.

In the Hebdomadal Council, opinion was balanced in favour of a single final School, and the division of Greats into two Schools of classics and philosophy. In February 1856 Liddell reported to Vaughan:

We have a committee sitting upon the examinations &c. In this we have carried that there shall be only one School necessary at the Final Examination, so that men may leave off their Classics after Moderations. Do you still adhere to the plan, or something like it, drawn out in the Report? I think the committee are prepared to recommend something like this: Schools (1) of Classics (2) of Mathematics (3) of Physical Science (4) of Law and History (5) of Philosophy. But they will require every man to pass through a preliminary examination in the 'Rudiments of Religious knowledge'. This is a sine qua non, and unless it is conceded there is not the slightest chance of carrying the other. Cardwell suggested to bring in some Divinity both at Responsions and Moderations and to establish a School of Theology by the side of the other five. This will be considered, but will not, I think, be carried. I doubt whether it is so good as the other . . . Michell and Gordon attend but little. Hussey alone opposed and *now* seems inclined to further the scheme. Scott does not know what to make of it. V. C. strongly opposed. The rest for. . . . You might do much even by an occasional speech in Congregation.[15]

Liddell continued to consult Vaughan, and on 21 April wrote to tell him that the School of Law and History was not to be

[14] J. M. Wilson to Vaughan, [1857].
[15] H. G. Liddell to the same, 13 Feb. 1856.

touched except that a more careful choice of books was to be recommended. He had, he said, carried that there should be Boards of Studies on which the professors were to be represented.[16]

The proposal to establish Boards of Studies found its way into the statute promulgated in March 1857, but there is evidence that the professors had already acted on their own initiative and organized themselves into an unofficial Board. The experiment was designed to deal with problems common to the whole professoriate rather than with those of particular faculties. The teachers of science were the prime movers, but Pusey, who had earlier poured scorn on the idea of faculty and general boards alike, showed now a remarkable anxiety to be present. In a long letter to Vaughan, Maskelyne, the Reader in geology, described the meeting which took place on 18 January 1857. It was not without an element of farce.

We had a professorial gathering to-day but a very small one. Walker, Daubeny, *Pusey*!, Wall, Price and myself. Acland and Donkin could not be there.

Pusey wished to be classed as a Divinity Professor! This was the cause of his coming. Ogle put himself down as: Anatomy and Physiology, Regius Professor for! I had been put down (not by myself) Assistant Professor of Chemistry, which I had erased.

Well the question was raised what was to be done about Pusey and Ogle. It was agreed that each Professor was responsible for the one line in which his name appeared, and as unfortunately at present there is no professorial organisation, such as could appoint a committee to manage the promulgation of this paper in a proper form, every Professor might appear under any name however ridiculous or put himself where he pleased in the list provided no other Professor or Professors of the same faculty or class were there to question it. So under a sort of protest against Pusey making it into a precedent at a future time, Hebrew appears as a Divinity subject, not as a philological one.

Your sensible letter was read and Pusey strongly supported the rejection of the Vice-Chancellor's name from the bottom of the paper, which was unanimously determined on. Daubeny made a move in the other direction and wanted to have the university teachers of

16 The same to the same, 21 Apr. 1856.

German and French put in. This I am happy to say we got rid of, and so poor little Frädersdorff will have to bluster loudly about the neglect of his dignity.

But the most important question raised was that of the number of lectures on which the certificate is founded. Wall and myself opposed the certificate altogether and prepared to make an effort to get rid of it, but it brings too much grist to the professorial mill and the feeling was too strong. Daubeny thinks *you* ought to give a certificate only for attendance on *two* courses of your lectures. Or the alternative is he must give courses of only 8 lectures on Chemistry! He also wished to know how you were certain that the men had attended all your lectures when you gave their certificate—in fact whether you required attendance on *all* your lectures for a certificate. He had it seems previously told Walker that you gave a ticket for 6 lectures' attendance—this however he denied when brought to book about it. I went at him —told him the attendance on your lectures was shown by the statistics of that attendance not to be influenced to any very paramount degree by the certificate system; that you were very particular about the giving of certificates, and that if a man said and his word was not a sufficient guarantee, I thought it was the best proof that any guarantee of attendance was wrong. I told him how many lectures are given on Chemistry organic and inorganic, viz 380 in 8 months in a German University by the same Professor, while the Professor of Botany gives 190 besides, and asked him if he thought a Professor of Modern History could lecture in this manner and if it would be good for anything if he did. The number of lectures given in German universities evidently startled some of the brethren, and Walker began considering how he should like to give so many. However it ended in the question being deferred to another meeting in term time.

To such another meeting the question was also deferred regarding the propriety of the adoption of the fee system adopted at Cambridge, each Professor being paid his share out of a common fund created by massing all the sums paid for attendance on professorial lectures.

I forgot to tell you that Hawkins and Cardwell both declined for the present putting their names on the list. They wish to remind the Professors that 'they do not constitute a Board.' Wadham, University and the Vice-Chancellor and I believe also the Dean of Ch. Ch. are in favour of the schedule of lectures we propose to put out, and we have determined it is to go out from the university press whether they will or no. Acland wants his name not put in, as not being a university

Professor. Ogle has in fact purposely called himself Anatomy and *Physiology* in order to tread on Acland's toes, and Acland is timid.[17]

Meetings of professors had taken place during the opposition to the Oxford Act in 1854, but the meeting described by Maskelyne is the earliest of which record survives of a meeting solely of professors within the university. The meeting was resumed in February, and 'after much talk', as B. C. Brodie put it, decided to recommend the continuation of the existing system of two compulsory courses of professorial lectures for a degree and that certificates should not be given for attendance at less than 15 lectures[18]—a measure which would have had serious consequences for Vaughan if accepted by the university. The professors duly submitted a memorial to Council, which accepted the substance of their recommendations.

The statute for the reform of the examinations was put to Congregation on 3 March 1857. It proposed to reform the School of Greats by transferring much of the history, ethics, and rhetoric to Moderations, and to divide it into two Schools, of classical literature and philology and of moral philosophy and metaphysics. The obligatory double Finals was to be abolished, and boards of studies introduced. The statute, however, was rejected, and a second attempt in which all the proposals were jettisoned except the abolition of the double Finals met with the same fate in the following term. The tutors would have none of it, and it was perhaps no accident that Michell and Gordon had not attended the committee of Council at which it was discussed. The fear that Liddell had expressed to Gladstone at the time of the Oxford Act that the tutors would block university reform seemed to be vindicated. Their opposition and the ineffectual attempt of the university commissioners to increase the professoriate were bitter blows to Vaughan at a time when his resignation was in the balance.

[17] N. Maskelyne to Vaughan, 18 Jan. 1857.

[18] B. C. Brodie to the same, 8 Feb. 1857. Compulsory attendance at professorial lectures was abolished in 1859.

14. Resignation

VAUGHAN resigned his professorship in May 1857. It was a decision not reached in haste, and he told Stanley that he had considered it for some time 'not without oscillations of feeling'.[1] He was then forty-six years old and apparently at the height of his powers. He did not resign in order to take up another appointment or in protest against some injustice real or imaginary, but to live quietly in London and subsequently in the remote countryside of Wales. What, it may be asked, were the causes of such an apparently inexplicable and self-denying act?

Goldwin Smith was not alone in attributing it in part at least to failing health, or rather, since he was seldom overgenerous in the attribution of charitable motives, to hypochondria.[2] Vaughan's health had never been robust, and it is probable that all the children of his father's first marriage suffered from ill health. In 1834 his aunt Amelia remarked that all that side of the family were very unhealthy except Vaughan's sister Augusta, and she might well have included Augusta who suffered from acute neuralgia.[3] His eldest sister Barbara was often ill and at one time feared for her reason.[4] Vaughan too suffered from some kind of nervous debility, the most conspicuous symptom of which was described by Sir M. E. Grant Duff as 'insomnia of the most terrible kind'.[5] It was accompanied by headaches and

[1] Vaughan to A. P. Stanley, 19 May 1857.

[2] G. Smith, *Reminiscences* (1911), 275.

[3] Letter from Mrs. Amelia Hughes to Sir C. R. Vaughan, 20 Mar. 1834 (All Souls College). Lady Barbara Halford wrote that Augusta's neuralgia 'comes on regularly every morning at 4 o'clock after which she can get no sleep' (Family letters).

[4] In an undated letter she wrote to Vaughan, 'If you should ever hear it said that my illness has caused my mind and intellect to be much weakened, I know that I had never a very strong intellect or mind, but it is no worse than it ever was. Pray *don't allow* any strong measures to be taken with me without interfering.'

[5] Sir M. E. Grant Duff, *Notes from a Diary, 1851–1872* (1897), ii. 302.

dizziness,[6] and the brief interludes of sleep were often tormented by nightmares. His habits were abstemious and temperate, and in view of the family history of nervous disorder it is possible that his malady was hereditary in origin. It resisted equally conventional cures and the nostrums of his friends. His friend Osmund Priaulx recommended him to try the seemingly dangerous treatment advocated by a speaker at the British Institution of pressing the carotid artery. His daughter Emma declared that he could not sleep because of Gladstone, but the soporific effect of Disraeli was no more perceptible than any other remedy. At times he suffered from prolonged prostration and depression, and after one such occasion in 1869 Priaulx wrote to him 'I had no idea that you could be so changed in so short a time and the worst is that so far as your bodily troubles go you seem to despair.' Although none of this could be described as hypochondria, Vaughan developed valetudinarian habits of an eccentric nature. Towards the end of his life, for example, he attributed his increasing deafness to 'faulty making of my night caps which leave all my back-head quite bare. I knew that the mischief was effected at night by the singing and confusion in my ears and head when I waked every day. I attributed it however to draughts or cold down from the roof for I could not see the back of my head.'[7] But grievous and incapacitating as his illnesses were, and although accentuated by other causes at the time of his resignation,[8] they were not in themselves sufficient to cause him to surrender his chair. For this the explanation must be sought elsewhere.

The ostensible cause of Vaughan's resignation was an obstinate refusal to reside in the university. For a reformer of such radical opinions it was an improbable and even at first glance a discreditable issue to produce such a serious consequence, nor need it have done so but for the fact that it touched a sensitive area of

[6] In 1869 his sister hoped that he had had 'no return of those unpleasant feelings about your head proceeding as I hoped they did from faintness'.

[7] Fragment of a letter without date or addressee.

[8] In his recollections of Vaughan, Liddell wrote that at this period Vaughan manifested 'great caprice and irritability in his intercourse with his friends at Oxford'.

Vaughan's experience and convictions. The residence of Fellows of colleges had not been an issue of importance among reformers, and indeed attempts to insist on it during the passage of the Oxford Act had been strenuously resisted by the radicals because of its tendency to increase the conservative complexion of Congregation, but after 1854 its importance increased with the reduction in the number of Fellowships and the performance of tutorial duties by those which remained. At the same time the long-standing scandal of professorial non-residence, which the Royal Commission had sought to curtail by insisting on strict residence for professors, was being removed as the professors were given a more active share in the work of the university. It was perhaps a consequence of Vaughan's own non-residence that he failed to appreciate how much opinion in the university had changed on this question. In February 1856 Congregation regulated several professorial chairs, though none of the regius professorships, and required their occupants to reside for six months in the year from October to July. It was an unmistakable sign of the way the wind was blowing.

Before a similar regulation could be framed for the chair of modern history, the question of Vaughan's residence came to a head when the university commissioners granted new statutes to Oriel in the following spring. In November 1856 Council had proposed that the stipend of the regius professorship of history should be increased by Oriel, which had previously been contemplating the provision of an endowment for a chair of Anglo-Saxon. The suggestion was taken up, but the college, perhaps rather than find that it was committed to electing Vaughan to a Fellowship and not unmindful of the circumstances of his deprivation in 1842, which Hawkins had recently resurrected, resolved unanimously to make its contribution in the form of a grant to a general fund on the grounds that the suppression of a Fellowship would thereby be avoided. Vaughan was indignant and described the proposal as a 'slap in the face'. It was, he said, an insult and injury 'to offer to annex a Fellowship or its value to a Professorship in some branch of learning connected with the studies of the place, and then to meet the proposal with regard to the Reg. Prof. of Modern History by offering to subscribe to a general fund rather than it specifically'.[9] Although his pride was hurt, he did not in fact wish to be elected to a Fellowship at all, for when Twisleton explained that the scheme would permit the professor to be elected a Fellow of any college in the university, Vaughan declared that he viewed with dislike the participation of professorial Fellows in college management and social life. A Fellowship, he said, gave the professor uncongenial duties, it involved him though an officer of the university in the interests of a particular college, and it jeopardized the chances of obtaining funds for the professoriate by forcing Fellows on colleges against their will.

But the main question was residence, which Twisleton assured him was likely to be insisted on as a condition of the endowment. In a persuasive letter he begged Vaughan to accept it.

I should deem it a noble object of ambition for the highest intellect that he should be at the head of the School of Modern History on its introduction to Oxford, and that he should impress his own direction on that study. This cannot be done through the delivery of 8 lectures a year (however excellent) by a Professor residing in London or its vicinity. The salary I know ought to be double £600 a year, but still the receiving such a salary ought not to be an essential condition of performing such a duty. Three fourths of the main arguments for Professors are cut away by non-residence, and your own non-residence renders it comparatively useless to quote you as an authority concerning the use of Professorships. Do go and become a resident King.[10]

Despite its friendly tone, the letter was a veiled ultimatum. Vaughan, who had good reason to believe that Twisleton shared his view of the matter, was wounded and distressed. As recently as 1853 Twisleton had expressed what Vaughan interpreted as approval of professorial non-residence. 'You are quite right', he had written, 'not to increase the number of your lectures, and I should regard the insinuations and the ravings of adversaries with equal indifference on this point.'[11] When Twisleton changed

---

9 Vaughan to E. Twisleton, 5 Mar. 1857.
10 E. Twisleton to Vaughan, 24 Feb. 1857.
11 The same to the same, 28 May 1853.

his mind, Vaughan felt betrayed not only because of their ancient friendship but because he believed that Twisleton's appointment as a commissioner was due to his 'earnest and repeated suggestion when the commission was first about to be issued'.[12] His experience of the commission convinced Twisleton that residence was necessary and prevented absolute uselessness in case of the non-delivery of lectures. He saw no reason why an exception should be made in favour of Vaughan, but whatever the claims of friendship might have been they were outweighed by the strength of the opposition within the commission to the whole professorial system. 'The *general* question was frequently raised which I was as frequently obliged to answer,' he wrote, ' "What is the use of having any Professors at all?" My answer invariably embraced two topics: 1st, the advantages of the delivery of lectures; and 2ndly, those resulting from the residence of able men in the University. [There was much incredulity, on the part of one Member of the Commission, as to Professorial Lectures being of any use whatever.]'[13]

He made a further attempt to persuade Vaughan to reside, even using the rather self-defeating argument that to do so would not cause any positive injury to the History School, but Vaughan was adamant. On 25 February 1857 a statute was framed requiring the professor of modern history to be resident for six months in the year from October to July. In March the Oriel Ordinance was issued. It endowed the professorship with the emoluments of a Fellowship to the value of £250 a year on condition that the professor was resident for six months in the year, and it empowered the college to elect the professor to a Fellowship.[14] On 11 May Vaughan sent in his resignation to Lord Palmerston.

At various times Vaughan produced a variety of arguments,

[12] This is probably true, but Twisleton's subsequent appointment in his own recollection was due to Lord Palmerston, Sir G. C. Lewis, and 'most essentially to the Dean of Christ Church'. Letter to Vaughan in the possession of Professor Quentin Bell, 3 Feb. 1860.

[13] E. Twisleton to Vaughan, 3 Feb. 1860. The sentence in brackets appears only in Twisleton's draft in the possession of Lord Saye and Sele. The incredulous member of the commission was perhaps Sir John Awdry.

[14] Stubbs was the first regius professor to hold a Fellowship at Oriel.

some more convincing than others, to explain and justify his
preference for resignation to residence. He maintained that it was
distinctly understood when he was appointed that he would not
reside. 'At Oxford', he wrote, 'it has been the rule that when the
statutes of the Professorship do not prescribe residence, the
Professor is not bound to reside. Arnold could not reside and
this was known when he was appointed. Milman, Keble,
Senior and Merivale did not. The minister pledged me to give
lectures at Oxford when he appointed me, then resident in
London, but not to reside at Oxford.'[15] Having lived in London
for eight years he saw no good reason why he should alter his
habits. When pressed on the alleged statutory requirements of
the chair, he replied with some legal subtlety that the stipulated
residence was introduced by the regulations issued to each professor of modern history by the secretary of state, and that these
had no authority because they infringed the procedure for
amendment laid down in the statutes.

At other times Vaughan claimed that he needed to be in
London for the sake of its libraries. The Bodleian Library he
found unsatisfactory compared with the London Library, of
which he was a foundation subscriber and life member. 'I have
tried reading in the Bodleian', he complained. 'It is not open more
than six hours out of the twenty four, and those during the day
when exercise must be taken if at all. In winter too the temperature is low, and I have found that even with a great coat and
railway rug I have been quite chilled by three hours consecutive
study. Having been for many years a student and a water drinker
I am perhaps more sensitive to cold than many.'[16] Neither his
complaint about conditions in the Bodleian Library nor his
strictures on the regulations governing his chair carry conviction,
for Vaughan had advocated the alteration of statutes when they
stood in the way of reform. No more convincing was his
argument that he could not afford to live in Oxford because
his Clerkship required his presence in London 'periodically and
occasionally' to discharge duties which could not be left to

---

[15] Vaughan to E. Twisleton, 23 Jan. 1860.
[16] Evidence submitted to the University Commissioners, Jan. 1856.

subordinates, and that the income of the office was 'more pro-portionately and positively than the salary of my Professorship'.[17] Not only did his duties as Clerk of Assize require his absence from London as much as they would have done from Oxford, but when he sat on the Public Schools Commission he did appoint a deputy, and in 1877 he employed the Welsh historian John Roland Phillips to assist him in a similar capacity.[18]

He also maintained that he could not afford to live in Oxford because the stipend of the chair was only £371 a year and did not carry with it a Fellowship and the benefit of rooms and meals which this involved. He had repeatedly argued that good men could not be attracted to professorial chairs unless stipends were increased substantially, and although he could not reside on a salary far below what he had advocated without repudiating his own argument and exposing himself to ridicule, his case was largely demolished by the Oriel Ordinance which would have raised the value of the chair to £620, which compared favourably with all professorships except those attached to Canonries of Christ Church.[19]

Although each of these reasons contained a grain of truth, they do not suffice separately or collectively to explain Vaughan's decision, and more compelling causes were at work. Goldwin Smith hinted at one of them when he said that Vaughan 'took it into his head that regular lecturing was intellectual slavery, not to be endured'.[20] Until 1855 he lectured regularly and de-livered an average of eight lectures a year, but the creation of the History School, and the still inadequate state of college tuition in history, reinforced the prevalent belief that it was the duty of the professor to teach undergraduates. In 1842, after representations by Arnold, the Hebdomadal Board had reduced the statutory number of lectures given by the regius professor of modern

17 Vaughan to E. Twisleton, 23 Jan. 1860.

18 In 1861 he appointed Richard Harington, subsequently deputy Clerk of Assize.

19 Vaughan believed that a first-rate professor ought to receive £1,200–1,400 a year, which was roughly the income of a Canon of Christ Church (Letter to E. Twisleton, 23 Jan. 1860).

20 G. Smith, *Reminiscences* (1911), 275.

history from twenty to sixteen. Many considered that Vaughan ought to deliver this number, and at the meeting of professors in January 1857 it was suggested that certificates should be given only for attendance at so many. To Vaughan a proposal which would have doubled the amount of lectures he gave and turned him into what he had once called 'a tutor of the third year' was quite unacceptable, and by engaging him actively in the instruction of undergraduates would have required almost constant residence. It ran contrary to his whole conception of the professoriate.

I think [he wrote to Twisleton] that you and others very much undervalue the possible effect of a few striking lectures. It is my personal belief founded partly on analogy and partly on direct experience of one kind or another that a few good lectures will give a tone and feeling, a mode of thought, a style, to those who listen. In fact they will reach the very soul of those who are in the earliest prime of their faculties and feelings, and that excellent teaching day after day would not do so much on the whole.[21]

In as much as a question of principle was involved in Vaughan's resignation it was to be found in his protest against the development of the professor primarily as a teacher and his assertion of the duty of study. It was a protest more keenly felt at this time because the great metaphysical work on the origin of moral behaviour, which was the central intellectual preoccupation of his life, occupied his mind during the crisis of the resignation with increased fervour. It was in 1856 that we hear for the first time of one of those extraordinary and recurring calamities when part of the manuscript of this work was lost.[22] History had fertilized the sources of Vaughan's philosophical thought, and so in a sense had served its purpose.

The conflict between lecturing and residence, between education and learning, was one reason for Vaughan's resignation, but there was another of at least equal force. The exchange with Twisleton at the time of the Oriel Ordinance suggests that Twisleton was prepared to accept Vaughan even if he lectured

[21] Vaughan to E. Twisleton, 5 Mar. 1857.
[22] H. G. Liddell to Vaughan, 9 Feb. 1856. See pp. 238–46.

no more frequently than in the past providing that he resided in Oxford. But Vaughan was inflexible: not only would he not lecture more frequently but in no circumstances would he even reside. Vaughan disliked Oxford and Oxford society, and the reason is not difficult to discover. Twisleton reached the heart of the matter when he wrote to Vaughan that his resignation 'did not arise from your denying intellectually the benefits likely to accrue to the university by your residence in it, but from your reluctance to make a plunge into an atmosphere which you so much disliked'.[23] He had good cause to dislike it for by 1856 there existed great personal animosity, sometimes amounting almost to hatred, towards him. He drew attention to it himself in a letter to Twisleton.

My own residence *under the present state* of Oxford and the Professorship is I believe from my heart a mere pretence when urged as a ground to discredit my opinions. I do not doubt that it *is* urged on such a ground, but urged partly by those who hate the objects which I have in view with regard to the endowment of learning and genius at Oxford, partly by Professors whom my success has made jealous, partly by Tutors who do not forgive the 'spreta forma' of my pamphlet, and partly by mere anti-reformers as a general objection against me, and partly also by half friends and timid friends, and credulous friends, who have not the sagacity and strength of mind to defend me as they might.[24]

Vaughan was once described by Twisleton as 'super-sensitive', and his touchiness once caused a wag to remark that he desired to be treated as a Special Revelation.[25] But if he manifested symptoms of persecution mania in his letter to Twisleton it was not without cause. By his contribution to the reform movement, by his influence on the Blue Book, by his personal identification with the dominance of the professoriate, by his criticisms of the tutors, by his quarrel with Pusey, by his inflexible opposition to the Oxford Act, by his attacks on the clerical element in the university, he had antagonized almost

[23] E. Twisleton to Vaughan, 5 Dec. 1859.
[24] Vaughan to E. Twisleton, 5 Mar. 1857.
[25] E. Twisleton to Vaughan, 5 Dec. 1859.

every shade of opinion. His enemies, who did not lack malice, attacked him whenever they could, and the occasions were not infrequent. Unlike other reformers, he was never a public examiner. In 1854, when the Vinerian Scholarship was reformed, he became an examiner by virtue of the statute, but when he protested that he had received no formal invitation from the Vice-Chancellor, Charles Neate told him roundly, 'The Vice-Chancellor does not want you. Nobody *wants* you, as there are enough to do the work without you.'26 In 1855 he was not consulted when the statute regulating the Stanhope Prize appointed the regius professor of history an examiner. Two years later his lectures were described by an anonymous critic as 'bawdry and the greatest trash'.27 The ill treatment he received during these years rankled for the rest of his life. He never set foot in Oxford after his resignation, and as late as 1884, when Freeman became regius professor of modern history, the old bitter memories remained. 'Freeman', he wrote to his son, 'passes me over spitefully [in his inaugural]—he has treated me in the same spirit for the last thirty-five years, in *every manner*, and I doubt not prompted Stubbs to do the same in his inaugural lecture.'28

His refusal to reside gave his enemies a powerful weapon which they were intent on using, but the final act of betrayal came when some of his Oxford friends came out in support of his residence. Only once did he state explicitly the reasons which caused him to resign, and his statement shows how keenly he felt their desertion. It occurred in a letter to Stanley.

A position in which I could not have the entire sympathy of a strong knot of the good and wise at Oxford I did not like to hold. More and more did I feel unwilling to pledge myself even to myself to the task work of any given number of lectures in the year. I could pledge myself to any amount of study almost after the next twelve months, but to lecturing under the legal and moral necessity of doing so constantly felt I have a dislike. I found it inconvenient in more than one

26 C. Neate to the same, [29 Nov. 1854].
27 Vaughan to E. Twisleton, 27 Mar. 1857.
28 Vaughan to W. W. Vaughan, n.d.

point of view. I might justify myself to myself in holding a Professorship on the terms of study only because I really believe that if the right
man be appointed so to prosecute his studies the lecturing might be
left to itself and *in the long run* the university and literature would
gain much by such Professors. But I could not reckon on similar
opinions amongst my friends, still less could I hope for a sacrifice on
their part of opinions more generally approved on behalf of myself.
The terms of my Professorship require, I believe, but four lectures per
annum, but even on this number hardly could I fall back without
assurance and sympathy on the part of the select at least of Oxford.
This view and feeling was the *chief* element in my decision.[29]

It might have been thought that this was the end of the matter,
but such was not the case, and there followed one of the most
remarkable and moving episodes in Vaughan's life. None of his
friends knew of his resignation until the deed was done. 'I
breathed my resignation to no one until the minister had accepted
it . . . I hardly mentioned it even then.'[30] When at last it was
known, the response of his friends demonstrated as nothing
else the extraordinary esteem in which he was held by some of
the most distinguished men in the university. 'I feel', wrote
Stanley, 'as if the best flower had fallen from my chaplet, and as
if my own position had lost in dignity by your retirement, if so
be, from the order . . . I know the annoyance you have received
from the snarling curs of this cynical place, but surely they are
not worth considering in comparison of those—many I hope—
but if few most select, who value your connexion with Oxford
as it deserves to be valued.'[31] J. M. Wilson, one of the staunchest
supporters of the professoriate, described the resignation as 'the
greatest blow to professorial interests', and begged Vaughan to
withdraw it and to give the statutory number of lectures 'residing
or not as you please'. 'I believe', he wrote, 'that your doing this
for a few years would have the effect of reconciling people
generally to the idea of *studying professors*. In the meantime I can
assure you that your threatened resignation has had the effect
of showing your friends and all liberals the importance of such

[29] Vaughan to A. P. Stanley, 19 May 1857.
[30] The same to E. Twisleton, 23 Jan. 1860.
[31] A. P. Stanley to Vaughan, [May 1857].

Professors. Rely on it they see clearly that giving lectures ad infinitum does not constitute a professor.'[32]

The resignation was a great shock to the university liberals, and it fell to Jowett to take the lead in an attempt to persuade Vaughan to change his mind. On 21 May he wrote the following letter to him.

I cannot express to you how deeply I regret the determination at which you have arrived. No greater loss could befall the university. It seems to me quite sad that seven years of your life should have been spent in an employment which is to produce no permanent result.

Some of your friends wish me to convey their earnest entreaty that you would reconsider your decision. I will express their feelings in the words of Grant, 'lecture or not lecture, reside or not reside, I think him an infinite loss.' Those who desire me to make this intimation to you are Stanley and Brodie, whose feelings you already know, Wilson, Conington, Maskelyne, Müller, Henry Smith, to whom let me add myself and Grant. Pattison is not here. Many others would no doubt join in expressing the same wish. But as we hoped that you might still be induced to withdraw your resignation it was thought undesirable to mention the subject further.

We want you to understand that we are too glad to have you on any terms, and that it is not your lectures or residence amongst us that we chiefly value but yourself; also we feel that work like yours is not to be measured out by the yard, and we do not wish to see uncongenial restrictions imposed upon you.

I was requested to beg you to confer with Twisleton once more on the subject. There is, no doubt, some inconvenience in retracting a step which has been already taken but we hope that the strong feeling which we have about it may be a sufficient reason for doing so both to yourself and to Lord Palmerston. And the inconvenience is of no consequence a few months hence. C. Lewis has been, I believe, already written to to get him to prevent your Professorship from being filled up.

Your employment with your 'opus magnum' seems to me quite a sufficient reason to the world as well as to your friends why you should in any particular year confine yourself to the bare requirements of the statute. I think he would be a hard-hearted person who refused to allow you to dispense with them altogether.

I cannot but think that you would be shaken in your purpose could

[32] J. M. Wilson to the same, [May 1857].

you have heard the very strong expressions of admiration and regret which have been used to me to-day, such as no one else here would have called forth.[33]

It would have been difficult to have resisted such a generous appeal, but it was not easy for Vaughan to extricate himself from the situation. Since it was too much to hope that Palmerston would make the first move, Jowett hit on the expedient of sending a memorial to him. It was signed by Jowett himself, Max Müller, Stanley, Brodie, Wilson, Conington, Henry Smith, Maskelyne, Grant, 'and several more . . . whom I cannot in this haste remember', and was accompanied by a letter from Goldwin Smith, who was already being mentioned with Froude as a candidate for succession to the chair.[34]

The memorial was couched in the following terms:

The undersigned friends of Professor H. H. Vaughan having heard the reasons of his resignation respectfully beg your Lordship to suggest to him the reconsideration of it.

Those reasons are that Professor Vaughan has been engaged for many years partly in writing a treatise on Moral Philosophy which is shortly about to appear; partly in original researches on English History which he desires to make the subject of an historical work. These occupations though not incompatible with his delivering the number of lectures required by the statute he finds inconsistent with frequent lecturing.

The undersigned believe that any writings of Mr. Vaughan will have a permanent interest and value. And they deeply regret that what they feel to be an unnecessary scruple should deprive the university of the ablest of its professors.

At the same time Jowett wrote to Vaughan that the strong wish of his friends was quite sufficient grounds for the withdrawal of his resignation, and that any explanation to Palmerston beyond

---

[33] B. Jowett to Vaughan, 21 May [1857]. Although Müller's name is mentioned in this letter, he was not regarded as an ardent reformer, but he owed a debt of gratitude to Vaughan to whom he later wrote, 'I know that I owe my present Professorship chiefly to your influence' (M. Müller to Vaughan, 12 Aug. 1860).

[34] Jowett wrote of Goldwin Smith's conduct in the affair, 'G. Smith has behaved most rightly and kindly about it. Though I cannot think him a good candidate for the M. H. Chair and disapprove of his conduct on many occasions, I shall always respect him for having acted as he ought, that is unselfishly, about this' (B. Jowett to Vaughan, 28 May [1857]).

an expression of his willingness to remain in consequence of this wish should be avoided and was likely to be misunderstood.[35]

The memorial was presented to Palmerston by Cornewall Lewis, but the Prime Minister could not act without some communication from Vaughan himself. Jowett begged him to write:

It seems hardly fair that I should ask you to do so. Yet how to accomplish otherwise what I believe to be of the greatest importance to the university and what your friends here are extremely desirous to effect I do not see.

Circumstances have changed in one respect since you sent in your resignation. You could scarcely have been aware that so strong a wish would have been felt that you should remain. It cannot lower the dignity or character of anyone to change his resolution on such a ground.

The position, the income, the occupation of a Professor, and perhaps even the society of Oxford may even seem desirable a few years hence. I shall always feel your withdrawal to be an irreparable loss to Oxford and the professorial body.

Should you, as I hope, request to withdraw your resignation it should be done immediately. At present there are no candidates in the field but G. S. and Freeman of Trinity.[36]

Vaughan was not persuaded to revoke his resignation without great mental anguish. Even though he was assured of the enthusiastic support of his Oxford friends, who were ready to welcome him on any terms, the underlying causes which had led him to resign remained unchanged. When Stanley visited him on 6 June, he found him 'in a highly recalcitrant state; very unwilling, almost determined not to take any step himself—and evidently very much averse to the notion of returning to the Professorship—perhaps in the same state as that in which he was before we roused him'.[37] It was with many misgivings that he eventually wrote to Lord Palmerston, and it is indicative of his indecision that although the letter was written on 3 June it was not dispatched until the 11th. Palmerston agreed to the withdrawal

[35] B. Jowett to Vaughan, 28 May [1857].

[36] The same to the same, 2 June [1857].

[37] A. P. Stanley to B. Jowett, 7 June 1857. Balliol College.

of his resignation, but remarked tartly that 'it is desirable that persons holding appointments under the Crown should well make up their own minds before they tender their resignation, lest when they change their intentions they should find that a successor has been appointed'.[38]

It was the hope of Vaughan's friends that once a respite had been gained by the withdrawal of the resignation, he might be induced to reside in Oxford and continue his lectures. Early in June, B. C. Brodie wrote to him that if he would but come and live in Oxford, and in addition to the four lectures he was required to deliver give some private catechetical lectures, all opposition would be effectually silenced.[39] Less than a week after Palmerston had accepted Vaughan's retraction, Jowett was writing to ask if there was any chance of him coming to live in Oxford. 'It would give great satisfaction to your friends here,' he wrote, 'and I really believe that both in Modern History and also in university business you would *now* find a field, but *that* was not part of *our* contract with you.'[40] On 19 July Jowett wrote again, having heard from Brodie that Vaughan was thinking of taking a house near Oxford, to tell him of two possible places.[41]

Whatever hopes his friends may have had that he would eventually reside, Vaughan had yielded to their entreaties on the understanding that it was on his own terms and he remained as intransigent as ever. Liddell and Twisleton, the two men who knew him best, saw more clearly into the matter than either Jowett or Brodie. Liddell had been recuperating in Madeira from severe inflammation of the lungs when the crisis occurred, and returned to England a few days after the memorial to Lord Palmerston had been dispatched. He wrote at once to Vaughan, but not at all in the terms used by Jowett.

Is it my business to advise you to recall your letter of resignation, which (I am told) is possible? I know not. I should indeed be too glad to think that you could even yet contemplate the work of honouring

[38] C. Barrington to Vaughan, 15 June 1857.
[39] B. C. Brodie to the same, 4 June [1857].
[40] B. Jowett to the same, 21 June [1857].
[41] The same to the same, 19 July [1857].

and exalting the university by continuing your lectures, for I feel, and many feel with me, that your occupation of the chair is an honour to Oxford, and, if this is possible, I beg and supplicate you with both hands to continue professor. But if this place and the work is loathesome to you, if your resignation now recalled would merely entail vexation of spirit, and if the same act would be repeated in the course of a year or two, I have nothing to say.[42]

Twisleton adopted an even sterner attitude and refused to sign the memorial to Palmerston. Two years later he told Vaughan, who until then was unaware of his refusal, the reasons.

In 1857, I was asked to sign a memorial to Lord Palmerston requesting him to invite you to resume your professorship. I never saw the memorial, but I declined to sign any document of the kind on the ground of your non-residence at Oxford. And I stated that notwithstanding my high opinion of your lectures, I could not in common honesty sign such a memorial, inasmuch as on the University Commission one of my main arguments for a professoriate was founded on the advantage which, independently of lectures, would accrue to the university from the habitual residence in it of men with first-rate ability.[43]

The significance of Twisleton's attitude was that it threw the weight of the commission behind those who were opposed to a non-resident professor of modern history. When Vaughan learnt of his refusal to sign the memorial a lengthy and occasionally acrimonious correspondence ensued ending in the abrupt termination of their long-standing friendship.

The autumn term had hardly begun before Vaughan's critics showed their hand. On 23 October Jowett told him that trouble was brewing in Council, and that Jeune had informed him that the malcontents were prepared to address the Crown. Jeune mentioned the matter to Liddell also, and said that unless Vaughan showed some intention of lecturing an endeavour would be made to bring the matter before the university. Jowett begged Vaughan to silence his critics by taking up residence.

---

[42] H. G. Liddell to the same, 8 June 1857.
[43] E. Twisleton to the same, 28 June 1859.

P

I want you to consider for your own good (excuse my speaking so plainly), whether you can come back and throw yourself into our university life. All your friends here desire it and will receive you warmly; it seems to me hard that you should refuse them. There was a time when you might have had the world at your feet at Oxford, and I believe you may still. The present clamour might be dissipated by the publication of your lectures, but not so completely as by allowing your friends to state your intention of coming to reside among us.[44]

Liddell wrote with even greater bluntness.

The misfortune is that you take such a view of your Professorship as is contrary to men's wishes here and incompatible with their designs. They have introduced Law and History into the cycle of academical studies and have made no provision for having them taught, and they expect the Professor to lend a hand in the matter, and are angry because he does not. Very little would be said about lecturing if you shewed any interest in the place or its studies. I do not mean that you *feel* none, but certainly you do not manifest any. In fact, the friendly feeling with which you were at first received, and (I may add) would be received again has by your continual absence given way to a sullen discontent which will (I doubt not) vent itself if ever an opportunity occurs. It is useless to reason with these men, and I lament that things should be so, but that they are so I fully believe.[45]

Vaughan remained deaf to all appeals, and branded the movement in Council against him as due to 'rancorous hostility'. Nevertheless he announced a course of four lectures within a few days of the receipt of Jowett's letter, though he subsequently cancelled it in place of a series of eight lectures which were to be given in the following Easter term.

[44] B. Jowett to Vaughan, 23 Oct. [1857].
[45] H. G. Liddell to the same, 19 Nov. 1857. It no doubt added to Vaughan's sense of betrayal that, like Twisleton, Liddell had changed his mind on residence. When the statutes of the Latin Professor were under discussion in 1853, he had defended Vaughan's non-residence to Jeune with the words, 'that it might be two centuries or more, before they would again find a man either with your great qualities or with your peculiarities, and that, admitting those peculiarities to be as great as ever he chose to rate them I would beseech the university not to take any steps towards you which might end in your resignation, for that you were worth more to the university as you are than any one else I knew could be'. Liddell to Vaughan, 2 May 1853.

The announcement of the lectures silenced the critics in Council, or appeared to do so, but early in December a broadsheet was circulated containing a violent attack on Vaughan. It was entitled *Modern History and Regius Professors* and was signed 'Academicus'.[46] The identity of the author was never divulged. One of the main reasons for reviving the professoriate, he wrote, was that 'our less immediate studies' must depend largely on the professors, since, so it was said, it was impossible for colleges to teach history and physical science adequately. Most of the professors of physical science accordingly gave one or more terminal courses of lectures. Not so the Regius Professor of History, who had expressed himself with more feeling than anyone else on the professoriate. In the School of history a professor who did not reside, lectured very little and recently not at all was calamitous, and the question was how the university could claim lectures 'even from Regius Professors, as its distinct right'. The writer offered two suggestions. First, Council might consult the Commissioners or take legal advice. It was, he said, inconceivable that only four lectures should be given, and the argument that the professor was paid inadequately was dismissed on the grounds that for so few lectures coupled with non-residence he was paid too much. The second solution was for the colleges to which professorships were attached to insist on due residence and lectures, and such a provision should be made in the case of the connection about to be made with Oriel. If professors were allowed to draw Oxford salaries and reside in London, coming down occasionally to lecture, chairs would speedily become 'one of the less respectable sinecures of Patronage'.

Vaughan refused to reply to an anonymous critic, but in the following month 'Academicus' returned to the attack and repeated his charges, claiming that the question was not whether he wrote anonymously but whether his statements were true.[47] Vaughan made no further answer, and tendered his resignation to Lord Derby on 6 March 1858. It was accepted.

[46] The broadsheet is dated 8 Dec. 1857.
[47] The broadsheet is headed simply, *Oxford, January 25, 1858.*

Thus the man who above all others had been the champion of the professoriate retired from the university because of his refusal to discharge what were seen as the duties of a professor. But Vaughan had really championed what Wilson had described as 'studying professors', whereas what the university needed if it was to provide instruction in the infant School of Jurisprudence and History was a teaching professor. The two things were not necessarily opposed, but an important question of principle was involved, for in the circumstances of the time it was by no means certain where the balance of emphasis in the duties of the professor, whether in education or in learning, would eventually settle. The university placed it on education, Vaughan on learning. Vaughan himself never claimed to have resigned because of a question of principle, and the mixture of motives leading to his decision make it difficult to describe him as a martyr for his beliefs. Inflexibility of temperament and an aversion to Oxford, for reasons which cannot lightly be brushed aside, prevented him from combining teaching and study as other professors then and subsequently have done, and when he came to apply himself to study it was not to history but to philosophy that his energies were directed.

15. London Life and Marriage

THE demands and vexations of university life were the principal but not the only reason for Vaughan's unwillingness to reside in Oxford. London was his home. He had spent most of his life there, most of his friends lived there, and there can be little doubt that he found the social and intellectual atmosphere of the capital more congenial than the comparatively restricted and predominantly ecclesiastical society of Oxford. Twisleton lived nearby and Liddell was at Westminster. In 1843 he met Carlyle, who, though not usually well disposed to lawyers, took an immediate liking to him.[1] In 1850 he was proposed for membership of the Athenaeum and elected under rule II which allowed the election of a limited number of men of eminence in science, literature, the arts, and in public service. In the same year Thackeray was passed over.

It was while he was at the Athenaeum that there occurred an event which profoundly influenced his social and private life. His daughter relates that

> One day, when my father was a middle-aged man and was sitting in The Athenaeum he received a message to say that Mrs Prinsep (of whom he had never heard) was at the door in her carriage and wished to speak to him. There he found a charming lady, half English, half French, who insisted on carrying him off with her to her home on the then outskirts of London. Her salon was renowned for the painters, poets, and men of science who frequented it. She had heard of my father and was determined to draw him in, no matter how unconventionally.[2]

In this way Vaughan was enlisted or pressed into the Little Holland House circle.

---

[1] J. A. Froude, *Thomas Carlyle* (1897), i. 334.
[2] Recollections of Miss Emma Vaughan communicated to the author.

Little Holland House was a bucolic Bloomsbury. As Holland House had provided a salon for the political aristocracy, so did Little Holland House for the intellectual and artistic middle class. It stood symbolically in the grounds of Holland House, and was a long low structure with large wainscotted rooms and long passages. In 1804 the original house had been enlarged by connecting it to an adjacent farmhouse, and it became the home of Lord Holland's sister, Lady Caroline Fox, until her death in 1845. Five years later in 1850 a lease of twenty-one years was granted to Thoby Prinsep, who made it his home until 1874.[3] Thoby Prinsep had spent some thirty-five years of his life in India and had eventually become a director of the East India Company. He was a wealthy man and would have been wealthier if he had not spent large sums in a series of contested elections. He was, wrote Mrs. Twisleton, 'a great six footer, not fat, with a fair complexion, grey hair, and a good broad forehead and a generally sunny expression. He is a generous, affectionate person who appreciates his wife, and likes to have her do just as she pleases and to have everybody at their ease and at home in his house.'[4] Mrs. Prinsep was one of the seven daughters of James Pattle, of the Bengal Civil Service, who achieved the remarkable distinction of becoming known as 'the biggest liar in India'. He married a daughter of the Chevalier Antoine de l'Etang, a penurious French émigré who claimed to have been a page to Marie Antoinette. Of James Pattle's other daughters, most made what would be called good marriages. Virginia married the third Earl Somers, and Julia married C. H. Cameron, the Indian jurist, and as Julia Cameron is remembered as a photographer of great distinction. Yet another daughter, Maria, married John Jackson, professor of medicine at Calcutta Medical College, and an authority on tetanus and the anaesthetic effects of mesmerism, and another married General Mackenzie, an officer in the Indian army.[5]

[3] Lord Ilchester, *Chronicles of Holland House*, 1937, 444. Little Holland House was demolished about 1875 and the site is now occupied by Melbury Road. A second Little Holland House was built by Val Prinsep in Holland Park Road.

[4] *Letters of the Hon. Mrs Edward Twisleton*, (1925), 132.

[5] The remaining daughters married H. V. Bailey and J. W. Dalrymple.

The tone of Little Holland House was set by Mrs. Prinsep. She was described by Mrs. Twisleton as 'the greatest cordial you can imagine. I never saw such exuberant cheerfulness and beaming kindheartedness in anyone as her manners express—she is rather stout and not handsome, but delightful to look at, and the sort of person one would like to live under the shadow of, or rather bask in the sunlight of.'[6] Neither she nor her husband went out much in society but at home entertained many of the most distinguished men and women of the day, amongst them Thackeray, Tennyson, Ruskin, Grote, George Eliot, Herbert Spencer, Gladstone, and Meredith.[7] Burne-Jones convalesced there, and G. F. Watts was installed in a studio on the upper floor, and as 'a reward, paints nothing but idealized figures and faces of herself, and her sisters, and their children'.[8] It was at Little Holland House that Watts met Ellen Terry, who said that it was a paradise in which all the women were graceful and all the men gifted.[9]

The salon has flourished less in England than in France, and the fusion of social and intellectual society at Little Holland House was no doubt due in part to Mrs. Prinsep's French ancestry and childhood in Pondicherry. All the Pattle girls were well educated, and Thoby Prinsep provided the background of wealth and emancipation in which their talents could shine. They set the style of Little Holland House by their vitality, their lack of formality, their directness, their unaffected interest in their guests and friends. They provided a society which, in its freedom from the conventions which increasingly stifled Victorian social life, and 'that time of dread, the conventional Sunday of the early Victorian era', offered 'a breezy Bohemianism'.[10] The atmosphere was relaxed, much more so, Leslie Stephen recalled, than at Sir G. C. Lewis's where 'one had

6 *Letters of the Hon. Mrs Edward Twisleton* (1925), 108.

7 *The Shaving of Shagpat* was said to be partly the result of Thoby Prinsep's oriental discourses (Leslie Stephen's Mausoleum Book).

8 *Letters of the Hon. Mrs Edward Twisleton* (1925), 117. See also the lengthy description of Watts's studio and his decoration of the house.

9 *Victorian Photographs of Famous Men and Fair Women*, by J. M. Cameron, eds. Virginia Woolf and Roger Fry (1926), 2.

10 A. M. W. Stirling, *A Painter of Dreams* (1916), 299.

to be ready to discuss metaphysics or the principles of aesthetic philosophy and to be presented to George Eliot and offer an acceptable worship'.[11] Perhaps above all there was feminine company of a kind rarely found in the Victorian household. It was, as will sometimes happen, misunderstood on occasion, and Liddell relates that

> in an unlucky moment my wife gave to this curious establishment the name Agapemoné,—an institution formed in Somersetshire (I think) by a Mr. Prince, and intended as a refuge for gentlemen and ladies who desired to live in society without the trouble of housekeeping or marriage. Of course, this gave rise to scandals—whether deserved or not I know not. But this was enough. The appropriation of the name came to the ears of Mrs. Prinsep, who was extremely angry and gave all the gentlemen notice to quit.[12]

Vaughan was a frequent visitor at Little Holland House. He was regarded with much affection by the Prinseps, and there was no one, it was said, they loved or admired more.[13] Thoby Prinsep was the author of a book entitled *Tibet, Tartary and Mongolia: Their Social and Political Condition, and the Religion of Boodh*, and it was perhaps as a token of his esteem, which the recipient might well have been prepared to do without, that the far from euphonious nickname of 'Boodh' was conferred upon Vaughan, indicating, according to Julia Stephen, omniscience.[14] With Mrs. Prinsep's sister Maria Jackson, who lived near Vaughan at Well Walk in Hampstead from 1851 to 1855 before she moved to Brent Lodge, Hendon, a close friendship developed. A friend of Coventry Patmore, Woolner the sculptor, and Holman Hunt, she was 'a tall, striking person, who has been a great invalid, and lives in complete retirement. . . . She has been a great reader, and has the greatest refinement and charm of manner—very quiet, not like Mrs. Prinsep, but equally attractive, in another line.'[15]

---

[11] Leslie Stephen's Mausoleum Book.

[12] H. G. Liddell's recollections of Vaughan.

[13] *Letters of the Hon. Mrs Edward Twisleton* (1925), 132.

[14] The name was at least no worse than that of 'Sheepskin' by which Vaughan was known to Jowett.

[15] *Letters of the Hon. Mrs Edward Twisleton* (1925), 116.

It was a mark of her friendship for Vaughan that she went up to Oxford for almost all his lectures.

It was at this time that Vaughan became romantically attached to a young lady, or rather, if Liddell is to be believed, a young lady became attached to him. 'He told me, I remember', Liddell wrote, 'that it had been conveyed to him that a young lady had fallen in love with him—handsome, clever, rich and in every way a desirable match. He found, however, that the union would be distasteful to the parents, and with the high sense of honour that always distinguished him he did not respond to the invitation he had received. He did not, of course, tell me the name of the lady, nor did I ever hear it; but I understood that the family stood high in the social scale.'[16] There is little information to be gleaned about the affair in Vaughan's papers, but enough to suggest that Liddell was mistaken in some particulars. The lady appears to have been Maria Farquhar, the sister of Sir W. R. Farquhar, with whom she lived at 18 King Street, Westminster. She was twenty-five years old. A letter from Vaughan survives in which he reproaches her for failing to announce their engagement as had been agreed between them, 'leaving Lady Farquhar a reasonable time to reconcile herself to our union'. If Maria made the first overtures, as Liddell recalled, she now began to have second thoughts in the face of Lady Farquhar's opposition, and, so it would seem, because of a disparity of wealth, and Vaughan noted a cooling off in her affections. 'You have caused me perplexity', he wrote in a tone more minatory than amatory, 'and doubt as to your affections, and doubt as to your wishes, and even doubt as to your simplicity of mind and our eventual happiness. Such a state is one of torment.' The engagement was never announced, and the lovers parted.

Almost immediately after the rupture with Maria Farquhar, Vaughan married Adeline Maria Jackson, the daughter of his old friend Maria Jackson. The ceremony took place at Hendon on 21 August 1856, and was performed by Liddell. Adeline was then eighteen years old and Vaughan forty-five. Goldwin Smith expressed the surprise of Vaughan's friends when he remarked

---

16 H. G. Liddell's recollections of Vaughan.

that the marriage was 'the most startling event of the kind since the marriage of Luther'.[17] At the time of her marriage, Adeline was a very pretty and engaging young woman,[18] but her life with Vaughan, particularly in his later years which were dogged by ill health and disappointment, cannot have been easy. Leslie Stephen, who was no admirer of Vaughan, remarked that Vaughan thought better of Carlyle's conduct than most when the *Reminiscences* were published, and that he could hardly be expected to condemn Carlyle's behaviour to Mrs. Carlyle in view of his own towards Adeline. Stephen, writing at the time of his own wife's death and resentful of what he regarded as Vaughan's selfish self-absorption at the time of Adeline's, described the marriage in terms of unusual bitterness.

This strange, self willed, proud recluse [he wrote] absorbed in his futile studies, barely sane in one direction and yet managing all his own affairs, sensibly enough I was told, keeping everything in his hands and ruling his family autocratically, was idolized by his gentle wife, who retained her belief in the genius of the man to whom she had looked up from her marriage at an early age. She was as devoted to him as my Julia was to me. Alas! I fear that her reward was a poor one. He was not, I believe, unkind; only wayward and crotchety; but he accepted her devotion as his due; frankly regarding himself as a superior being and rarely unbent or condescended to caress her.[19]

Adeline bore two sons, Henry Beauchamp and William Wya-mar, and four daughters, Augusta, Margaret, Millicent, and Emma, all of whom were christened at the Halford family seat at Wistow. Henry Beauchamp died in infancy, and William Wyamar, whose birth his father in a fit of absent-mindedness omitted to register, became a distinguished headmaster of Rugby. Of the daughters, Millicent married Sir Vere Isham, eleventh Baronet, and Augusta one Robert Croft—a marriage 'not very gratifying to anybody except, I hope, the Crofts themselves'.[20]

By his marriage, Vaughan entered a remarkable family circle.

---

[17] G. Smith to H. G. Liddell, 15 Aug. 1856. Christ Church Archives. MS. Estates 117, f. 22ᵛ.

[18] H. G. Liddell's recollections of Vaughan.

[19] Leslie Stephen's Mausoleum Book.   [20] Ibid.

His father-in-law Dr. John Jackson had two other daughters. One of them, Mary Louisa, married Herbert Fisher, who tutored the Prince of Wales at Oxford, and was the father of Admiral Sir William Fisher, of H. A. L. Fisher the historian and Warden of New College, and of Florence who married the historian F. W. Maitland. His other daughter Julia married first a barrister named Herbert Duckworth, who died young, and secondly Leslie Stephen—whose first wife was Thackeray's daughter—and was the mother of Virginia Woolf. Vaughan's son William Wyamar married a daughter of J. A. Symonds, and was the father of Dame Janet Vaughan, Principal of Somerville College.

After the stimulating society of Little Holland House, with the inmates of which he was now connected by marriage, Oxford had few attractions for Vaughan, and in weighing the reasons for his resignation in 1858 it may be assumed that his marriage had no inconsiderable influence.

16. Public Schools Commission

1861

VAUGHAN'S last contribution to education was made when in 1861 he became a member of the Royal Commission appointed by Lord Palmerston to inquire into the state of the public schools. Sir M. E. Grant Duff, who had actively pressed for the commission, has related some of the circumstances leading up to its appointment and the invitation to Vaughan.

All through this spring [he wrote] I was much occupied in urging the expediency of a Royal Commission to inquire into the Public Schools, circulating a paper of reasons in favour of it to all members of the House of Commons, and communicating with Northcote, the two Russells, the Head Masters of Harrow and Rugby, etc., besides Gladstone and Sir George Lewis, who were the members of the Government who took most interest in the matter. After much negotiation all ended amicably, and the Commission was issued. It was in connection with this matter that I went with William Spottiswoode one day to see Mr. Halford Vaughan, who was then living at Hampstead. He showed us, I recollect, a copy of Euripides, which had belonged to Milton, with manuscript notes in the poet's own hand.[1]

On 15 June a formal invitation was sent to Vaughan by the Home Secretary, Sir G. C. Lewis. The commission to which he was thus appointed was composed of men of great and in some instances of outstanding ability. At its head was the Earl of Clarendon (Cornewall Lewis's brother-in-law), and with him the Earl of Devon, Lord Lyttelton, Sir Stafford Northcote, W. H. Thompson, and Edward Twisleton. Lyttleton, who, within a month of the announcement of the commission, was voicing

---

[1] Sir M. E. Grant Duff, *Notes from a Diary, 1851–72* (1897), i. 157.

his doubt whether it could ever reach unanimity, wrote to his brother-in-law Gladstone, 'Northcote and Lord Devon are the only Commissioners who seem to me unexceptionable. Thompson is indolent, though very able and philosophical. Vaughan (exceedingly clear) and Twisleton are rather crotchety, especially on religious questions.'[2]

The commission was appointed to inquire into the finances, administration, and studies of Eton, Winchester, Westminster, Charterhouse, St. Paul's, Merchant Taylors', Harrow, Rugby, and Shrewsbury Schools, and it took additional evidence from Marlborough, Wellington, Cheltenham, and the City of London School. None of these schools was in a state of decay or decline. On the contrary, as places of education they were among the leading schools of the day, and all of them were or had recently been presided over by headmasters of exceptional ability. The number of public schools was rapidly increasing, however, and it was as much the object of the commission to present a body of detailed information which might be drawn upon by them as to suggest changes which would make both the old and the new schools more serviceable to the middle class. If the schools were to supply enough men trained for the needs of the Civil and Colonial Services, the army, and the universities, it was necessary to broaden the basis of studies and to raise the general standard of attainment. Although the public schools stood less in need of reform than the universities had done a decade earlier, the Public Schools and the Oxford and Cambridge Commissions pursued similar educational objects. Both sought to open their respective institutions more widely to the middle class, to encourage merit and reward intelligence rather than to assist indigence, to extend the curriculum, and to remove obstacles which stood in the way of these goals.

Vaughan was well qualified to serve on the commission. His experience in connection with the Oxford University commission had made him familiar with the educational problems of schools and universities, and it was indicative of his public reputation on

2 Add. MS. 44239, f. 159.

such matters, which stood higher outside Oxford than within it, that he was invited in 1854 to address the Royal Institution on the state of education in the upper, middle, and lower classes. He had declared his belief in the importance of broadening the basis of education, particularly by the inclusion of natural science, and his effort to encourage scientific studies in schools was without doubt one of his most important contributions to the proceedings of the commission. He threw himself with enthusiasm into its work, and gave up as much as he could of his legal duties. He was regular in his attendance, and questioned witnesses frequently and often in considerable detail. The whole of the account of Rugby, his own school, and part of that of Winchester were written by him.

Because he saw the schools as the nurseries of the universities, the one commencing the education which the other continued, Vaughan applied many of the principles he had advocated at the time of the Oxford commission. He pressed,[3] for example, the award of scholarships by open competition, and argued against the restriction of places on the foundation of schools such as Rugby to the children of local residents. He produced the scheme for reorganizing the Governing Bodies, a conspicuous feature of which was the nomination of some of the governors by the Crown. The anticlericalism which had previously contributed so largely to his belief in university government by an oligarchy of professors figured in his recommendation that the supreme authority in schools should be vested in lay governors. To Lord Clarendon he wrote:

I venture to express a hope that Government will not unnecessarily abandon the ground taken up as to maintaining the Governors of Schools in the Supreme Authority which the constitution of nearly all the Schools and the Bill itself as now framed give to them. One consideration on this point out of many I would urge. I am not suspicious of the English clergy—nor indeed distrustful of their liberality and good sense on the whole—but is not the intelligent laity of the Upper Classes of society to have any voice either direct or indirect, either in exercise or in *reserve* as to the principles in which their

[3] P.R.O. H.O. 73/57.

sons are to be taught or the discipline to which they are to be subjected in Public Schools. The Clergy supplies all the Head Masters. The laity appears only in the governing bodies and therein not exclusively.[4]

Lyttelton wrote admiringly of Vaughan's labours to Gladstone, qualifying his praise with a note of criticism which the latter would no doubt ruefully have recognized, 'Of all the wonders of laborious industry, fertility of thought, and subtlety of expression, your old friend Vaughan is about the greatest I ever knew, but his practical wisdom is not commensurate. His Rugby Report, which is not yet finished, will be read by few, but it is a writing sui generis and quite a marvel of elaborate and minute statement and investigation.'[5]

Vaughan's views on the reform of the curriculum, and particularly on the teaching of natural science, are of enduring interest. Except at Rugby, science was either not taught at all in the schools which came under the commission's view, or occupied a position subordinate to music and drawing, the traditional Cinderellas of education. At Charterhouse and Winchester a few lectures were given, and at Harrow a prize was awarded though there was no teaching in the subject, and at none of these schools was a boy's progress influenced by his ability in scientific studies. At Shrewsbury, Kennedy had established beside the classical education given by the school a non-classical education, chiefly for the benefit of the townspeople, but science formed no part of it. Science had been introduced at Rugby by Tait in 1849, and was studied voluntarily in the Middle and Upper School as an alternative to modern languages. In general, the headmasters examined by the commission were hostile to the teaching of science, and unwilling to concede that it had much educational value. When asked whether physical sciences were not valuable as mental discipline, George Moberly, the Headmaster of Winchester, replied, 'As a matter of education and training of the mind, which is our particular duty as instructors, I do not feel the value of them.'[6] Even at

4 Vaughan to Lord Clarendon, 1 May 1865.
5 Add. MS. 44239, f. 235.
6 *Public Schools Commission* (1864), iii, Evidence, pt. 1 345.

Rugby, where science had a firmer foothold, Temple considered
that its value fell far below that of classics, and the following
exchange, illuminating for the ideas of both of them, occurred
between him and Vaughan:

VAUGHAN: You consider that neither mathematics nor physical science
touch the strictly human part of our nature. Do you not think that
they tend to produce many wholesome moral emotions? I am speaking now of natural science, such, for instance, as wonder and
admiration at the order of the world and so forth?

TEMPLE: I think that in the present state of civilisation, physical science
to a very great extent tends to cultivate and refine all the emotions
connected with the love of order and beauty; but I think that it never
rises to touch the sense of personality or responsibility, the sense of
being yourself a person and having to deal with other persons.

VAUGHAN: Do you not think that the contemplation of the physical
laws of the universe tends to produce a high degree of awe and
admiration, and, of course, so far as that is connected with the
workmanship of an Omnipotent Being that it tends to produce
feelings towards Him of a very high order?

TEMPLE: I think physical science does that very much, and that is what
I meant by speaking of it as cultivating the love of order and beauty,
which rapidly leads to a sense of religion; but I do not think it can
be compared for one moment in the power of cultivating those
emotions, with the body of literature . . .

VAUGHAN: Do you think that in any point of view literary studies
produce that state of admiration and awe, and so far of worship,
which physical science tends to produce? Do you think it brings
before the mind works and evidences of a nature to produce the
same moral emotions, or in the same degree?

TEMPLE: The study of literature appears to me to cover almost all
that physical science could cover, and very much more besides.
There is hardly anything you will find in physical science, which
you will not find in different departments of literature. There is no
sense of awe or love of beauty which you will not find, I think, more
powerfully brought to bear on the mind from the study of poetry
even than from the study of any science.[7]

[7] *Public Schools Commission* (1864), iv, Evidence, pt. 2, 270.

Temple concluded his evidence by assenting to the proposition that 'classical attainment necessarily involves a greater knowledge of the laws of the intellect and of the human mind than scientific attainment'. Vaughan dissented strongly from this view. A good classical scholar himself, he believed in the value of classical studies, but he opposed the predominant and exclusive position they occupied in the schools and universities, and held that the humanities and the sciences ought to go hand in hand, each complementing the other. In the Public Schools Commission he continued the campaign for a wider definition of a liberal education which had been one of the central issues in the dispute between him and Pusey. The classical scholars who doubted the value of science were equalled by the scientists who were sceptical of the value of classics. Vaughan sought to heal the growing breach between the disciplines by asserting that all knowledge was a unity, and he applied his belief with considerable ingenuity to the principal purpose of education, which was the training of the mind. The manner in which he set about the task avoided sterile arguments based on utility and met the objection of the headmasters that any great extension of the curriculum was impossible without injury to the classics. Vaughan argued in essence that different kinds of mental discipline were appropriate at different stages of mental development, and that in the structure of education the sciences and humanities were locked together like an intellectual jigsaw.

The first step was to demolish the exclusive claims made for the study of languages. In his minority report to the commission he remarked,

Language has been already in our earliest years mainly the object, and almost exclusively the instrument of instruction. Languages have been studied in and for themselves; ideas have been formed and conveyed mainly through language, as well as by language compared, reasoned on, and connected. Facts have been represented, opinions and judgments have been communicated and determined through words, objects so far realized at all have been realized chiefly through words. There has been no want of intellectual activity, nor of intellectual discipline of one kind. But in minds so trained as well negatively as positively, this verbal and ideal education has had its effect, not in all respects advantageous. Of the objects, properties, and laws of the material world among educated men, there has prevailed too general an ignorance. Of the senses as direct instruments for the perception of truth and acquisition of knowledge, there has been a too prevalent disuse, ending in loss of activity and power. Even the purely intellectual powers, the memory, the imagination, and the judgment, having been stimulated, directed, and confined by words, have been affected by the verbal instruments and objects with which they have been so largely and exclusively occupied.[8]

Vaughan held that classics and science not only provided mental disciplines of different kinds, but were suitably studied at different ages according to the stage of development of the faculties. He had advanced this argument as early as 1852, when he stated that

the years of education between seven and twenty-one should be in some degree methodically distributed and allotted to the different studies of which the whole educational course is to consist. It seems advisable that a certain order should be preserved—that the compulsory prosecution of a certain class of subjects should be brought to a close before the whole instruction is finished—and that a certain other class of subjects should be taken up when the former is relinquished . . . I am far from laying down that the study of the natural world ought necessarily to *follow* that of the ancient languages. I do not contend now for any particular order, but it seems quite necessary that some should be commenced before others; and, indeed, that some should be advanced almost to completeness before others are entered on.[9]

He developed his ideas a stage further in *Oxford Reform and Oxford Professors*, where he attacked the premature study of grammar 'before the powers of reflexion are nearly strong enough to master and appropriate its principles, which are of a nature highly abstract'.[10] The result was often mechanical learning by rote without understanding. There was, he said,

no study which could prove more successful in producing often through idleness and vacancy of mind, parrot repetition, and sing-song

[8] *Public Schools Commission* (1864), i. 332. See also *Oxford Reform and Oxford Professors* (1854), 27.

[9] *Report of the Oxford University Commission* (1852), Evidence, 84.

[10] *Oxford Reform and Oxford Professors* (1854), 28.

knowledge,—to the abeyance and destruction of the intellectual powers, —as well as to the loss and paralysis of the outward senses,—than our traditional study and idolatry of language. Thinking as highly as a rational being can of the discipline which may be given to good natural faculties, well ripened, by linguistic studies, I protest against the one assumption—not uncommon—that no other studies could minister a discipline to the reason.

In his minority report Vaughan elaborated his argument. Drawing on evidence supplied by Hooker and Faraday he maintained that between the ages of eight and twelve the study of natural science developed the faculties of observation and reasoning. At that age the mental faculties were better sharpened by material objects than by abstract thought. In order to make way for the study of science in the curriculum, it was necessary to sacrifice other studies, but which studies and how were they to be determined? Every subject, he said, possessed two distinct kinds of educational value—its disciplinary power as an intellectual exercise and its utility and applicability as an acquisition. Any single language had both characteristics, but, the structure of all languages being basically the same, any additional language after the first was only of educational value from the point of view of utility. Since mathematics and science possessed value as discipline and as acquisition, room for their study might best be found by omitting some language, and the only question therefore was which language ought to be retained. Vaughan gave the preference to Latin because of its value for the teaching of grammar and its relationship to the tradition of European culture.

But Vaughan's theory of the different stages of mental development allowed him to introduce science without the permanent sacrifice of languages. Turning to the study of Greek, French, and German, he remarked:

One of the languages might be deferred for five or even six years, without fear that the temporary omission need involve any sacrifice of it eventually. If begun comparatively late, it would be commenced with all the advantages of an intellect matured by age, developed by kindred studies, freed from the demands of many other concurrent and distracting studies in subjects quite unknown, and in the case of able and industrious youths stimulated by the novelty and the interests of a more intelligent curiosity. Such conditions would in themselves go far to compensate for the later start and the apparent loss of time which it involves. Four years of concentrated study begun at such a period, and extending through the very prime of a student's life (so far as the powers of acquisition are concerned), if well bestowed, ought to give a fair degree of scholarship in any language commonly studied at school.[11]

When the study of Latin grammar had been mastered, French, being based on Latin, might follow, but Greek should be postponed until the difficulties of both languages had been overcome. A boy of 12 might be required to study Latin and French, arithmetic and natural science. At 14, having mastered Latin and advanced well in French, he might commence the vigorous study of Greek, remitting his attention to Latin and French, and continuing with the same amount of arithmetical and scientific studies as before. The schoolboy thus arrived at the university with a thorough liberal education prepared for the more specialized studies to follow.

Had Vaughan not disagreed with one of the commission's recommendations, he would not have had occasion to write his minority report setting out his educational ideas. The disagreement occurred over the provision for the study of science. The members of the commission were almost unanimously well disposed to scientific studies, Twisleton and Lyttelton enthusiastically so. But faced by the opposition of the headmasters to any diminution of the pre-eminence of classical studies, they recommended in the Report that the study of classical languages should be the basis of education, and confined themselves to condemning the exclusion of natural science as 'a plain defect and a great practical evil' which ought to be rectified. Vaughan objected that this was inconsistent with the recommendation that there should be an entrance examination in classics, arithmetic, and French or German. Not only, he maintained, would preparatory schools ignore a subject not required for the entrance

[11] *Public Schools Commission* (1864), i. 336.

examination, but when admitted boys would frequently prefer to continue studies in which they had received instruction rather than embark on new. The solution he urged was either to drop the recommendation altogether or to admit natural science as a further option at the entrance examination.

Vaughan fought hard for his amendment and in May 1863 proposed that any general principles applicable to all schools should be approved by the vote of the whole commission. Having been defeated, he drew up his minority report, and insisted, much to the annoyance of Lord Clarendon, who referred to him as 'the intolerable Vaughan',[12] on inserting footnotes in the Report directing attention to it. His efforts were largely wasted, and neither of the main reviews in the *Quarterly* and the *Edinburgh Review* referred to him.

Vaughan's contribution to educational theory does not rest simply on his recognition of the value of natural science, which had other equally persuasive advocates. What distinguishes him is the breadth and coherence of his view of education. The unity of knowledge which was expressed by classical studies in the sixteenth century had been shattered by the scientific revolution of the later Renaissance, and in the nineteenth century was further fragmented under the influence of utilitarianism. Vaughan believed that it was possible to restore unity by combining the humanities and sciences in a truly liberal education. All his writings on education distinguish between education and knowledge, and it was by the application of this distinction that he was able to justify his belief and to point the way to its practical realization. His educational theory had a moral basis. Most of his intellectual life was devoted to the exploration of man's moral nature, and his inquiries led him to investigate the basis of ideas in language and observed phenomena, the generalization of ideas, the formation of judgement, all of which combined to express man's conception of morality. Education sought the same end, and its purpose was not to instil facts—though he recognized a utilitarian element in it—but to train the mind and discipline the faculties to form judgements and to discriminate between facts, whereby

[12] Add. MS. 50036, f. 133.

the intellectual foundation of morals was revealed. The humanities and the sciences were equally important in education because they provided different but complementary methods of achieving this end. The relationship of both disciplines to a common end enabled him to distinguish between their suitability for study at the various stages of development of the child's mind. It was a fertile line of thought which in 1864 he could do no more than sketch in outline.

It was the opinion of H. A. L. Fisher, who as a former President of the Board of Education was well qualified to speak on the subject, that Vaughan's most outstanding work was done on the Public Schools Commission.[13] But English education did not follow the lines indicated by him. The Public Schools Commission missed its opportunity, and the dichotomy between the humanities and sciences remained. As facts became more numerous, attention was devoted less to the training of the mind than to the acquisition of knowledge, a development which Vaughan would have regarded as destructive of the idea of a liberal education.

[13] I owe this illuminating comment to Sir Gyles Isham.

Epilogue

IN 1867, his exhausting labours on the Public Schools Commission concluded, Vaughan moved from London to Upton Castle in Pembrokeshire. It was to be his home from which he seldom stirred, except on matters of legal business, until his death in 1885. The parish of Upton is situated three and a half miles from Pembroke, and in 1840 had a population of six souls. Despite his interest in the Welsh language and history, the choice of this remote part of the country was probably dictated rather by its convenience for the discharge of his duties as Clerk of Assize on the South Wales circuit and by the mildness of the climate which suited his precarious health than by any sentimental consideration of supposed Welsh ancestry. The castle, which he rented from J. Tasker Evans, stands on an elevated site above the creek of Milford Haven, and its ancient gateway and bastions were incorporated into the house. From it there was a superb view over the green rolling countryside, and Vaughan used to tell his children that they might travel the world over without seeing anything so truly beautiful as Upton and its setting. Here he lived the life of a country gentleman, surrounded by his books, engaged in desultory and ineffectual farming, and in the evening playing his violin to a not always appreciative family. It is not difficult to picture him in the 'good strong velveteen shooting jacket with old fashioned pockets holding a little game and buttoning up to the chin', which he purchased soon after his arrival. Vaughan was not gregarious by temperament and the empty Pembrokeshire countryside suited him, though for his young wife, separated from the vital society of Little Holland House, rural society may well have been more than a little dull.

It was a strange life that we led in that old Welsh castle [his daughter recalls], completely isolated from our relations and the

friends of our parents. To children of the present day it would seem
to be intolerably monotonous. In those days of no motor cars, no
bicycles, no telephones, it was terribly remote. The nearest railway
was four miles away, a distance that would be easily overcome
nowadays. We had no carriage of our own. If calls had to be paid or
the railway reached, a landau and pair of horses were ordered from the
county town. My father being a great deal older than my mother,
judged things by very old-fashioned standards. Not being well enough
off to keep a carriage complete with coachman and footman, he
would tolerate nothing else. He would have thought it highly
improper for his daughters to be seen driving themselves about the
country lanes in a pony-carriage. Things had to be done in state or
not at all.[1]

Very occasionally Vaughan entertained on a lavish scale. 'For
months and years my parents would live in almost complete
seclusion and then suddenly my father would decide on an almost
devastating exhibition of hospitality. The whole of the country
would be invited, a regimental band invoked, refreshments—
to include most marvellous ices—would be sent from Gunter's.'[2]

There can be little doubt that one of the principal motives
for Vaughan's retirement to the inaccessible countryside of
Pembrokeshire was his hope that the freedom from interruption
and the claims of friendship which it afforded would enable him
to complete the metaphysical work which had come to dominate
his intellectual life. Considerable fragments of this work survive,
but it was never completed for reasons which perhaps can now
never be fully explained. He began to work on it before he
accepted the chair of modern history and it continued to occupy
him until about 1880, and the greater part of the remaining
manuscript was composed at Upton. At first he made good
progress, and in a draft will, found among papers dated 1840–50
and certainly written before his marriage in 1856, he bequeathed
all his 'goods, chattels, and property whatsoever' in trust to
Twisleton and Liddell for its publication. Jowett believed that
one of the causes of his resignation was the desire to complete it,

[1] Recollections of Miss Emma Vaughan communicated to the author.
[2] Ibid.

but the Public Schools Commission subsequently took up so much of his time that he was obliged to put it aside until he settled at Upton.

The subject of the work was the causes of man's moral nature. Liddell, who was one of the few people to see any part of the manuscript, wrote that 'while he [Vaughan] was at Hampstead, he undertook a treatise, of which I forget the exact title, but the subject was the Development of Moral Character in Man. He read me portions of it, and I thought it most striking. He began with earliest traits of what is now called Anthropology, and traced the ascent of man's mind to the "Moral Sublime", as expressed in the life of Jesus Christ.'[3] The unfinished state of the work permits only tentative conclusions to be drawn of Vaughan's intentions, but he seems, taking as his starting point the writings of the eighteenth century English moralists, to have endeavoured to explain morality without recourse to religious revelation. In a letter to Stanley, conjecturally dated 1846, Jowett wrote that 'He looks upon morality as having its roots in pleasure and pain, the flower which it bears being the work of imagination or reflection on those first impressions. His great object seemed to be to find out the origin of our moral ideas—looking for them, however, only in the individual, not in the history of the world.'[4] As the work progressed, Vaughan broadened the individualistic basis of his philosophy as described by Jowett, and in his philosophical studies as in his historical the influence of Hume steadily diminished. The study of history had a profound influence on him, and caused him to seek the origins of morality in society rather than in the individual, and the study of natural science led him to seek the origins of society before the dawn of history. His aims and methods were perhaps not dissimilar to those found in J. M. Wilson and T. Fowler's *Progressive Morality* published in 1886 and 1887, and it is possibly significant of this connection that while he was still professor Vaughan became so alarmed on hearing that Liddell had communicated to Wilson 'views which

---

[3] H. G. Liddell's recollections of Vaughan.

[4] *Life and Letters of Benjamin Jowett*, eds. E. Abbott and L. Campbell (1897) i. 123.

I had on two occasions communicated to him' that he wrote a
lengthy letter to Wilson in which he remarked

Under these circumstances therefore if it should turn out that you
published on this subject and that your publication contained principles
identical with mine it would naturally occur to me that owing to our
mutual intimacy with Liddell I had lost the advantage of apparent
originality and priority in the entertainment of opinions emanating
from myself. . . . From something which Liddell has let fall I am
inclined to think that you may be entertaining the idea of publishing
on the same subject . . . and for the reasons which I have mentioned
I hope that you may not have made up your mind to do so.[5]

Wilson's work was eventually printed in 1875 but not published
until after Vaughan's death.

The extensive remains of Vaughan's work consist of lengthy
passages, often dated and in more than one version, and with
some sections transcribed by his amanuensis George Rigby,
concerning the nature of ideas, and in particular language,
memory, judgement, and the generalization and classification of
ideas.[6] Although he spent at least thirty years of his life on it, and
a large part of that time without other major intellectual preoccu-
pations, no part was ever published. An explanation of Vaughan's
reticence in this respect was given by Leslie Stephen, who as the
husband of his sister-in-law might be supposed to be well informed. In his life of Vaughan in the *Dictionary of National
Biography* he wrote, 'A good deal was written, when unexplained
accidents happened to the manuscript; and for whatever reasons,
it was never completed.' Behind this bald statement, with its hint
of matters undisclosed, lay a drama of tragi-comic calamities. At
intervals so frequent that even Vaughan lost count of them
large sections of the work vanished. The mishap which overtook
Carlyle's manuscript of the *French Revolution* was as nothing

---

[5] Vaughan to J. M. Wilson, n.d. Fowler paid tribute to Vaughan's influence
on him when in the introduction to *The Principles of Morality* (1886), vi, he wrote,
'No University Professor during my own undergraduate career, unless it was the
late Professor H. H. Vaughan, exercised so powerful an influence in Oxford
[as Wilson].'

[6] Bodleian Library MSS. Eng. misc. c. 364–73.

compared with the constant bereavements suffered by Vaughan. The first reference to a loss occurred in 1857 when Arthur Butler heard that an octavo volume of manuscript, 'a portion of the work which has been announced as forthcoming', had disappeared through the dishonesty or carelessness of a servant.[7] Two years later Vaughan told Conington that he had suffered the loss of a quarter of the book by two acts of spoliation in the previous two years. But worse was to come. In 1881 he informed Lord Selborne that substantial losses had taken place in 1867, 1871, 1875, and 1879–80.[8]

An examination of the remains of the work throws little light on the extent of these losses. Considerable sections, including one of over 300 foolscap pages, appear to be complete, but in the absence of a plan of the intended scope of the work it is not possible to determine what parts are missing. When he examined the manuscript at Vaughan's death, Leslie Stephen found that 'Nearly all that I read was in the nature of an attempt to write the opening chapter, written and rewritten and written over again; but I could not even make out what was their drift or guess at the main purpose of the book.'[9] The only definite evidence on the nature of the supposed losses was provided by Vaughan himself, who in 1872 offered a reward of £25 for the return of papers on 'the nature and construction of the logical forms of judgment, and . . . upon language generally, particularly in reference to the expression of the logical forms of judgment'. That the losses were great is suggested by their frequency and by Vaughan's remark to Lord Selborne that 'the bulk in each instance was too great not to suggest that the writings were for some purpose deliberately and carefully kept by me'.[10] Carefully kept they certainly were. While Vaughan lived at Hampstead they were stored at the head of his bed in a locked box which he always took with him when he went on circuit, and at Upton they were kept in a locked bookcase in the library, which adjoined the

---

[7] A. G. Butler to Vaughan, 31 May 1857.
[8] Lambeth Palace Library MS. 1867, f. 219.
[9] Leslie Stephen's Mausoleum Book.
[10] Lambeth Palace Library MS. 1867, f. 235.

insomniac Vaughan's bedroom.[11] He was firmly convinced that the losses were due to the deliberate malignity of his servants, and suspected 'one constant plot to appropriate or destroy'.[12] To Lord Selborne he wrote, 'All I *believe* to have been done by maid-servants—the motives doubtful and perhaps mixed.'[13] Liddell has recorded the circumstances of one such loss as related by Vaughan. 'One day, it seems, he left it [the box] unlocked, and the next time that he had occasion to examine the contents he found that a large number of the sheets were missing. He attri-buted the loss to the spite of a housemaid, with whom he had found fault.'[14] In 1873 Vaughan tried without success to obtain a warrant to search the home of Jane Shears, the daughter of a smith in Pembroke dockyard, who had been dismissed and whose baggage was searched by him before she left Upton. In 1881 he wrote to another former servant, Marianne Edwards, accusing her of having stolen 'very nearly' all the contents of the drawer in the library in which the manuscript was kept. 'You had before leaving', he wrote, 'made a demand on me for money, in order, you said, to pay something which you had promised to young Davies. Not seeing the reasonableness of this demand I declined to pay it.'

It is possible that one of these disasters was caused by the negligence or malice of a servant, but it is scarcely credible that all of them could have been so without assuming a state of endemic revolution in the Vaughan ménage. If, on the other hand, the losses were not caused by servants, it is difficult to see what other explanation there could be for them, assuming them to have occurred at all, save that Vaughan himself was directly respon-sible. Leslie Stephen had no doubt that this was the case,[15] and it was suggested with great delicacy by Osmund Priaulx who wondered whether Vaughan might have caused the losses by sleep-walking (perhaps when sleep had been induced by pressing the carotid artery as Priaulx had proposed).[16] That Vaughan

[11] H. G. Liddell's recollections of Vaughan; Vaughan to Marianne Edwards, 20 Oct. 1881.

[12] Lambeth Palace Library MS. 1867, f. 236ᵛ.

[13] Ibid., f. 236.   [14] Recollections of Vaughan.

[15] Mausoleum Book.   [16] O. Priaulx to Vaughan, 18 Aug. 1873.

sincerely believed his own explanation cannot be doubted. It is not consistent with what is known of him that he would have perpetrated a saga of lies spread over twenty-five years and more, or that he would have sought to bring police proceedings against a servant whom he knew to be innocent. There are, however, some grounds for supposing that during the Upton period Vaughan suffered from delusions of an irrational character. In 1881 he reported the loss not only of the inevitable section of his philosophical manuscript, but also the manuscript of a course of historical lectures he had prepared at Oxford. To Lord Selborne he disclosed his suspicion that it had been stolen at the instigation of Freeman, A. W. Haddan, Mountague Bernard, or even Stubbs. The motive was plagiary and the evidence had been destroyed to conceal the plagiary. This was a strange charge to level against such distinguished historians, and was not sustained nor could be by any evidence, but against Freeman, Haddan, and Stubbs Vaughan had real or imaginary grievances of long standing—if Bernard had offended the cause is now unknown. Taken with the accusations against servants of theft, the episode may be thought to hint at some kind of persecution mania.

The most likely explanation of Vaughan's losses is either that he caused them himself but could not bring himself to accept the fact, or that no losses actually occurred and that the periods when the thefts were alleged to have taken place were times when Vaughan found himself intellectually unable to proceed with the work. If this is true, the supposed losses were a scapegoat in which Vaughan needed to believe.

Although this must be supposition, there is some reason to believe that Vaughan never expected to complete the work. Leslie Stephen once wrote to him, 'I rather wonder (if I may venture to say so) that you do not put some of it at least beyond the reach of such misfortunes by having it printed.'[17] Vaughan considered doing so on at least three occasions, but in every case posthumously. The first occasion has already been mentioned and occurred in the will made before his marriage. In 1861 he made another will leaving the sum of £300 to a competent

17 L. Stephen to Vaughan, 23 May 1882.

person to undertake publication. In 1872 he wrote a memorandum appointing J. M. Wilson to publish 'my philosophical work on "the intellectual system" . . . even as a fragment' in case he should not live to do so himself. It would, he said, comprise four octavo volumes, of which two were already transcribed by his amanuensis, and a further volume and a half were ready for transcription.[18] In view of Vaughan's symptoms of hypochondria this repeated provision for posthumous publication may signify no more than unfounded intimations of mortality, but it may also reflect the early conviction that the work would never be finished even given the longevity usually accorded to valetudinarians. It is at least remarkable that with so much of the work apparently completed in 1872 Vaughan should have taken no steps to publish any part of it if he seriously intended publication to take place at all.

The evidence of the wills is not the only ground for suspecting that Vaughan may have found completion of the work difficult. The subject was of such complexity that it would have been remarkable had there not been periods when avenues of inquiry proved fruitless or the scope and design in need of revision. This was Vaughan's experience, and although his accounts of the changes occasioned by the alleged thefts are contradictory they establish some coincidence in time between the thefts and large-scale recasting of the design of the work. In a letter to J. A. Froude in 1872, he referred to recent losses and added that 'So long as ten years ago I had all but finished another manuscript in part the same but *on a plan rather more comprehensive*.'[19] But in 1881 it

[18] This document was written on 20 Aug. 1872. In his account to Lord Selborne of his losses, Vaughan mentions a loss in 1871 but not in 1872. If the date of the letter is correct it is surprising to find the manuscript so well advanced a year later. Vaughan makes no mention of a loss in 1873, in the May of which year he tried to procure a search warrant against Jane Shears. This loss may have taken place in a previous year—in the handbill offering a reward Vaughan says all the lost papers were dated prior to 1872. If this theft, in view of its alleged gravity, occurred as early as 1871 it is even more remarkable that so much of the manuscript was ready for publication. If it occurred in 1872 it is equally remarkable that it did so so soon after the manuscript had reached such an advanced stage of readiness that Vaughan was making provision for its publication.

[19] Vaughan to J. A. Froude, 23 Jan. 1872. My italics.

appears from a letter to Lord Selborne that far from the earlier manuscript having been more comprehensive than the later, the reverse was the case. 'In the case of my philosophical writings', he wrote, 'I at first tried to lessen the sense of loss by somewhat enlarging the plan or details of the work, but this had the effect of making the scheme more voluminous and so subjecting the work to more chances of spoliation as well by its greater size as by the longer lapse of time in reaching a conclusion, and it has so turned out that while finishing the last portions I have been deprived of the earlier.'[20]

If, as has been suggested, Vaughan was unable to bring his work to a conclusion, the reasons remain a matter of speculation. A letter which he wrote to Richard Congreve towards the end of his life suggests that what had once been fresh and vital in his ideas had been overtaken by the passage of time and the investigations of others. 'I still possess', he wrote, 'considerable *fragments* of philosophical writing, in which the public would take, I dare say, very little or no interest even if they were complete. . . . Being aware how unprogressive and unaltered has been my mind and temper and interests during the last twenty-five years, and how different probably from your own mind and that of others in this respect, I really do apologise for bringing these distant matters again before you.'[21] In a remarkable passage of his recollections, Liddell suggested on Vaughan's own authority that there was a decline of intellectual power. Vaughan, he relates, 'told me he felt an increasing defect of brain-power and doubted whether he could rewrite what had been destroyed, certainly not, he said, with the same spirit and fire that had formerly animated him'.[22] This conversation must have taken place no later than about 1856, after which date the two men were not to meet again. In view of the friendship which existed between Liddell and Vaughan it is unlikely to be a fabrication, but there was certainly no obvious sign of waning powers during the time Vaughan sat on the Public Schools Commission a few years later.

[20] Lambeth Palace Library MS. 1867, f. 236ᵛ.
[21] Vaughan to R. Congreve, 8 July 1881.
[22] H. G. Liddell's recollections of Vaughan.

During the Upton period it is possible that there was some diminution in Vaughan's intellectual powers. The move to Upton, which was intended to have precisely the opposite effect, was probably one of the most important reasons for Vaughan's failure to complete the treatise. Jowett wrote that he would probably write a better book for not having read the German philosophers, 'but unless a man could, like Descartes, pluck out one by one the ideas he already has, I do not see what gain there can really be in travelling alone, and probably losing the way on the same ground with the German thinkers'.[23] Vaughan was a solitary thinker and he was able to pluck out his ideas one by one, but in order to do so he needed to respond to some external stimuli. His inaugural lecture, his evidence to the Oxford University Commission, his controversy with Pusey, his contribution to the Public Schools Commission were all produced in this way. At Upton he had the solitude he needed, but he was denied the stimulation which catalysed his thoughts and brought them to the point of definition. Leslie Stephen acutely observed that in his Upton period Vaughan was 'intellectually smoke-dried by his long seclusion from any intercourse with contemporaries of equal ability or familiarity with the course of modern thought'.[24]

Whatever its reasons, Vaughan's failure to finish the treatise was a great personal tragedy which clouded the last years of his life. In 1881 he wrote in moving terms to Lord Selborne of

the ineffectuality of my life now coming to its close. I speak in this way quite sincerely, recognising a plain fact, without imputing to myself an amount of faultiness which quite corresponds with my great shortcomings. I have not spent my days very much amiss in the way of work, and employment of faculties, but for the last twenty-five years I have had much to bear in the loss—I must add spoliation, of the little which I have been able to achieve . . .[It] has left me with the sense that I am fit for little but to 'crawl toward death'.[25]

This note of defeat, which coincided with the death of Adeline,

---

[23] *Life and Letters of Benjamin Jowett*, eds. E. Abbott and L. Campbell (1897), i. 123.

[24] Mausoleum Book.   [25] Lambeth Palace Library MS. 1867, f. 218ᵛ.

did not appear until his last years, and the retirement to Upton was by no means the renunciation of the world by a broken man but the act of one who prized his solitude as the instrument of further endeavour. Vaughan was constantly active during the years at Upton in many fields in addition to philosophy, but, like Job, he had many afflictions to bear besides the loss of his manuscripts. After losing money in railway shares, he made a brief excursion into journalism at the suggestion of Priaulx, who persuaded Sir Francis Doyle, a friend and contemporary of Vaughan's at Christ Church, to ask Philip Harwood, the editor of the *Saturday Review*, to accept contributions from him. Harwood readily agreed, and Vaughan duly sent him an article which, it comes as no surprise, failed to arrive. Two months later the same or another article was sent dealing with the case of a murderer named Hinton, but it was unfortunate that the article protested against Hinton's execution since the *Saturday Review* was one of the journals which, according to Priaulx, 'rejoiced' at it. Vaughan had no experience of journalism and Priaulx found his article too solid. He wrote with an unintentional irony which was, one may hope, not lost on Vaughan, 'I suspect that of late years you have avoided the labour of writing.' Harwood was not so impressed by his experience of Vaughan's journalistic prowess that he wished to repeat it, and in a conversation with Doyle let it be known that 'no communication from you [Vaughan] would have much chance with him'.

Vaughan had also been in the habit for some years of noting variant readings of Shakespeare's plays, and in 1876 the 'repeated, and destructive, yet not final, spoliations of another manuscript work',[26] decided him to publish them. In 1878 appeared the first stout volume of *New Readings and Renderings of Shakespeare's Tragedies*, a title which was something of a misnomer since the book dealt only with the historical plays, including *Cymbeline*. A second volume was published in 1881 to be followed in 1886 by a third, and more would have followed but for Vaughan's death.[27] When the book appeared Shakespearean studies had been

[26] *New Readings and Renderings of Shakespeare's Tragedies*, i (1878).
[27] Material for a further volume is in Bodleian Library MS. Eng. misc. c. 373.

greatly influenced by the republication of the quartos, which brought in its wake a reaction against textual emendation of the old school. Although Vaughan made use of the quartos and folios, he belonged rather to the tradition of Dryden, Pope, and Johnson. He was, however, a cautious and conservative commentator, who strove to give sense to apparently corrupt passages by the smallest change possible and in many instances he removed emendations introduced into the text by earlier commentators. His notes on the meaning of the text, as opposed to his emendations to the text itself, are often valuable and continue to repay study.

Although the most valuable part of his work consists in his commentary, unfortunately, in common with most other commentators, he suffered from the effects of an athletic stable of hobby-horses. He was inclined to reprove the poet for his faulty grammar and to amend his scansion, and from time to time he indulged in what Leslie Stephen called 'most singular instances of misapplied ingenuity'.[28] An example occurs in his emendation of Shakespeare's description of an ancient fortress as a 'worm-eaten hole of ragged stone'. Theobald had altered 'hole' to 'hold' on the ground that a fortress was a hold and could not very well be called a hole. Vaughan went further, and, having solemnly observed that worms do not eat stone, suggested that the line should read 'war-beaten hold of ragged stone', though the original reading was vouched for by the quarto and first folio texts. In *Henry IV*, he took the king's well-known address to sleep, in which winds,

> Who take the ruffian billows by the top,
> Curling their monstrous heads, and hanging them
> With deaf'ning clamours in the slippery clouds

and offered the uncompelling suggestion that the last line should read 'With *deafing* clamours in the *slobbery* clouds'.

Vaughan's attempts to improve Shakespeare's scansion earned him much ridicule, and it may be thought that many of them were misplaced, but what in an amateurish fashion he was seeking

---

[28] N. Annan, *Leslie Stephen* (1951), 296.

to do was to reconcile the text of the plays with Elizabethan pronunciation, and he deserves considerable credit for drawing attention to a neglected aspect of Shakespearean studies. In a letter to Kinglake, for example, he refers to the pronunciation of the word 'air', which he insisted, much to the scorn of his critics, had been pronounced as a double syllable.

This part of Wales [he wrote], anglicised by colonial immigration about a century after the completion of her conquest throws in my path sometimes amusing illustrations of Elizabethan language and pronunciation too, as I believe. Some habits of pronunciation seem to throw light on peculiarities in English orthography. For instance, the monosyllable 'air' (the atmosphere) is articulated here by *old* men 'ay-er' and 'field' 'fe-ild' or 'fe-eld', in such a manner as do give active function to the letter 'i' which is quite 'otiose' (as the classical grammarians say) in our modern utterance.[29]

The book received a mixed review, varying usually from hostile to patronizing. The *Saturday Review* pronounced it 'one of the most amazingly silly books which we have ever come across', but other papers were disposed to discover some merit in it. The *Spectator* remarked that, 'His conjectures may not be of much value—conjectures very seldom are—but the utility of his comments and suggestions of meaning, suggestions which not unfrequently tend to support commonly received readings, is beyond question.' The *St. James's Gazette* commented ambiguously on his emendations that the reader 'may not often take them down for purpose of serious reference; but they will afford him abundant topics for discussion'.

New Readings was not a financial success: one bookseller told Leslie Stephen that the only man who ever bought a copy from him was Disraeli, and the first volume ran into a second edition, not because the first sold out, but because it was destroyed in a fire at the publisher's in 1883. According to figures supplied by Kegan Paul on Vaughan's death, four copies of the first volume were sold,[30] three of the second, and fourteen of the third. Vaughan's last work was a translation into English verse of

29 Vaughan to W. Kinglake, 29 Mar. 1881.
30 The figure presumably refers to the reprint of volume 1.

Welsh proverbs. It was begun in 1884, but he did not live to complete it and it was edited and published by his son in 1899 under the title *British Reason in English Rhyme*.

Vaughan died at Upton on 19 April 1885. To the end the great book which, as Matthew Arnold wrote to him, would 'lay hold of the world and . . . make it think of you as your friends have always thought of you and will always think of you', eluded him.[31] Although he had lived in seclusion for twenty years and had produced almost no work apart from his almost still-born commentary on Shakespeare, his death revived old memories for his friends. The obituary notice of him in the *Daily News* closed with the words, 'the testimony of those whose opinion is of most weight pronounces him to have been among the most highly gifted men of his day'. The *Oxford Magazine* declared that 'no history of Oxford in the nineteenth century will be complete without mention of his influence'. In the *Oxford Review*, the writer said that Oxford had lost one of her greatest disciples and most inspiring teachers. His career, it continued,

was a remarkable one, not so much, perhaps, from its positive achieve-ments, for there have been men who have accumulated a longer list of prizes, but from the impress which it stamped on the best men of his day, from the evidences which it betrayed of a rare and commanding intellect, from the promise of its beginning, from the enthusiastic appreciation which met it at its close . . . Mr. Vaughan was possessed of all the qualities which go to make a great intellect—completeness of grasp, accuracy of research, nice and discriminating judgment. A less fastidious and painstaking man would have made himself a greater name; he would not, for all that, have been as completely and gener-ously made as was Mr. Halford Vaughan.

Vaughan possessed the qualities of intellect which the author of his obituary in the *Oxford Review* attributed to him, but his life was so empty of achievement that he himself described it as ineffectual, and Goldwin Smith went so far as to say that it was 'one of genius, mournfully, almost tragically, thrown away'.[32] The contrast between the exuberance of promise and the paucity

---

[31] Matthew Arnold to Vaughan, 3 Apr. 1881.
[32] G. Smith, *Reminiscences* (1911), 274.

of achievement is so great that it may be thought to point to some defect or unresolved conflict in Vaughan's character, but the evidence is too slight to subject him to the dubious benefits of psychological hindsight. His personality may elude the historian, but a remark made by his old friend Priaulx after his death has an authentic ring of truth. 'I loved him', he wrote, 'not so much for his great intellect as for his noble and lofty character. . . . It was his guilessness, his simplicity, his single-heartedness, his kindly gentleness, his dislike of all pretension and of everything low and false, it was these qualities illuminated by his intelligence which made him the most charming of companions and endeared him to his friends.' Vaughan was a man who was brought to the point of intellectual action by external events and too often the challenge was wanting. Early in life he obtained financial security, and he had little appetite for the conventional goals of social position, power, or wealth. Yet a man who devoted some thirty years of his life to a philosophical treatise can hardly be said to have lacked ambition, and it was the failure of this enterprise that he had in mind when he described his life as ineffectual.

Although his philosophical work failed to reach completion, there came out of it his ideas on education and learning. He offered a rational basis for integrating knowledge and healing the growing breach between science and the humanities, and in so doing laid down principles of education which have lasting value. In the history of Oxford, where the best years of his life were spent, he occupies an honoured place with Mark Pattison as the man who reaffirmed the duty of the university to be the pursuit of truth, and his final monument lies in his own doctrine of 'search all things'.

A. P. Stanley's Account of Pusey's Lectures [1854]

Dr. Pusey's Lectures

IN the years 1845 and 1846, I attended courses of the Lectures of the
Regius Professor of Hebrew at Oxford. I did so, mainly with the view
of compelling myself to maintain the recollection of the very slight
knowledge of the Hebrew language which I had acquired in the previous long vacation, and which my pressure of engagements as tutor
of University College prevented me from pursuing in any other way.

I never shall forget the shock of surprise which I then experienced.
The whole atmosphere of the Professor's lectures breathed the spirit
of Germany to a degree, which I am convinced could have been found
in no other Lecture-room in Oxford, Professorial or Tutorial. There
was of course much that was peculiar to the theologian—the long
digressions, and the fanciful theories drawn from the writers of the
4th and 5th centuries. There was still more that was peculiar to the
man, the kindness, the sweetness, the unaffected devotion which no
one who has ever witnessed it can ever forget. But all that related to
the interpretation of the part of the Scriptures on which he was
lecturing—in this instance it was the Book of Psalms—was both in
matter and manner almost entirely German. The table was piled with
German commentaries. They were quoted freely, often of course
with deprecation yet often with commendation. I heard there the
names of more German writers than in the whole course of the
instruction given in my whole stay in Oxford. Their explanations
of the language, of the customs, of the allusions, of the Psalmists were
constantly adopted, and far beyond proportion to those of the theolo-
gians of any other country. The Professor's mode of lecturing was
exactly what I remembered in the very fine lectures of Professor Nitzch
which I once attended in the University of Bonn—the same solemn
and continuous flow, the same endeavour to exhaust the text in all

its bearings, even the very same peculiarity of brief and systematic reference to other interpretations, versions, or parallel passages. The only apparent variations from the German mode, and the only sense in which it could be at all termed catachetical, was that the auditors in turn read and construed the verse on which the Professor proceeded to lecture, that very rarely, perhaps once in four lectures and then chiefly to a younger student who had gained a Hebrew Scholarship, the Professor put a passing question on some minute point of criticism. I say 'apparent' variations, for I am told that both these exceptions may be often found in the smaller classes of German Professors.

To these Lectures I certainly look back as to the most instructive[1] which I attended in Oxford—as to those, the notes of which are still most useful to me. And it is certainly not from agreement with the peculiar views which the Professor extracted from the Fathers, but from the combination of the personal character of the man with great research and ardour of criticism. Of all the Professors in Oxford there is none who has more frequently recurred to me as the example of what a German Professor is, and of what an English Professor might be than the present Regius Professor of Hebrew.

[1] I cannot refrain from adding one course which in their more limited sphere I attended with perhaps equal advantage and which though delivered in a college lectureroom were essentially of the same character—those of the Rev. R. Scott on the tragedies of Aeschylus.

Vaughan's Memorandum to the Parliamentary Commissioners[1]

Holly Mount
Hampstead
7 Jan. 1856

My Lords and Gentlemen,

When the letter of your secretary reached me I was officially and completely occupied. I have since my liberation from such duties applied myself to execute your wishes so far as time permitted, and I beg to present to you the results in the following sheets.

I have the honour to be
My Lords and Gentlemen
Your obedient servant
Henry Halford Vaughan
Her Majesty's Professor of Modern History at Oxford

The Commissioners for the Improvement of the University of Oxford.

———

[Endorsed, Received 8 Jan. 1855]

Index of Contents

1. Existing duties of professor of modern history.
2. Advisable duties of professor of modern history. Principles determining them and consequences.
3. Residence during term in Oxford, what it implies in the case of a professor of history.
4. Means of encouraging the study of modern history.   1. Devotion of Fellowships; general reasons for; scholarships; special reasons for in case of modern history; method of devoting Fellowships and reasons against partial application of the principle.   2. payment of

[1] At Vaughan's request, this paper was returned to him by the Parliamentary Commissioners.

expenses in the lecture room.   3. Modification of tutorial system.
4. Organisation of professoriate in modern history, principles,
their application, distribution of functions.

I have received an invitation to express my opinion on the duties
which I conceive ought to be attached to my professorship.

It is now five years since I answered the Oxford Commission of
Enquiry on the same subject. I have during that time found no reason
to change my opinion on the main points. I therefore refer to it.
The portions of my evidence before the Commissioners to which I
beg to call attention are these. 1. On the different subjects of professorial
teaching and the different duties of different professors. Evid. p. 273,
274. Suggestions offered on the best method of encouraging modern
history as a study (p. 277). On the propriety of giving professors *a*
voice in the nomination of Examiners (Evid. p. 87). On the creation
and endowment of professorships (Evid. p. 88). On the method of
appointing professors (Evid. p. 89). On the modification of the
present tutorial system p. 91, 92. I will, however, speak also more
summarily upon the topic.

The regulations affecting my professorship are contained in the
original deed of endowment. They require from the professor four
solemn lectures annually. As professor of modern history I have also
every year read and given a voice in the decision of the Arnold Prize.
I also take a part in the examination for the Vinerian Scholarship now
awarded (in consonance with my suggestion to the Commissioners of
Enquiry) to the most proficient Bachelor of Arts in Law and History.
A recent statute of the university ordains that the Regius Professor of
Modern History should also be one of the judges to decide on the
Stanhope Prize. Such occupations as these occurring every year con-
sume some time and some energy which are thereby directed from
other pursuits. In practice I have hitherto given eight solemn lectures
annually.

It is, I conceive, quite necessary before saying a word on the subject
of professorial duties to have arrived at a definite conclusion on another
point. The tutorial system is at present a part of the university system.
If it be intended to preserve this, in any form it must have its appropriate functions in university instruction, and the assignment of such
functions must affect the duties of the professoriate both in their nature
and in their range. A professoriate in a university where the professoriate
is the sole organised instrument of instruction should, I conceive,
have a more extended sphere of action in teaching (though not in

general devotion to the subjects taught) than a professoriate aided and supplemented by a tutorial system.

Assuming, therefore, for the occasion that the tutorial system is to be preserved, I may venture to conclude also that the teaching of modern history is a function in which the tutors can take a beneficial part. Subjects differ very much in their aptitude for tutorial teaching, and on this point I have entered at length in the evidence to which I refer. The tutors have given instruction in the history of the Old Testament and in Ancient History, and therefore if they have the requisite knowledge they can do so in regard to Modern History. In all there are text books on which the tutors can catechise and comment. I think, therefore, I may pass on to a further assumption that modern history may be taught in part by tutors.

Under such circumstances, therefore, I conceive that the most important duty of the professor will be to deliver solemn lectures on historical subjects. The advantage of such an institution to the university as a place of instruction and of learning is manifold. First, such teaching may constantly impart animation to the student and to the tutor, and will keep up freshness of thought and interest by the constant accession of new knowledge to that already presented in text books and traditional instruction. It is not possible even if it were desirable that all who teach should be on the search for new truths whether of special facts or of reasoning on facts. But it is most beneficial even with effect on the student that he should come into contact with some mind charged with the knowledge of original documents and authorities and able to exhibit a proper use of them. I believe that the effect of such an influence on the intellectual character of some students is such as hardly can be measured. The effect upon the tutor or teacher is also most salutary. It constantly reminds him of a knowledge beyond the common range of second hand authorities and text books however good, and suggests views of history, of the importance of historical periods, of the nature of historical characters, and of historical authorities, which must in many ways stimulate a wise curiosity and a noble ambition.

Such teaching will on the whole sustain the character of the university as a seat of learning, and it can only be a matter of grief to me, speaking of the general state of things, when I say that with regard to Oxford this is a position which she has to gain rather than to support.

If the professor's duties, therefore, should be mainly those of public lecturing, it remains to consider what amount of lecturing should be required of him. The real and valuable return which the university should desire from the professors in addition to natural ability is industry in reading and reflecting and in throwing the result into lectures. 'Much labour' bestowed upon lecturing is, however, a thing totally distinct from 'many lectures'. Many, laudably anxious that the professoriate should not be an endowed and idle institution, have, I think, often confounded the two terms and two ideas which are totally distinct. They have proposed to prescribe many lectures on the assumption that to require much industry from the professor is synonymous with requiring from him many lectures. There is no such necessary connexion between them as that the fulfilment of the one condition at all implies the satisfaction of the other. A man labours in lecturing in the most precious sense of the term who throws much reading, and the exercise of many faculties, reflexion, judgment, and imagination into his lectures. A man labours in another and very different sense who writes many lectures, and a man may only *seem* to labour who yet delivers lectures frequently. But the second kind of labour is precisely that which in a tutorial university is least required upon such a subject as history.

Now very much lecturing, i.e. the writing as distinct from the mere delivery of lectures, is inconsistent with the best object which we all have in view. It substitutes the wrong kind of industry for the right one. It makes industry and research and thought, digestion and arrangement, impossible, because it exacts the treatment of many subjects within a short time and the writing and delivering of many words within a short time. Its best fruit can but be that which books and tutors are imparting without its aid, and meanwhile it is a substitute for energy of a better and more useful description. One thing indeed can be said in its favour. It is an outward activity and therefore rules and laws can enforce it. The other and better industry, it may be urged, eludes all statutes and can not be the object of any outward guarantee. This must be admitted, but what does it establish? It only leads us to feel that by legislation we can secure any number of *Parliamentary Lectures* and nothing beyond this. But in such an university as Oxford where teaching in the common sense on such a subject may be otherwise provided, lectures of such a description, if not out of place, had, I think, better not be supplied by any expensive organisation. There is a guarantee for labour and lecturing such as I have described. A moral guarantee which will fail perhaps in particular instances, and will surely succeed in the general result. This guarantee is the proper choice of a professor. A man whose natural abilities and tastes have prompted him to a life of thought and study during the restless years which precede thirty is not likely to find a life of active study and composition from thirty to sixty other than a natural energy requiring little self command for its continuance.

Under these circumstances I am of opinion that if it be desirable that the professor should devote his whole time to the professorship, it will not on the whole conduce to the benefit of Oxford university that any addition should be made to the number of lectures which he is at present *required* to deliver. Dr. Arnold has recorded his opinion generally to the same effect in very emphatic language. He says that if he had nothing to do with Rugby and devoted himself to Oxford he could not profitably give more than 8 lectures annually. 'Eight lectures a year would, I am sure, be as much as any man could give with advantage.' Stanley's Life of Arnold, vol. 2 page 298. But *if* any thing further be exacted from him by law, I am of opinion that it should be catechetical instruction. His more profound acquaintance with the subject will enable him perhaps to be of service to a few students in this way. But to produce a full effect, the lecture must be actually catechetical, consist of question no less than of comments. Such lectures will not be resorted to by many, first because men, unless they are thoroughly in earnest, will not offer themselves to be constantly examined; secondly, because, unless they have a consciousness of superiority, they will shrink from the eyes and judgment of those who attend the class with them. One catechetical lecture in the week will be sufficient to test the reading of a fortnight, and therefore if one catechetical lecture in the week be required of the professor this would answer all purposes.

It is of course *in itself* a thing desirable that professors should reside during term. But there should be no mistake as to what such residence really means if it be proposed to enforce such residence in the case of the professor. It means residence generally through the whole astronomical year and not merely through the academical year. Residence for any portion of the year, if exacted from the professor at the expense of his studies is not a benefit to the university but the contrary of a benefit. Therefore, of course, it is intended that the professor should reside and study and work during his residence. If so he must reside at Oxford altogether. I know from experience that a studious professor can not have two homes. He must always be surrounded by his books. His books of hourly reference in the common sense of the term are too bulky and voluminous for frequent removal. He can not borrow such, even from the most public libraries so as to command them at all times, and unless they are constantly with him to meet the need of the moment they are comparatively useless. Again, to a professor all his books of authority become more and more books of reference. One fact explains another, the statements of authors must be compared. The longer he studies, and the more he knows, the more frequent and necessary will be his reference from the pages which he is reading to the pages which he has read. A professor student is always reading in this way a great many books at once for he is always consulting, and getting at the truth by comparison and convicting error by the same process. As a man is learned does his library become to him a single book. The young student finds his book in the volume before him: the professor student finds his book in the library around him. It is this fact which leads the professor student to form a library which is as needful to him almost as his roof and his fire. And his own margins often are as needful to him as the text. This is the rationale of a fact to the truth of which I can speak from experience. A professor of history must reside constantly in one spot, and on the same account I am compelled to add that the most unprofitable hours which I have spent are those passed within the walls of the university during term. I have tried reading in the Bodleian. It is not open more than six hours out of the twenty four, and those during the day when exercise must be taken if at all. In winter too the temperature is low and I have found that even with a great coat and railway rug I have been quite chilled by three hours consecutive study. Having been for many years a student and a water drinker, I am perhaps more sensitive to cold than many. But some must resemble me in his degree, and all in the fact of such sensibility. The Bodleian I found, therefore, on all accounts an insufficient substitute for my own study. I began by residing four months in the year at Oxford. For various reasons I have more and more narrowed the period of my residence till it has now dwindled down to visits to Oxford on university business and to deliver lectures. This has been my course during the last twelve months.

Let it be remembered, therefore, that residence *means* i.e. involves, residence generally i.e. not merely residence through the term (though the latter only is expressed) but whenever he studies his subject. As to the best means of encouraging the study of modern history in such a manner as shall give to it no improper advantage over other branches of learning and permit no improper prejudice to its prosecution, those which lie most directly within the power of the Commission seem to consist in the appropriation of a proportion of Fellowships and Scholarships, especially the former, to the highest proficiency in the subjects of the modern history school, that is to modern history, the elements of common law, and civil law, and political economy.

In my answer to the Commission of Enquiry I pressed this topic upon their attention, and as they deemed my proposal worthy of adoption into their Report I think it best to extract the statement which I then made and the commissioners then quoted [quotation of pp. 90–1 from Report].

I should observe that I am more anxious for the appropriation of Fellowships than for the appropriation of Scholarships, not as thinking the latter as the less powerful inducement to the cultivation of modern history but because I think that the later period of the academical status pupillaris is the best for devotion to such a subject. I should be content to dispense with the Scholarships, therefore, if the other new Schools should stand on the same footing, but if they are admitted to a share of the Scholarships I fear that it must act very unfavourably on the subsequent cultivation of history if this branch be excluded from the same advantage. Men will be encouraged thereby to begin the mathematical and physical studies at the earlier period in order that they may obtain a scholarship. They will be encouraged rather to continue their mathematical and physical studies at the later period rather than to resort to modern history because they have advanced as far on their way toward honours and Fellowships by the reading for Scholarships, and therefore the transference of their attention to a different branch of learning will prove a waste of time and trouble in the university career.

I must observe in regard to Fellowships that in no branch of learning are such inducements more wanted than in that of modern history. Physical sciences must be taught mainly by Professors and their assistants owing to the want of college apparatus and theatres. In modern history the Fellows of colleges can give more effective aid, and therefore it becomes the more advisable to ensure the existence of efficient instructors in this branch by the devotion of specific Fellowships to it.

I do not advocate any *distinction* in favour of modern history, but I can not help pointing out this peculiar reason which gives an additional claim of modern history to a share in such arrangements. This School had greater difficulty in establishing itself than any other. The proposition to organise an examination in physical science was approved and adopted by the university at once. The proposition of the same kind for the introduction of modern history and law was at the same time negatived. This was done by the efforts of two parties unfriendly to its introduction, some on educational grounds, others (I think) on grounds political or religious. It required a great effort and a second trial to succeed in establishing the School. I believe that it would be quite rash to infer that the same hostile feeling is now extinct, and although the School will I trust succeed under fair terms of competition yet it will sink if it be excluded from a due share of emoluments, and there will be no prosecution of it as a study by elder members of the university.

It may be thought on the first consideration perhaps that however desirable it may be to give due weight to modern history in the examination for Fellowships, this end may still be effected without the devotion of specific Fellowships to such a purpose. The colleges, it may be said, may be required to make modern history and law a *part* of every or of some Fellowship examination. But such an arrangement will not answer the end desired for two reasons. First, I know from my experience as a Fellow of Oriel College that, unless the Fellows of a college personally understand and value proficiency in a given subject, the mere apportionment of a paper or two in the examinations to it does not secure for it weight and influence in the competition. In such case they keep their eye on the other favourite subjects, and with so much to read through as a college Fellowship examination imposes on the examiners a very slight bias in favour of one subject is sufficient to determine the elections in accordance with proficiency in that branch exclusively. Now as the whole arrangement under contemplation presupposes, and is provided against, a strong leaning in favour of a knowledge of such branches on the part of the actual and existing Fellows of colleges, any remedy or provision which, even without combination or a very distinct and deliberate purpose, will be invalidated practically by the predilections and partial knowledge of the examining Fellows, must fail to carry out its object. It will be defeated almost without a struggle or perhaps even without the consciousness of favour and preference. In the second place no one ordinary examination can combine scholarship, moral science, and ancient history, the subjects of the classical school, and also comprise modern history and the elements of civil and common law with political economy, the subjects of the modern history school. There must be a paper on each of these subordinate subjects at least, and two papers at least on pure modern history proper. The assignment of a fewer number will involve the devotion of only one or two questions to each, and the result of this must be that the examinations are partial in their nature and unfair in their result. A very few questions on a subject must leave the larger part of it untouched, therefore also the real proficiency of the candidates in depth and range of knowledge and in power of treatment unascertained. Fortune may throw such questions within the limited range or superficial knowledge of a man comparatively ignorant, and even out of the wide range and more accurate recollection, and the more able treatment, of the man in all these points comparatively superior. A certain number of questions is necessary, to equalise chances, to exhaust knowledge, and to test acquisition and natural power, and it would be extremely difficult, almost impracticable, with the best intentions and fairest temper to do justice to proficiency in one school so long as the examination comprises many schools. The only plan then for ensuring to modern history and law a proper share in the Fellowships on which reliance can be placed seem that of devoting specific Fellowships to the successful candidates in a special examination confined to this branch of knowledge.

It has been suggested that one examination may include many subjects by making the examination sufficiently comprehensive and sufficiently searching in each branch of knowledge, and by assigning to each subject a specific and given number of marks. But, in the first place, this system is very difficult to arrange upon equitable principles. Secondly, the system is extremely cumbrous and difficult to carry out in itself. Thirdly, it is a system of which the effect has never yet been justified by experience.

First, it is very difficult to conduct such an examination on equitable principles. Say that a paper in modern history and a paper in classical knowledge are valued at 500 marks each paper. Different examiners will probably set the questions and the questions must in all probability be framed on different scales of difficulty. The 10 questions in paper A may be answered satisfactorily without more reading than 5 questions in paper B. Yet the respondent to one will get 250 marks, while a respondent equally meritorious to the other gains 500 marks. I put these numbers simply as an illustration. Again if all the questions in each paper are answered, still one examiner or set of examiners has a different scale of approval from the other. A and B think that their paper is sufficiently answered as to all questions and mark up accordingly; C and D with a higher standard of excellence are less easily satisfied and mark down. Suppose however that the examiners have a bias towards one subject, and the arrangement presupposes something of this sort, the effect of such obstacles to an equitable competition will be much increased.

Secondly, the system is exceedingly cumbrous. It involves the devotion of some ten days at least to every examination for a Fellowship, for a Fellowship in which the examination in two schools is involved, and of twenty days at least, for every Fellowship in which an examination in four schools is involved. It would require also for every such vacancy two or four sets of examiners, a great expenditure of power.

The uncertainty as to the result too would, I think, be an evil. The Vinerian Scholarships is now given by means of a historical and legal examination. The mathematical scholarships are given for a mathematical examination. The theological scholarships are given for a theological examination. I believe it would be very prejudicial to some of these studies if one long examination were to be given for all three scholarships including all three subjects. Such a system sacrifices one great advantage in all competitive examinations, a common and single standard of comparison. The merits of a theologian are without difficulty tested in a struggle with a theologian. So of a mathematician with a mathematician, so of an historian. But to test the merit of a theologian and of an astronomer in their several branches as against each other is as difficult and as pregnant with injustice as to award a prize to the competition of a dancer, a wrestler, and a musician. There is no common point of comparison and where this fundamental condition is lacking, any numerical tests, however plausible and imposing, must fail in securing a fair result when applied with the best intentions and fairest spirit, and where there is no security for perfect freedom from favour towards a particular subject, I fear that such expedients would only tend to disguise from ourselves and others for a season the partialities which in the case of college Fellowships would constantly turn the result of the examination.

The fact that the system which I deprecate in case of college vacancies has been this year adopted apparently by the framers of the East India Service examination does not invalidate my objections. First because the whole circumstances attendant on the trial for Writerships are different in some essential particulars from those attendant on the competition for Fellowships. Thus in the first place, the whole plan is new, and no bias generated by long habits and established predilections could be imputed to the whole body of examiners for the Indian Service. In the second place, the number of vacancies is very large indeed. Upwards of twenty Writerships have been the object of competition in a single examination. This circumstance alone supplies a point of important difference between college and Indian examinations. In such a case it is possible and expedient to organise and throw into action an elaborate machinery consisting of very numerous examiners and a multifarious examination. The result is worthy of so complicated and cumbrous an arrangement, which would be out of place if one or two (at the outside) college Fellowships were the only object of competition.

Again, where so many prizes are the rewards of success, there is not a competition between the different branches of learning for the same single reward. The struggle is not exclusive nor jealous to the same degree. There is, to use a common phrase, 'room for all' in each examination. Compromises can be made. The examiners in each department are content with the distribution of a few prizes to encourage those who prosecute the subject, even although the number of such prizes is not strictly in accordance with their view of its claims on public reward. The most eager examiners again are not desirous of monopolizing more than what will appear to the public a moderate and reasonable share of prizes. The inherent defects of the system, therefore, do not work themselves out as they would do in an examination where the examiners are supposed to have a bias, where the prizes are so few as to make such a machinery preposterous, and where they are also so few as to give a character quite exclusive to the success. I may also be permitted to observe in conclusion that the single trial afforded to the East Indian scheme can not be yet pronounced as successful even with all these circumstances and conditions in its favour.

For weeks after the close of the examinations the newspapers were full of letters complaining, blaming, and pointing out mischiefs. These letters were not written apparently by mere meddlers or disappointed friends only, but by men honourably placed in the educational managements of the country. At last, if I remember correctly, a Fellow of Dublin university wrote to prove and apparently did prove that the number of Writerships given to each department of knowledge bore the same numerical proportion to the whole number of Writerships competed for as the number of examiners in that department bore to the whole number of examiners employed in conducting the examination. In other words that as the tendency and inclination of each examiner was to give Writerships to his own subjects, the prizes were in effect distributed (so far as subjects of examination were concerned) according to the degree in which each subject was represented by voting examiners. I can not vouch for the perfect accuracy of my recollection. Still less do I assert that the system did not work out a fair result. I must be content to say that its success is not established as yet by experience, that its success if established would not give a bias for its application to college examinations, that there are great inherent difficulties in doing justice with it of which I do not see the remedy in any case, and of which I do see in the cases of college Fellowships probable consequences prejudicial to the success of the School of modern history at Oxford.

I think that all expenses incurred by the professor in providing apparatus for his lectures should be defrayed by the university or by funds set apart for this purpose. These disbursements can not be very large but they may be sufficient seriously to tax the private income of the professor. I can illustrate this from my own experience. My first lectures were given in the Taylor Institution. As my audience became too large for the accommodation I was compelled to move to the Sheldonian Theatre. This move has cost me nearly thirty pounds for each course of lectures. I was requested, although my lectures were gratuitous, by the university and the Curators of the Theatre to pay the keeper of the Theatre one guinea per lecture for his trouble and expense in cleaning up the Theatre after each lecture. I was compelled to have benches also introduced at my own expense: some existing benches were too few and had no backs to them, thereby occasioning inconvenience and discomfort to those who on such seats had to look upwards to the lecturer. Maps too I was obliged to have prepared on a scale large enough to be descried by the most distant of my auditors. I might, I do not doubt, have raised amongst those who resorted to my lectures more than sufficient to defray these expenses. But such a course was distasteful to me, and I preferred to furnish them at my own cost.

I think that it would conduce also to the successful prosecution of historical studies amongst the younger members of the university if the tutorial organisation were somewhat modified so as to permit colleges to aid each other in furnishing tutorial instruction. As I in my evidence to the Commissioners of Enquiry proposed a scheme of modification I beg leave to refer to it here. Commission of Enquiry. Evidence p. 91–92.

The propriety and expediency of creating and endowing a new professorship in modern history must depend upon two conditions mainly. First, the possibility of furnishing incomes to two Professors on such a scale as is likely to attract and retain the services of men fit for such a post. In knowledge of life, knowledge of human nature, knowledge of municipal and other laws, knowledge of the principles of political economy, in powers of sympathy, judgment, and imagination and in acquaintance with authors and facts are to be found the main conditions which will qualify a man for such a post. Considerable powers of composition also will, I think, ever be found requisite to fix the attention of hearers. One important consideration therefore must be: how can such abilities and accomplishments be attracted to the offices of Professors hereafter if professorships are preserved and created?

If the Commissioners have at their disposal adequate funds to give a salary to professorships such as will secure the devotion to them of the proper talents and knowledge, and if it is deemed advisable to add to the number of Professors in other branches and subjects which are taught also by tutors, the existence of another professorship would be beneficial. On consideration I think that the assignment of one professorship to the histories of England and France, and of another professorship to Italy, Germany, and other European history would be the most reasonable distribution of provinces to two professors. A division into a professorship of English history and a professorship on European history would, I think on reflexion, cast too much within the sphere of the latter and too little (comparatively) within that of the former. And this being so, the histories of France and England from the reign of Edward the Confessor have been so constantly and closely connected by all international relations of peace and war that they would naturally collect themselves into one province. No single *professor* would be likely to master both these subjects. But the single *professorship* might: that is of three or four professors in succession some would naturally turn in the main to one country and some to the other, so that in a few years both would be adequately treated.

On the other hand, Italy and Germany have been closely connected since the days of the Carolingian dynasty, and these two countries with the remainder of Europe would give ample occupation to the second professorship in a similar manner.

I think it right to say that another division upon a different principle naturally and reasonably suggests itself. A professorship of modern history embracing all Europe from the fifth century to the fifteenth and a professorship of recent history embracing all Europe from the fifteenth to the nineteenth century. There would be advantages in such a distribution. On the whole, however, I incline to the first which I have suggested, if two professorships be the desired number.

But as I said before the propriety of a new professorship in modern history seems to me to depend upon economical considerations in part, which do not lie within my knowledge. If an attempt is made to provide much professorial work out of small means and therefore out of inferior materials, the result, I fear, would be the failure to obtain any professorial work at all in the sense in which it is most required on such a subject as modern history in such a university as Oxford.

I am of opinion that the professor of modern history should have a voice in the nomination of examiners. But this perhaps is a point not the most likely to fall within the legislative functions of the present Commission.

Index